Beyond the Dream

Fig. 1: First Purchase: Fahy Ranch Property and Outlying Parcels, 1991
Aerial photo courtesy of Bandon Dunes

Chrome
Lake

Randolph Road

Round
Lake

Cut Creek

Fahys
Lake

Fahy Road

Bullards Beach
State Park

Coquille River

100-Acre
Parcel

Hwy 101

Lighthouse

Bandon
Waterfront

Beyond the Dream

BANDON DUNES

BRUCE JOHNSON

JOHNSON STREET PUBLISHING
Portland, Oregon

Johnson Street Publishing
Portland, Oregon

Printed in the United States of America

ISBN 978-0-692-23282-8 (paperback)

Book design by Jennifer Omner, ALL Publications

Note: Unless otherwise indicated, all photographs and drawings are courtesy of the author.

For Howard L. McKee

Howard, a business partner with Mike Keiser, was the point man for the Bandon Dunes project. With the help of others, he obtained the necessary development approvals and led a consultant team of professionals who planned, designed and built the infrastructure that makes extraordinary links land golf possible at the resort.

CONTENTS

ILLUSTRATIONS

ACKNOWLEDGMENTS

Although I have a lot of institutional memory about the subject matter covered in this book, the book would not have been possible without the contributions of many other individuals. Many times I have felt I was simply an actor playing a role in a play called Bandon Dunes: a play that has had over a twenty-year run, wowed audiences and will continue to wow them. Over time, this play has had a large cast of actors that has grown into a family.

Each played their role to the best of their ability. Howard, as the director, orchestrated their time on stage, and gave direction to the overall performance of the cast.

If Bandon Dunes is a play, Mike Keiser is the producer. Many thanks to him for the opportunity to have shared the stage set of this World Class Act.

Thanks to the wonderful cast of players who have contributed to the realization and success of Bandon Dunes, many of whom I interviewed for this book. They include: Al Johnson, Ben Crenshaw, Bill Church, Bill Coore, Bob Johnson, Hank Hickox, Josh Lesnik, Corinne Sherton, David Leland, David McLay Kidd, Dave Zinkand, Don Stastny, Don Ivy, Erik Stevens, Frank McNew, Janet Rogers, Jim Urbina, Ken Hattan, Ken Nice, Matt Leeding, Phil Sabold, Ralph Christenson, Roger Redfern, Scott Craig, Tom Doak, Tom Jefferson, Tor Flatebo, Warren Felton, Wood Sabold, and the Bandon Dunes resort staff; key individuals from Walsh Construction—Bob Wilde, Eric Stevens, Matt Leeding—who, under Bob Walsh's leadership, joined the team and ensured that this effort was accomplished with finesse and success; as well as a local Bandon construction company that was also responsible for project construction efforts. All were encouraging during my research work and graciously offered answers and insights to my many questions. Each has contributed, large and small, to the Bandon Dunes story.

I would be remiss in not acknowledging the special contributions of six individuals: Al, Bob, Warren, Don Ivy, Harry and Don Stastny. Al Johnson—he led the legal team and, in partnership with Howard, provided the legal strategy that kept our ship on course. Bob Johnson—a real estate broker who facilitated the acquisition of the property and has advised the resort owner on the purchase of other properties that will eventually lead to the long-term preservation and conservation of environmentally sensitive coastal lands along the South Coast of Oregon.

Warren Felton—a jack-of-all-trades, he was the caretaker and on-site manager at the Pistol River Ranch, a Keiser-owned property, before the acquisition of the resort property. At the onset of the Bandon Dunes project, Howard enticed Warren to relocate to Bandon. Warren proceeded to prove himself invaluable to the team, eventually becoming responsible for the management and operation of the resort's wastewater treatment plant. His fingerprints are all over miles of underground piping that crisscross the resort property.

Although not a member of the consultant team, Howard relied upon the advice and counsel of Don Ivy—the cultural resources coordinator for the Coos-Coquille Tribe—in gaining important knowledge and an appreciation about the tribe's concerns regarding their ancestral lands from Cut Creek to Whiskey Run Creek. Don was extremely helpful in providing background material on aspects of Native American prehistory.

As Howard's understudy and replacement, when Howard had to step aside and relinquish his leadership role, Don Stastny—at a critical juncture—stepped up to the plate, and the show continued at the highest level of performance.

I also owe a debt of gratitude to all the regulatory agency personnel who reached back into their memories to add to my understanding about events that occurred during the permitting phase of the project. There were private citizens and others who shared their views about Oregon's land use planning system and continuing conservation programs in Oregon. Notable among the group was Harry Hoogesteger—he provided me with an appreciation and understanding of what it actually takes to accomplish habitat restoration on the South Coast.

My narrative about how staff manages and operates the resort came from discussions I had with KemperSports personnel. Josh, Hank, Jim, Ken, Tom, Matt and others, thank you for the thoughts you shared with me.

At the last minute, when circumstances dictated changing the first chapter of the book, fortune smiled on me. What Dick Youngscap accomplished at the Sand Hills Golf Club, and its influence on what later occurred at Bandon Dunes, ushered in the idea of minimalist golf course design. The opportunity to interview Dick allowed me to move ahead when I could have stalled. Thanks for the great chat, Dick.

And last, but not least, special thanks are due to Martha Bergman, and Kathryn Hurd. The former was instrumental in prodding me to get the storyline right. Kathryn, my editor, helped me reorganize early drafts; her suggestions about the story flow vastly improved the final manuscript.

A decade ago, I was in Minneapolis, Minnesota, visiting family, and I had the occasion to speak with Roger Martin. Roger was the director of the landscape architecture program at the University of Minnesota in 1966, where I was one of three students who began the program. Roger listened intently as I described what I was doing as a consultant to the golf resort. When I finished, he asked me, "Why don't you write a book about it?" I ducked the question and said something about not having the time or interest. Roger, here's the book you suggested I write.

To all, thanks again.

Bruce Johnson

2014

INTRODUCTION

For everything has a past
and a future reason for being.
—Michael Murphy, *Golf in the Kingdom*

The flat floodplain and landscape of the Red River of the North sits beneath a sky dome. Potholed lakes dot the landscape. After settlement, agricultural fields of wheat, oats, soybeans, corn; the occasional treed windbreak; and scattered copses of spindly hardwoods replaced what was once tall grass prairie. The horizon seems to recede forever. This is the landscape of my youth.

In stark contrast, as an adult, I found my way to the emerald, evergreen forests and ocean coastline of the Pacific Northwest. Here the horizon ends, and the sky dome is absent. Each landscape is beautiful. Both still retain their natural intrinsic qualities, even though man has interceded and changed the natural order.

In 1971, with a recently acquired master's degree in landscape architecture, I arrived in Portland, Oregon. There I met Howard McKee, and he hired me for my first professional job. I worked with him in the offices of Skidmore, Owings and Merrill for four years. Then I took a job in Australia for another four years. When I came back to the United States in 1979, Howard coaxed me back to work with him at Skidmore.

After a while, I left to work for myself, but in 1991 he called and said he needed help. A friend of his—Mike Keiser, a developer from Chicago— had just purchased over 1000 acres of coastal property in southwestern Oregon. Mike wanted to build a golf resort. Could I help them out?

I listened to Howard's spiel—designing a golf resort sounded challenging. I'd never worked on a golf resort project, but neither had he. At the time, neither of us even played golf. Howard, a natural born salesman, made the project out to be a great adventure. So I took the job.

For five years, Howard and I traveled to Bandon, Oregon, while we prepared a resort master plan. We then spent another four years building the basic facilities so the resort could open for business. I ended up spending twenty years, half of my professional career, working on the Bandon Dunes Golf Resort. During which the picturesque landscapes of the Pacific Northwest captivated my soul. Unfortunately, Howard died before we completed our work, and by 2009 I felt the job we had been hired to do was nearly complete.

A few years earlier, a book had been published about the making of the resort. After reading this book several times, I decided the story was incomplete.

So I decided to expand the story. Taking myself off the resort planning and design team, I became a fledgling author. I have collected my observations and recollections, and now I will tell you the full story behind how difficult it was to get development approval for the resort concept; what and how the necessary infrastructure was put in place to support the golf activity; what distinguishes this golf resort from other golf resorts, especially community-oriented golf resorts; and how the vision of "Dream Golf" was augmented to include a regional approach to coastal conservation.

To turn a vision into a permitted development meant confronting a complex land planning and public review process prescribed by state law. After obtaining an initial development approval, the team proceeded to design and oversee construction of the destination golf resort. Over the years, the resort grew and expanded beyond its original design program. When most of the pieces of the master plan were in place, the owner came up with a surprise. He wasn't finished with his dream: he wanted to build one more golf course—something special—but it wasn't allowed in the master plan. As the story unfolded, resulting changes produced an unforeseen outcome that took the initial dream golf vision beyond the dream.

The planning and construction process also produced a surprising outcome about how local Native Americans felt about the finished resort. Howard had anticipated serious objections from Coquille tribal members because of their ancestors who had lived on the resort property until the mid-1850s. Instead, a cordial relationship developed due to open communication and the resolution of tribal concerns about potential damage to native artifacts. The land planning process we embraced produced a resort design that reflected shared human values about gathering, celebration and a purposeful use of the land. While there were dissimilar cultural contexts and worldviews, we were able to *bridge* these cultural differences with mutual respect for the natural resource values and the spirit of the place at this beautiful coastal site.

Beyond the Dream is a story about how it feels to be part of something bigger than anything you thought it could be while also trying to respect the natural order and spirit of the land.

CAST OF PRINCIPAL PLAYERS

Al Johnson	Land Use Attorney
Ben Crenshaw	Golf Course Architect, Coore and Crenshaw
Bill Church	Architect
Bill Coore	Golf Course Architect, Coore and Crenshaw
Bill Grile	Coos County Planning Director
Bob Johnson	Real Estate Broker
Bob Wilde	Walsh Construction Company
Bruce Johnson	Landscape Architect, Author
Christopher Smith	Speed Golfer
Corinne Sherton	Land Use Attorney
David Leland	Marketing/Real Estate Consultant
David McLay Kidd	Golf Course Architect
Don Stastny	Project Director
Doug Spiro	Landscape Contractor
Eric Stevens	Walsh Construction Company
Grant Rogers	Resort Director of Instruction
Hank Hickox	Resort General Manager
Harry Hoogesteger	South Coast Watershed Council Coordinator
Howard McKee	Project Director
Janet Rogers	Naturalist
Jim Haley	Golf Course Shaper
Jim Urbina	Golf Course Architect
Josh Lesnik	KemperSports President
Ken Brooke	Caddy Master
Ken Hattan	Architect
Kristie Jacobson	Resort Human Resources (Acting Director 2014)
Matt Allen	Resort Director of Golf
Matt Leeding	Walsh Construction Company
Matt Winkel	Bandon City Manager
Mike Keiser	Resort Owner
Shorty Dow	Ranch Manager

Cast of Principal Players

Tom Doak   Golf Course Architect
Tor Flatebo   Civil Engineer
Troy Russell   Golf Course Superintendent
Warren Felton   Utilities Manager

and a few others....

PART ONE

DREAM GOLF

We all appreciate an architect who will try to
let the land dictate the style of the course.
—Mike Keiser, Chicago, Illinois

Fig. 2: Links Land at Bandon Dunes

Chapter One

Looking Back

History doesn't repeat itself, but it does rhyme.
—Mark Twain

NOSTALGIC RECOLLECTIONS

On March 10, 2014, a late night conversation with Bob Johnson triggered memories of his childhood and events we had shared in the past. Bob was a good friend of mine whom I had met in the early 1990s while preparing a master plan for a destination golf resort along the southwestern coast of Oregon. That night we discussed the beginning chapter in a book I was writing about the development of the Bandon Dunes Golf Resort and its relationship with other golf courses in America.

I had asked Bob about the Prairie Dunes Country Club, a private golf course located in Hutchinson, Kansas. Bob knew about the course because he had played it several times a few years ago while visiting family near Wichita. What he remembered was that Salinas, Kansas, where he'd spent his early childhood, was a town about sixty miles north of Hutchinson. And he hadn't become a golfer until much later in life.

Our conversation drifted back to one of the times at Bandon Dunes when he and I had been at a dinner hosted by Mike Keiser, the developer of the resort. Mike had invited several of his golf buddies out to look over the property and offer advice about his project. Included in the group was Dick Youngscap, an architect and developer, who, at the time, was actively planning a golf course in the Midwest.

As the night progressed, Bob and I spoke about how our involvement in the Bandon Dunes project had introduced us to the game of golf. When we both started working on the project, neither of us were golfers. I'd played a little in high school but had never taken up the game. Bob eventually took the game up primarily because he spent lots of time at the resort since he was Mike's real estate agent. Being around the resort as the number of golf courses expanded was a great incentive for both of us to take up the game. Bob was serious; he practiced a lot, I didn't.

In time, Bob found himself playing golf at several courses on visits back home to Kansas, among them Prairie Dunes. Near the end of our conversation, I related a story a golf course architect had told me about Prairie Dunes. As I finished the story, Bob sighed and commented, "Life really is a circle; everything is interconnected."

KANSAS TO NEBRASKA TO OREGON

Bob's reminiscences about the Prairie Dunes Country Club reminded me of a conversation I'd had with Bill Coore. Bill, a golf course architect, had mentioned Prairie Dunes when I interviewed him about the golf course design work Coore and Crenshaw had done for two golf course developers—Dick Youngscap and Mike Keiser.

Bill was familiar with Prairie Dunes because he had been in East Texas at the Waterwood National Golf Course, where he met Ron Whitten for the first time in 1977. They ended up having hamburgers in the club grill. While talking about golf, Ron happened to mention that he thought the best land for golf in America was in Nebraska. Bill had never considered Nebraska as prime land for golf, but he filed the information away. A couple of years later, while in Hutchinson, Kansas, at the Prairie Dunes Country Club, Doug Peterson, then the golf course superintendent at Prairie Dunes, told Bill the Sandhills of Nebraska was an ideal location for a golf course.

What really sparked my interest was what Bill had to say about Prairie Dunes, Sand Hills and Bandon Dunes. At some point during our conversation, Bill said that some people in the golf community consider Prairie Dunes to be the "grandmother or matriarch" of site-driven golf course development in America. It is his belief that you can draw a direct line, historically, from a golf course built in Kansas before WWII to two courses built in Nebraska and Oregon in the mid-1990s. These three golf course developments all share a common golf lineage, primarily based on three factors: remoteness, sand-based golf course construction, and personal relationships among various individuals who were involved in the planning and development of all three courses. These relationships constitute a "historic arc" in the evolution of contemporary American golf course design.

In 1935, the Carey family hired Perry Maxwell to design a nine-hole course on 480 acres of land near Hutchinson, Kansas. It's been written that Perry found "there are 118 holes here, and all I have to do is eliminate 100." At first, only nine holes were built and opened in 1937. Later, Perry's son, Press, added another nine holes, and the result was a golf course that is considered an American original today.

Geographically, Hutchinson is located in the Great Bend Sand Prairie region of the Great Plains. Locals would also describe it as on the edge of the High Plains, and the 640-acre Sand Hills State Park is located a few miles north of Hutchinson. The windswept sand dunes with rolling hills were an ideal location for a sand-based, links land style course evocative of the ancient courses in Scotland.

In the early 1990s, Sand Hills and Bandon Dunes were both in their initial stages of development. Both Dick and Mike had purchased properties that also had sand-based ground. In both instances, many in the golf course industry felt both locations were too remotely located to succeed.

Historically, up to WWII, golf course design had been site-driven. This changed from the 1950s onward, when golf course design became market-driven. Most courses built afterwards were in proximity to urban centers where there were concentrated populations of potential customers. The idea that you could build a golf course at a remote location was considered crazy and foolhardy by most in the golf industry. As Dick has said, "Sand Hills kicked the door back open for site-driven golf, again."

The Sand Hills Golf Club was built in the Sandhills near Mullen, Nebraska. In 1981, Geoffrey Cornish and Ron Whitten co-authored a book called The Golf Course. The book included a small photograph of sand dunes in the Midwest. The caption read: Links land far from the ocean in

Nebraska. On the same page, a photograph of the Machrie Hotel GC in Scotland takes up more than half the bottom of the page. You could easily miss the smaller image tucked into the upper left top of the page.

Bill and Ben, that's Ben Crenshaw the other half of Coore and Crenshaw, were invited by Dick to view his land. Both of them flew out to Nebraska and began walking the land to discover its potential. It's been said that it took them two and a half years to design and build the course. However, seasonal weather limited their time on-site to half the year, as the winter climate is harsh.

Similar to what happened during the design of the first course at Prairie Dunes, Bill and Ben found 137 holes that they whittled down to eighteen holes at Sand Hills. They took as much time as necessary to design a course that fit the local landscape. Bill remembers having a local rancher tell him how grateful the local community was that the final product fit in with the local culture and lifestyle.

The Sandhills are a semi-arid landscape composed of a gigantic sand dune field located in the north-central part of the state, sometimes referred to as the "last prairie" in America. The region is a stark, beautiful landscape spread out over 20,000 acres sandwiched between the Niobrara and the Platte Rivers. Essentially a system of hills and valleys, grass-covered, stabilized sand dune formations rise to heights approaching 400 feet and can extend for lengths of up to twenty miles. Except for the river corridors, the landscape is virtually treeless.

Golfers at Prairie Dunes see a different landscape setting compared to what a golfer sees at Sand Hills. Both courses were built on sand, and golfers at both venues experience wind conditions. However, although Prairie Dunes has native grasses that define the fairways, the overall appearance has a manicured feel to it. By far, the most prominent difference is the presence of trees on the Prairie Dunes course. But these differences don't diminish the historic connection between the two courses.

In Oregon, Mike Keiser found a seaside property that included several hundred acres of sand dunes. The landscape setting wasn't anything like the courses in Kansas and Nebraska; each has its own distinctive character. At Bandon Dunes, the landscape is a more complex eco-system because of the upland conifer forestland that covers half the property. However, like Sand Hills, it is at a remote location, and the design approach Mike embraced was also site-driven. He and Dick Youngscap had similar attitudes—building linksland golf courses would be the harbinger of a different and higher quality experience for golfers. In Mike's case, he felt the focus should be on the retail golfer.

Bob and I ended our conversation that night, and we made plans to meet at Bandon Dunes, where he and I have spent many nights discussing how and why this remarkable resort came into being. It's these discussions and conversations I've had in the past that led to this book. This story is about a golf resort and about the people who took on the various tasks needed to build and operate what is in essence a small community—a village of sorts—that offers a special experience to guests who continue to travel from all over the United States and from offshore locations to play golf at Bandon Dunes. If a guest lives out-of-state, getting to the resort requires planning—sometimes multiple legs of air travel, as there are no non-stop flights to the North Bend Airport, and then the final leg is accomplished by rental car or shuttle bus. If you live in Oregon—in Portland, for example—it's a five-hour drive, both ways.

By 2014, the Bandon Dunes Golf Resort offers golfers many choices: four eighteen-hole courses; a thirteen-hole Par-3 short course; a nine-hole practice course; a forty-acre practice facility with multiple driving ranges, along with a separate chipping area and an oversized putting green; and a special putting facility—the Punchbowl—that officially opened for play on May 20, 2014. And there is an outside chance additional golf courses under Bandon Dunes management might be built in the future, just south of the City of Bandon.

To tell this story, I have to go back in time. That's when the seed for Mike Keiser's vision for Dream Golf took root, and he's been watering it ever since.

Chapter Two

Mike Keiser

Do the right thing, at the right time, in the right place.
—Harry Gordon Selfridge, Department Store Developer

BEFORE THE VISION

At mid-life, Mike Keiser had a dream. He was a successful entrepreneur, but what he really wanted to do was build real Scottish links golf courses in America. A passionate golfer, his interest in golf began during his high school years. Summers, he caddied. Thinking back on that experience, Mike has said: "I learned more than I learned in school at that time." As a caddy, he learned how to get along with different people and to smile a lot. If you spend time with Mike, you learn to appreciate that broad smile and his easy way with people. In communicating, he exhibits a simple approach: his choice of words is selective, to the point. His written communications are usually kept to half a page or less. These traits served him well as his dream became a vision.

As an undergraduate, Mike had played golf on the Amherst College golf team. Eventually, he became a serious student of the game and soon became interested in golf course design. By the mid-1980s, he had played courses all over the United States and some of the ancient courses in the British Isles, like St. Andrews Links and the Royal Dornoch Golf Club. He liked the feel and experience of playing on linksland courses.

Years before he conceived of Bandon Dunes, Mike bought sixty acres of land in New Buffalo, Michigan as a defensive purchase to protect a lakefront property he and his wife, Lindy, owned on Lake Michigan. The property was a wooded parcel that later engaged Mike's budding interest in golf course design. On weekend outings, he and his family hit golf balls in sandy areas scattered among the trees. At the same time, Mike began to clean out the noxious weed growth that ran rampant in the woodland understory.

This desire to clean up a place is rooted in Mike's upbringing. Growing up in East Aurora, about twenty miles from Buffalo, he watched his father convert an apple orchard on their rural property into a tree garden. The orchard was removed and replaced with about 500 trees, mostly Pine species. Watching his father create this special garden instilled in Mike a fundamental value to "always improve the place you're at." Later in life, this blossomed into an interest in conservation.

Some weekends, Howard McKee joined him, and together they worked to clean up the place. Howard was a friend Mike had met when Howard moved to Chicago to plan the 1992 World's Fair. Their families became close when their children attended the same school.

In the late 1980s, Mike decided to build a golf course. The land he bought to protect his lake property investment wasn't large enough for a golf course, but fate intervened and afforded him an opportunity to build a course in his front yard. A thirty-acre parcel contiguous to the sixty acres he already owned came up for sale. He bought it. Now he had enough land for a compact nine-hole course. He liked the courses at Pine Valley, so that became his model. The result was the private Dunes Club, which is acclaimed and nationally ranked by many as the best nine-hole course in the USA.

Both Mike and Howard were dazzled by the transformation of a woodland parcel that went from just another patch of forest to a unique golf course. Prior to the design of the course, Mike solicited Howard's opinion. He didn't use it but, in so doing, laid the groundwork that led to their future partnership and adventures.

A VISION AND PROGRAM

The dream was now a vision. When asked about the origin of his vision, Mike would say, "The vision evolved. My initial thought was: I built the Dunes Club which Howard and his wife Kennon and others appreciated. It was successful, and it was fun (to do and play)." It was not successful in commercial terms, but it was successful in attracting members (in 2013 it had 105 members) and, according to Mike, it could have 200 if he so desired. Mike has also said: "Because the Dunes Club was built by Lake Michigan, on sand and successful in my eyes, I wanted to do one more of these links courses. I also wanted to do it on an ocean side site instead of the Midwest."

The vision was simple, but he needed the right land, and he needed help. So Mike approached Howard. He told him he had looked for land on the East Coast and couldn't find anything acceptable. Would Howard consider helping him find land on the West Coast? Howard was familiar with the Oregon coast because he and his wife still owned a summer home they periodically visited near Lincoln City, Oregon.

But Howard wasn't sure Mike was serious, so he asked him to write out a design program. A few weeks later, Howard got his answer. Mike wanted a minimum of 1,000 acres with breathtaking views. He had also made a list (the Appendix describes the original document) of amenities and critical conditions pertaining to acceptable geographic locations and other general criteria. Simply put, Mike wanted a site by the ocean and the ability to build on sand. Add fescue grass to these two features and you have a true links course.

THE LAND

On his first trip to see the property that became Bandon Dunes, Mike hiked a ridgeline trail to a high point and looked out over a windswept landscape of dunes. It was 1991. What he saw reminded him of links land he had seen playing golf in Scotland, and it brought a big smile to his face. On the spot, he made the decision to buy the property. His gaze wandered over open sand, undulating dunes, waving beach grass, a dark green band of Shore Pines in the distance, and finally the ocean and the horizon. He had to turn his head in both directions to take it all in. The view was stunning. Just right for a golf course. That unforgettable view remained fixed in his memory. Years later, after building several courses elsewhere on the property, he recalled this scene. Maybe, he thought, I'm not done building courses.

Fig. 3: What Mike Saw

FIRST PURCHASE

The land Mike bought had once been part of the Fahy Ranch. Although logged earlier, about half the property had dense stands of second growth timber, primarily marketable Douglas fir and some Sitka spruce. When the Fahy family sold the ranch, it was purchased by a group of local businessmen. They held it for seven years and then sold it to the Bandon Partners, a Seattle-based investment group led by Duke Watson. Plagued by bad luck over the next twenty years, the group tried unsuccessfully to develop the land (they even thought about a golf resort).

When Mike Keiser decided to buy the 1215-acre property, the asking price was five million dollars. Fortune smiled on Mike, and he bought the property for $2.75 million. He had checked off the first axiom for successful development: buy the land at a discount.

Mike was now committed to his vision. He'd thought about what he wanted to do, but the path was unclear. The vision now became an odyssey—one that turned into a series of adventures that never quite seemed to end.

Years later, sitting with Mike, I asked him how big a gamble he thought he was taking. He initially thought he had a "1 in 3 or maybe a 1 in 5 chance of success." But he also had a model for the first course—the Royal Dornoch in Scotland. At the time, he didn't know if he would follow the model, but he knew it had been done before. "I had played the courses and saw lots of golfers playing there. I knew what I wanted; hence, there was a general plan." His plan was simple: build several golf courses, keep Randolph Road as a graveled entry road, install a doublewide trailer for a clubhouse and open for business.

To that, Howard replied, "Where are they going to stay? And then we need a presentable entrance—a nice paved road—and interior roads, bridges to get over creeks, a waterworks (how are we going to flush the toilets?), what are they going to drink? (A potable water supply was needed)." Howard's view was that there had to be a critical nucleus of support facilities designed to a high qualitative standard in order for the place to have a chance to succeed. The attractiveness of the resort needed to reflect a distinctive aura. Guest experiences after playing golf were just as important as their experiences on the golf links. Initially, Mike had been prepared to commit five million of his personal money to the project. On reflection, Mike has admitted that he grudgingly went along with Howard's recommendations. By going along with Howard's views, he gambled twenty million.

In 1999, when the resort opened with 10,000 rounds the first year, Mike knew "we needed all those facilities." Did Mike have doubts? Sure, but he had a backup plan. Denied a development permit, Mike would have built a cheap version of Royal Dornoch. He'd have fenced the land, created pastureland and put out a mob of sheep, as allowed under existing agricultural zoning. The course(s) would have had no irrigation and no clubhouse. Golfers could have come and played a rudimentary form of golf on a private Sheep Ranch, like the origins of the game. They could have stayed in Bandon, Coos Bay or elsewhere. It wouldn't have been as "polished" as what Mike actually built, but it was a viable plan. In truth, Mike viewed the proposed resort as something between a "speculation and a folly."

SECOND PURCHASES

Mike wasn't finished buying land near the resort. Around the same time as his purchase of the Fahy Ranch property, Mike also bought a ninety-seven-acre parcel on the Bullards Beach Spit along the west side of the Coquille River estuary from Moore Mill, a local company. Howard had begun discussions with the Oregon Parks and Recreation Department (OPRD), aka State Parks. State Parks were interested in the parcel, and Howard thought it could be useful in a potential land trade. It was purchased with the intention of conveying it to ORPD at some future date. Later, it became part of a potential land trade with the State Parks as part of another golf course facility Mike was thinking of building south of the city of Bandon.

As the proposed resort became public knowledge, land speculators began to buy nearby land parcels. In response, Mike began proactively buying outlying parcels as defensive land purchases. Two of his first purchases were industrial zoned properties—a twelve-acre concrete batch plant and a ten-acre parcel with a wetland pond and a low-level gold extraction operation—located immediately south of Weiss Estates, a rural residential subdivision situated on the south side of Fahys Lake. Acquiring the properties gave the resort a water right, an off-site storage area and, most importantly, protected the resort from future industrial development along Highway 101.

During the 1996 public hearing on the resort's development permit application, Mike bought 400 acres of land (the Schuman property). Originally part of the Fahy Ranch, the property expanded the resort boundary to the north. The purchase was a linchpin: the southern portion allowed greater flexibility in the routing and design of the Bandon Dunes course, and the remaining acreage became the Pacific Dunes course.

From 1997 to 2003, additional properties were purchased for varying reasons. The acquisition of several properties along Randolph Road between Seven Devils Road and Highway 101 allowed for a re-alignment and improvement of Randolph Road as the main entry to the resort. Other land acquisitions along the west side of Seven Devils Road south of Randolph Road expanded the resort boundary, ultimately providing building sites for resort staff housing. Mike wasn't done. Without the purchase of the PP&L property, there would have been fewer golf courses at Bandon Dunes.

In the 1970s, Pacific Power & Light (PP&L) owned 700 acres that straddled Whiskey Run Road, a local road located north of the initial resort property. Mike had tried to buy the south portion (325 acres), but a local company, Mast, purchased the land for its timber value. After Mast had harvested the timber, Mike bought the land in 2000 to fill out the resort property ownership north to Whiskey Run Road. A few years later, the Old Macdonald course found a home on this land.

Shortly thereafter, Mike and another Chicago businessman purchased the remaining 375 acres located north of Whiskey Run Road. It's referred to as the Sheep Ranch. The resort employees sometimes refer to this parcel as Area 51—no one is supposed to go there. A couple of years after this purchase, Mike had Tom Doak (the architect for the Pacific Dunes) design a wilderness golf course on the ocean side of the property. You tee off, hit balls until you reach a green and call it good, and then play the next hole. You can make the game as serious as you want, or only play for the pure pleasure of walking along a great scenic stretch of coastline.

There were other defensive or opportunistic purchases. A 120-acre cranberry farm, located along the eastern edge of the resort adjacent to the driving ranges, was acquired in 2001. It has a well and a water right. It's been used as a plant nursery and is extremely useful as a storage yard for construction materials. Mike has spent millions of dollars outside the resort in order to protect his original investment and, in the process, has preserved some of the rural character and natural beauty of the surrounding area.

PROJECT FEASIBILITY

Market research didn't affect Mike's decision to build the resort. He'd bought the land based on a personal assessment, and now it was time to get on with it. Howard, however, wanted a second opinion, and he turned to a consultant he knew in Portland.

David Leland was an old friend from twenty years ago. Dave's firm, the Leland Consulting Group, had golf resort development experience both in Oregon and nationally. Howard's decision was calculated. He knew he needed some type of marketing study in order to satisfy statewide land use goal issues and questions about the economic impact of building the resort. Getting an assessment from Dave was valuable in defining the parameters for more detailed market analysis that was needed later. As soon as Mike closed on the land sale, Howard introduced Dave Leland to Mike.

Everyone recognized that the chosen property was off the beaten path. It was remote from the major metropolitan centers in Oregon—Portland, Salem and Eugene. Access by air was limited. The local airport only handled small airplanes. The closest major airport was in North Bend, a coastal community almost half an hour away by motor vehicle. However, the planned resort was accessible directly off Highway 101—Oregon's scenic coastal highway. Interstate tourists traveling south from Canada and Washington State, or north from California, would have direct access to the resort entry road. Still, getting people to the resort appeared to be a major problem.

Mike, without revealing his vision for the property, had Howard hire the Leland Consulting Group to undertake a feasibility study for an eighteen-hole golf course. The consultant concluded that the probability of getting sufficient rounds of golf at a high enough rate would be extremely difficult. The property was too remote from metropolitan markets in Oregon and nationally. Golfers needed to take multiple flights to reach North Bend from outside Oregon. Dave felt it was improbable that golfers would put up with this kind of inconvenience, and then have to rent a car or take some form of shuttle service for another half hour trip to reach the resort.

The feasibility study was not encouraging; the findings did not support building a golf course near Bandon. Mike's response, as Dave recalled, was something to the effect of: "Well, I play golf, I have some friends that play golf, I think I will build it anyway." Years later, Mike gave a speech to the business community in Portland. Responding to a question about how to accomplish golf development, whether or not a market study is needed, and why he didn't get a market study for the Bandon Dunes project, Mike's response was: "Why should I spend $50,000 on having a market survey done to tell me there is no market, when I'm going to build it anyway?"

Chapter Three

Howard McKee

He always had his eye on the prize.
—Don Ivy, Coos Bay, Oregon

PERSONA

Building golf courses requires land, money, design talent and permits. At this point, Mike had the right land and enough money. Talent came in the form of Howard McKee.

Building the Dunes Club was simple; Bandon Dunes wasn't. Permitting—that's where simple became complicated and difficult. In Oregon, building golf courses meant Mike had to build a destination resort as defined by state statute. He and Howard would need lots more talent, especially legal.

Howard had years of large-scale planning and design experience but no experience in golf resort development. Like many successful men and architects, Howard had an enormous sense of self-esteem. He was intelligent, self-confident and had a dual personality. In his stage persona, he appeared to be highly extroverted; his charisma did not go unnoticed, and he used it effectively to accomplish his professional agenda. In contrast, his private, introverted persona reflected strongly-held personal values. As he formed a work plan and agenda for the proposed resort, Howard examined his internal values and came face to face with his soul.

Bandon Dunes became, for him, "soul work." There is much in contemporary literature about the soul. As a subject, it arouses curiosity and is difficult to define. Many people who worked with Howard were interviewed for this book, and each had their own way of defining soul work. To understand why Howard considered the odyssey as soul work, one has to look at the values he held. First, one has to examine his early life.

He grew up on a small farm in rural West Virginia in the 1940s and was the youngest of four siblings. Left to his own devices, he was always outside playing in the woodlands, meadows, or a sandbox. Speaking about his childhood, Howard always said this sense of freedom to do what he wanted in his early years made him curious. His "sandbox" was a world filled with nature, farm fields, and not store-bought toys. This curiosity propelled his explorations and allowed him to shape and create his childhood play world. Little did he know that these early experiences and attitudes would blossom and lead him to discover a larger world.

Howard found himself in the shadow of his older brothers and sister, who was fifteen when Howard was born. His sister married early, in her twenties, and soon had children. Howard often said that he felt closer in age and relationship to his sister's children than to his siblings. His brothers' and sister's interests tended to focus on family and, in the case of his brothers, high school sports. Although he had the tall, lean build of an athlete, Howard never took to sports. Instead, he excelled at academics.

His father owned a painting company, and his mother was a homemaker. His father died when Howard was in high school. This put some financial pressure on the family household. In addition, the family lived in an era when coal mining was one of the main industries and employment opportunities for young men out of school. These experiences, coupled with the economic, social and cultural setting he grew up in, gave Howard an appreciation of nature firsthand and an awareness of the hardscrabble life found in West Virginia.

However, his character traits, along with his native intelligence, formed a foundation for early growth as a leader. Howard was the class president of a small student body in high school. Encouraged by his teachers, he sought and won a college scholarship, becoming the first in his family to go to college. Dropped off on the steps of Columbia College by his older brothers, who drove him up to New York City, Howard found himself competing with students who had enjoyed educational opportunities that were not available to him. Mentored by many of the professors who encountered his intellect and interest in life, he blossomed intellectually and socially during his college years.

New York City was a treasure box for Howard. There he found unlimited resources to expand his base of knowledge and cultural experiences beyond his imagination. He now saw a vast array of opportunities available to him. It was a much larger sandbox than he enjoyed back home. He spent ten years at Columbia, earning various degrees. Graduating with degrees in economics, architecture, urban planning and design, and after finishing a scholarship at the école des Beaux Arts in Paris, Howard was ready to go to work.

The next twenty years found him working for Skidmore, Owings and Merrill (SOM). He started in New York City, and later assignments took him to many metropolitan cities across the United States.

Howard had his own vision in mind when he began working on the proposed destination resort. Trained as an architect, Howard was not interested in solely designing buildings. He was more interested in broader issues, such as how a building fit into its surrounding environment. His intellectual curiosity led him to question the purpose and function of a building or the relationships between multiple buildings that make up a complex. This background, enhanced by student travels in Europe, propelled his professional career in a unconventional direction compared to architects who seek success and fame due to their building design style. The power of his vision manifested itself in his leadership style. His managerial skills grew out of his role in two major freeway projects.

A major urban design and freeway study in Baltimore, Maryland gave Howard the opportunity to lead and manage an interdisciplinary design team. As a protégé of Nat Owings, one of the founders of Skidmore, Owings and Merrill, Howard worked with an Urban Design Concept Team (UDCT) from 1966 to 1971. This project was a stepping-stone and led to another freeway project in Portland, Oregon.

The UDCT project used an interdisciplinary and collaborative approach to transportation and community problem solving and design. The team was tasked with a mission to design a freeway integral with the urban fabric of the city. It was highly experimental and sought to create a high-quality design, and minimize neighborhood disruption while maximizing social and economic benefits for local residents and businesses.

The UDCT project provided Howard with a clear and deep understanding of the benefits gained in a design team approach. Here was where he learned to create conditions in the workplace that fostered collaboration. This project was accomplished in a highly charged political atmosphere; this gave Howard keen insight and experience on how to maneuver and guide a controversial project through a maze of political minefields. Project completed, he took on another freeway project.

Under the auspices of SOM's Portland office, Howard formed a design team—the Environmental Study Group—to study the proposed Mt. Hood Freeway. The team he assembled in 1971 challenged conventional thinking regarding freeway and public transportation solutions. Howard's presence brought a new, outside perspective that resonated with local government officials and with his professional colleagues. The Environmental Study Group published several reports on the proposed freeway and on alternative modes of public transit. When reviewed by the City of Portland and all concerned, public opinion opposed building the freeway. It was never built.

An economic downturn in Portland resulted in the demise of the SOM Portland office in the early 1980s. Howard initially considered relocating to the New York office as a new partner. However, Nat Owings advised Howard to take on a World's Fair project. So Howard moved to Chicago, where he led the state of Illinois's planning study for the proposed 1992 World's Fair in Chicago. Unfortunately, the World's Fair ended up being highly controversial. The state scrapped the plan in 1987.

Howard remained in Chicago, but he left SOM and became a private consultant. A local construction company—McHugh—called and asked if he would go to Russia and help them out on a proposed bank project. Howard took on this overseas assignment and would travel back and forth between Russia and the U.S. until the mid-1990s. The work was financially rewarding, but Howard became disillusioned. The Russians were only going through the motions in order to obtain international funding to support proposed projects that were bogus.

His friendship with Mike Keiser altered the course of Howard's life. In the late 1980s, Mike purchased two properties in Oregon prior to buying the Fahy Ranch land. These earlier projects allowed both men to establish a working relationship that blossomed when they turned their joint attention to the proposed destination resort. One of the properties was a cattle ranch, and there was plenty of room for golf courses.

CASCADE RANCH

While searching for suitable golf course land out west, Howard first looked at a cattle ranch near Medford, Oregon. Howard was not initially impressed with the land, but he reconsidered, called Mike, Mike flew out and, in 1988, Mike bought about 12,000 acres of rangeland. They renamed it Cascade Ranch.

Under the previous owner, the land had deteriorated. The property had been heavily logged, and the pastureland had been leased to local ranchers who had overgrazed the property. Mike now got a firsthand look at a degraded landscape.

On the positive side, the ranch was blessed with a system of open channels that conveyed water from several lakes for irrigation use on ranch pastures. It was a million-dollar system, but it was in disrepair and defunct. Over time, the irrigation system was repaired and the pastures improved, resulting in a viable cattle operation. Mike now got to see Howard's skills being put to actual use on the ground. Watching Howard, Mike gained an understanding about macro-scale land restoration. With this knowledge, Mike's interest in land conservation grew.

Howard was also thinking about development opportunities. The property was unusual: it included the small, unincorporated rural community known as Lake Creek. In time, Howard decided to prepare a master plan, and he asked me to assist in this effort. In many ways, this planning effort foreshadowed the process and master planning for Bandon Dunes. We envisioned adding a few more residential structures to encourage limited cottage industry use in an expanded Lake Creek Center. It already had a village atmosphere owing to the presence of a rural fire station, grange and historic museum. The plan also incorporated a proposed recreation lake, a conference center, a vineyard and winery, recreational vehicle park and limited campsite development.

With a preliminary master plan in hand, Howard approached the Jackson County planning department to discuss the idea and see if the county would support it. The county responded by advising Howard that the ranch was zoned exclusively for agricultural and forestry (the Bandon Dunes property had the same zoning). We were advised to file an application for a zone change. However, the planning department decided they needed to hold a public information meeting as a preliminary step in the application process.

On the day of the scheduled public meeting, Howard and I spent most of the day exploring the resort property. Late in the afternoon, we drove to the North Bend airport. We were supposed to meet Mike and a party of golfers who were flying in from back east. As the Learjet touched down on the airport tarmac, Howard and I walked out to meet Mike. We exchanged hellos and boarded a plane that would take us to Medford—a flight that normally took about one hour.

Settling into leather chairs, we were each handed a beer. This was going to be an OK trip. The plane turned around, taxied to the end of the runway, and the pilot pushed the throttles forward. The jet, increasing in speed, was just about to leave the ground when there was a loud clank and bang from outside the aircraft. The pilot aborted the takeoff, taxied back to the terminal, got out and inspected the right engine. Looking out the window, we watched as the pilot tried to turn the turbine blades. Nothing moved.

A bird had flown into the engine and had jammed the intake fan blades. Luckily, the plane had not left the ground. A Learjet with engines mounted on both sides of the fuselage needs to be several hundred feet off the ground if an engine is lost during takeoff. The pilot needs sufficient air space in order to recover from the spin that occurs from the unbalanced engine thrust. The next morning at breakfast, the pilot told us how close we had come to a fatal air accident.

Howard and I still had a meeting to attend. Another aircraft was found, pressed into service, and we took off again. Howard called ahead to inform the county planners we would be delayed. Arriving at the Medford airport, a limousine was waiting to take us to Lake Creek—a trip that took half an hour.

We were late, but the assemblage had waited. We entered the meeting hall, and Howard calmly walked to the front of the hall, turned, faced the audience and proceeded to give a twenty-minute summary of our proposed master plan. Then he asked for questions.

All he got was a heavy load of pushback. Instead of questions, most people rose and attacked the plan because they felt the proposal violated the existing zoning. Many believed bringing city folks to the area would cause traffic congestion on the local rural road system. A county official, possibly one of the commissioners, stood up and spoke against the proposal. At that point, Howard knew he had lost the argument and application before we could write it and submit it. The notion of a mixed land use plan that sought to blend together agricultural, forestry, recreation and cottage industries was dead on arrival that evening.

There was nothing more we could do to advance a development plan for Cascade Ranch. We went to bed, got up in the morning and flew back to North Bend, and then drove back to the resort. As the airplane lifted off the ground, Jackson County and Cascade Ranch (Mike later sold the ranch for a profit and redirected the funds into building out Bandon Dunes) were no longer of interest to us. All our energies would now be concentrated on preparing a development and re-zoning application for the Coos County Planning Department.

Chapter Four

Development Philosophy

Bandon Dunes wasn't a project for Howard, it was soul work.
—Kennon McKee, Chicago, Illinois

PLAYING IN THE SANDBOX

Professional work can be demanding, yet rewarding. Past experience working with Howard had taught me it could also be exciting and immensely pleasurable. Collaboration can be an exciting process if people buy into the process. When you get people engaged and committed to what they are doing, they take ownership and pride in the shared products they produce.

Sometimes, however, collaboration is just a buzzword. People talk about collaborating and working with other people and other firms. Working on the Bandon Dunes project, I experienced collaboration in about as pure a form as possible. It is difficult, if not impossible, for members in a multi-disciplinary team to set aside their egos. Fortunately, when people are encouraged to put forth suggestions and unconventional ideas—good and bad—freely, there is a sense of joy and freedom of expression that, many times, is missing in the problem-solving process.

Problems arose, but we fixed them immediately. Sometimes it was due to bad information; other times it resulted from poor communication and coordination miscues. But, for the most part, team members refrained from pointing fingers at each other. Nobody made excuses, mistakes were admitted immediately, problems solved and the project moved forward. Things still went off track at times, but productivity and progress continued. Best of all, the resulting design was better.

Howard had an impressive set of skills. He was a visionary, and he was articulate in communicating his vision to others. Among his many talents was the ability to instill a sense of *esprit de corps* within the team. You always had the feeling you were working with him and not for him because he was exceedingly careful about how he dealt with people, what he said to them and how he said it. He was always challenging people to do their best. But if you said something stupid, he'd call you on it.

There was another aspect to this notion of challenging people. It can be a two-way street. One of the problems associated with corporate organizations is that people can get too comfortable with their colleagues and supervisors. Sometimes everyone begins to think along the same lines and reinforce each other's attitudes and decisions. This can have terrible consequences. Howard, in challenging team members, was also inviting his co-workers to "think" more deeply about our design process, our products and the outcomes. He definitely had an agenda, but sometimes it didn't turn out exactly the way he imagined.

In team meetings, when discussing various ideas or approaches to a problem or a design issue, occasionally a stupid idea was put forward. Howard would yell out, "Air Ball!" Immediately, the room would fill with laughter. And the group would move on to another idea that might provide an insight and, perhaps, resolve the issue at hand. Other times, a bad idea sparked someone else to build a better idea on it and move the discussion forward. Howard wanted thinkers, not followers, contributing to the process.

Howard truly enjoyed his role, but he was also thinking about Bandon Dunes in a different light. Howard realized he was nearing the end of his professional career. He knew it would take several years to realize a final product, and he might not be around to see the end. Was he thinking about what he was doing in terms of legacy? I don't think so, but he was becoming more introspective, more philosophical in his work. This was soul work.

SOUL WORK

Author Thomas Moore has written about the soul as that place within us that seeks experiences that have "genuineness and depth." These tend to be experiences we remember and those memories we desire because, as Moore has pointed out, they "touch the heart." Defining the soul is not easy. Most lexicon definitions refer to the soul as the spiritual or immaterial part of us.

If our soul is immortal: where does it come from and where does it go when we die? One view is that our individual soul is residue originating from a well of consciousness—an awareness or perception that there is something underlying our human, physical existence. This perception can become a desire in our life—an attraction to reconnect with that consciousness which is universal in nature.

This was a topic Howard could speak about for hours. He did. And, for me, these conversations reflected his personal search for a sense of "connectivity" and purposefulness in his life. While these conversations were philosophical, he was also searching for archetype symbols attached to the mythology associated with a belief in the universal consciousness. He would find a symbolic metaphor as the project progressed.

Pragmatically, his soul work had to do with his personal value system— what he deeply felt and believed in. Until now, he had always considered his professional work in terms of "projects." The freeway studies; a twenty-block urban design project in Calgary, Alberta; the Chicago World's Fair; planning and building a new town in Saudi Arabia; and, later, private consultant work in Russia: all of these projects had engaged him on several levels. Bandon Dunes was different.

First of all, he had no experience in planning a golf resort; he brought no preconceptions or a design template from previous work. Second, the acreage was extensive. Third, our investigations had revealed the sacred quality attributed to the land by the Native People. And fourth, this was the first time he had an opportunity to design a project in a setting dominated by nature. Bandon Dunes was a project unlike anything he'd done before.

If it wasn't just another project, what was it? It was artwork. This was an opportunity for him to "sculpt" a work of art using the land as his base material. He wasn't an artist in the conventional mode; he didn't paint or sculpt in stone. But he admired artists and had bought several paintings and sculptures in the past. He also began to think about how artwork could enhance the guest experience, and he planted the seed for an eventual artwork program and collection at the resort.

At Bandon Dunes, Howard found his values aligned with previous values held by the Native People; his values resonated with their values. It was an opportunity to find his "true nature" through his exploration of the nature and spirit of the landscape setting. Without a doubt, he became spiritually in touch with this coastal site. Spiritually, there is a belief that every place has both tangible and intangible aspects that define the particulars of that place. Howard's respect for how the Native People had managed their lands was important to our task. It found expression in how we thought about land stewardship, but, first of all, about the idea of placemaking.

PLACEMAKING & STEWARDS

Were we into placemaking? Absolutely. Placemaking is a contemporary term used by urban designers, city planners and architects when they are referring to the creation of interesting places for people. Most of the time it's in the context of community design. However, at Bandon Dunes, Howard was keenly aware that a "place" of significant value to people was actually in existence. He knew that people develop a sense of a place through personal experience and knowledge of a particular place. This insight would become a first principle in the way we prepared the resort master plan and later designed the infrastructure for the resort.

Professional planners and designers, more so in the past than today, have always talked about wanting to infuse a project or space with a "sense of place." Bandon Dunes already had a sense of place. In the master planning phase of our work, we did not have a conscious placemaking goal in mind, but we did want to preserve the "sense of place and spirit" that existed.

And we came to believe this meant restraint in architectural design and sensitivity in the placement of buildings in the landscape.

The landscape architectural profession refers to this sense or spirit of the place as the *genius loci*. Every landscape has a distinctive *genius loci*. As we became more aware of what we were observing and how we felt about the site, both of us recognized there was an intangible quality present that was of prime importance to our site analyses.

Land planning is both science and art. Besides collecting data, you have to walk the land and pay attention to what is actually there. It's really about developing a feeling for the land and trying to understand the factors that formed the landscape setting.

This recognition resulted in our examination of the property's historical record. We wanted to know how the land had been used in the past and know more about the relationship of the Native People to this particular piece of land.

Early in the project, Howard contacted the Coquille Indian Tribal office in North Bend. Don Ivy, the Tribal Cultural Resources Program Coordinator, wanted us to do an archeological survey because Native People had used this part of the coast for summer encampments. The tribe was concerned about potential harm to cultural artifacts that might be disturbed or damaged during future resort construction.

We agreed to their request. As part of the survey, we investigated mitigation measures to protect archeological resources. This concern became a major issue when golf course construction was proposed along the edge of the terrace bluffs overlooking Whiskey Run Beach, just north of Cut Creek. Later, when several golf holes were located along the bluff edge, we had to find a way to satisfy the tribe's concerns.

S tewards take care of things. When applied to the landscape, stewardship implies that someone is looking after the land and inherent resource values. Nowadays, everyone is talking about stewardship, conservation and that buzzword—sustainability. Everyone wants a sustainable marketing approach for his or her product or service. Impressed by the beauty and the spirit of the land, Howard began to think of himself as a land steward in the context of his mission. The last thing he wanted was to despoil this site, to overpower the land with cars, buildings, and people. To do so would diminish the natural resource values that gave the land its beauty and spirit.

PART TWO

THE PLAN

We went in having nothing, we had no cards (to play).
—Howard McKee, *Dream Golf*

Fig. 4: Main Lodge & Clubhouse and Resort Core Facilities, 2013
Aerial photo courtesy of Bandon Dunes

Chapter Five

Due Diligence

TOGETHER AGAIN

After Mike Keiser purchased the resort property, Howard needed a site survey. It wasn't a legal survey. What he needed was a natural resources inventory. That's why I was hired.

Sitting in my Portland office in the fall of 1992, Howard and I put together a work plan and schedule. Later, we drove down to Bandon. I walked the land, saw what was there, took pictures and made notes. This knowledge and an understanding of the relationships among the resources allowed us to make decisions about what uses were best suited at various locations on the property. This information formed the base data used in our site analysis. The master plan for the resort was grounded in this inventory.

It took several months to accomplish the inventory, organize my impressions, analyze my thoughts and arrive at some conclusions. After completing the inventory and an analysis of the data, I prepared a series of drawings that illustrated key site constraints and development opportunities for specific uses. These summary drawings gave us excellent graphic tools, which became useful in explaining to regulators, citizens, environmentalists and decision-makers how we arrived at the proposed master plan.

Time spent during the inventory also allowed me to rekindle my relationship with Howard, a mentor earlier in my professional career. Both our careers had taken us in different directions, but now our life paths had come full circle. Unknown to either of us, Bandon Dunes became the capstone to both our professional careers.

We formed an odd couple because we thought and processed information differently. Howard was a logical, linear thinker. His style was to present an idea, the facts of the matter and the rationale that supported the idea. This was his way of convincing people his idea was the right one.

On the other hand, I thought about things more intuitively. The five-hour drives to Bandon from Portland often became work sessions. To Howard's dismay, I sometimes interrupted him before he was finished, jumping to his conclusion or suggesting an alternative. This irritated him to no end.

But, to our surprise, there was a hidden benefit in our exchanges. It was an unconventional method of discourse, but we made it work to our advantage. It became a very efficient and effective method of exploring alternative ways to deal with project issues. We were able to cut through mushy thinking. This became our personalized way of communicating and getting to a solution in the shortest time possible. We could have a harsh dialogue without bruising each other's egos.

Most of the time, we used this communication technique privately, but sometimes we lapsed into this verbal jousting in public. When others were present, I often wondered what they thought was happening between us, considering the fact we were good friends. However, we were in complete agreement on our immediate need to build a consultant team. At this point, we needed a land use attorney.

HOWARD'S GANG

Years ago, a marketing consultant told me there were three key axioms to successful development: buy the land at a discount; hire the best planning and design talent available; and prepare a superlative plan and design. Mike had already checked off the first box. Now we needed the best people.

Ordinarily, resort developers hire firms that have established records for planning and designing successful resorts. This didn't happen at Bandon Dunes. Howard didn't want or need a big-time firm. He immediately ruled out hiring a major firm as the overhead and administrative costs would be too high. As important as fees were, Howard (a minor partner in the venture) also wanted to minimize the layers of communication and review that result in large fees and lengthy timeframes. By handpicking seasoned individuals, he assembled the team piecemeal, and in so doing checked off the second box—hire the best talent.

Howard made a few calls in his search for a land use attorney. He didn't want just a good attorney; he wanted the best person he could find. He ended up short-listing three individuals. All were well qualified, but Al Johnson stood out.

Like Howard, Al liked difficult challenges, and the fact that Bandon Dunes could become a controversial project did not faze him. Al had always wanted to be a land use attorney. After graduating from a Midwest college in the mid-1960s, he was recruited to work on a weekly newspaper on the East Coast. During the three years he lived in Connecticut, he developed an interest in land use law. Like many young people in the 1960s, Al found himself attracted to the environmental movement. At the same time, as a young journalist who couldn't afford to live in the town where he and his wife worked, Al was struck by how often environmental rhetoric was commandeered by privileged suburbanites—liberal as well as conservative—to exclude affordable housing, keep busing away from their school districts, and generally confine the costs of living in megalopolis to the region's cities—like Bridgeport, Danbury, and Norwalk. He found it fascinating to see the civil rights movement and people's territorial interests collide and reshape societal trends. One of his last editorials before leaving for law school was entitled "American Apartheid."

Al was also smitten with Oregon. He had visited Oregon in 1963 during a break from college when he delivered a taxicab to a forest ranger who lived in Enterprise. Remembering the scenic beauty of the Wallowa Mountains, sometimes referred to as the "Alps of Oregon," Al returned to Oregon in 1970 and enrolled at the University of Oregon. He studied law, graduating three years later, and rapidly transitioned from general practitioner to a concentration on land use, administrative law, and appellate work. The transition was speeded along by a three-year stint hearing appeals for the state's new Land Conservation and Development Commission, during which he drafted dozens of opinions, including leading cases on the topic that got him started: affordable housing. His diverse clientele included developers of market-rate and affordable housing, industrial and commercial developers, nonprofits and churches, local governments, interest groups, and state agencies. Much of this work was in southern Oregon, and along the way he had met Bill Grile, the planning director for Coos County.

Al had served as special counsel to Coos County at one time, and he had worked with other local government authorities. He knew the land use landscape, the environmentalists, and the political decision-making climate on the South Coast. He was a natural choice. As the project progressed, Howard would say, "Al was unflappable." Generally true but, as we shall see, there were exceptions.

When asked why Howard hired him, Al replied, "I don't know, he talked to quite a few people." On reflection, besides Al's experience in land use matters and political connections on South Coast, he had an amazing ability and agility with words, both vocal and written.

It's also been said Howard liked Al because of his low-key appearance. Al occasionally wore a sweater and looked "down valley" as opposed to a suited attorney from Portland. The truth of the matter is that Al got the job because he was the best-qualified person.

Now we had a team of three. With Al onboard we began discussions with the Coos County Planning Department and Bill Grile, its director. We needed to establish the ground rules as well as the exact application requirements. There were issues Al needed to resolve in order to ensure all the legal procedures were followed to the letter. A misstep could spell disaster since land use decisions in Oregon can be appealed.

Therefore, as we began our diligent, background studies, we looked at the past natural and cultural history of the property. Because we spent so much time in Bandon talking with various individuals, we came to appreciate and understand the dynamics of the local community. All of this was critical to shaping our interactions with people and businesses that would be affected by the proposed destination resort.

NATURAL AND CULTURAL HISTORY

Nature and time shaped the South Coast of Oregon. A billion years ago this land did not exist. In the beginning, there was one continent, and at some point it broke apart. As time passed, the earth's crust broke up into pieces; islands were formed; they changed location geographically, and, over hundreds of millions of years, additional land mass was added to the west coastline of North America. The coastline of North America was once situated somewhere between present-day Idaho and Montana.

Then, around sixty million years ago, tectonic plate movement caused uplifts; multiple episodes of volcanic eruptions and sedimentary depositions followed. In more recent geologic time, glaciers formed and melted, causing significant fluctuations in the sea levels. The West Coast saw sea levels lowered to depths several hundred feet below present-day sea levels. This geologic activity culminated in the emergence of uplifted marine terrace formations that are a distinctive feature along Oregon's South Coast.

These marine terraces are platforms on which dune systems formed, due to continual deposition and erosion of base materials that created extensive layers of sand composed of igneous or metamorphic rock, usually granite. Wind and water shaped these coastal sand dunes with a little help from temperature fluctuations. Ocean tidal fluctuations also played their part. At high tide, breaking waves scoop up sand and deposit it on the beach. Then, at low tide, the water recedes, ocean breezes pick up the sand and the wind carries the sand inland, forming dunes.

These dunal formations and associated marine terraces extend along almost half of the Oregon coastline. One particular formation—the Whiskey Run Terrace—has historical significance. Named for a coastal creek and the presence of gold mining during the early 1850s, this local coastline between Cape Arago and Cape Blanco was home to many Native American bands and tribes, including the Coquille and Coos people thousands of years before the European settlers came west.

Coastal physiographic features, such as headlands and terraces, were significant to the indigenous people. The first occupants, the Native People embraced a "worldview" much different from worldviews held by later European settlers. The native worldview was strongly tied to the land and what they could see in their view shed. Headlands became spatial markers, defining boundaries for native bands and tribal groups. Native People also felt they couldn't and didn't own the land; they were caretakers.

How the original occupants arrived along the southern coastline is debatable. There are two theories to consider: the dominant theory can be termed "the inland corridor theory." The overall thesis and archaeological evidence suggest that pre-historic man came to North America in the late Pleistocene or early Holocene epoch, approximately 30,000 BC, using a migration corridor in the Aleutian Islands when sea levels had exposed what is known as the Bering Strait Land Bridge. These migrations, moving from north to south and west to east, occupied and settled North America and, eventually, Central and South America.

Another theory, "the coastal migration theory," has emerged to explain how Native People may have settled the Pacific coastline. This theory is attributed to Dennis L. Jenkins, an archaeologist who works at the University of Oregon. In his capacity as the field school supervisor for the Oregon State Museum of Anthropology/Museum of Natural and Cultural History, and also the director of the University of Oregon's Northern Great Basin Field School, Dennis has undertaken field studies and site excavations that have led to revisions in the dating of human settlement in North America. He believes early man may actually have migrated southward along the North American coast using skin boats or other watercraft.

In the past, around 15,000 to 13,000 BC, the coastline of North America was perhaps as many as ten miles farther west, and the exposed coastal land mass could have been as many as 300 to 450 feet lower. This may have occurred during a geologic era when much of the northern North American continent was covered with ice. As the glaciers melted, sea level rose. The fluctuation in the rise and fall of sea level over time presented an opportunity for intermittent migration along this early littoral zone. An available and diverse abundance of ocean resources found in the intertidal zone provided a ready supply of nutritional sustenance for these nomads as they sought out new lands to occupy.

This hypothesis is difficult to prove since there is, as yet, little or no physical evidence. As with other coastal areas thought to have been inhabited, such as the former "Doggerland" connecting Great Britain with the European mainland, any evidence of earlier settlement in the fluctuating littoral zone was submerged when the ocean levels rose over time. However, the diversity of language, oral history and traditions among the native coastal bands and tribes tends to support the notion that both inland and coastal migration routes are valid theories.

The European "discovery" of the Northwest Coast saw the collision of two disparate cultures. Europeans recognizing the rich natural resources came to trap, trade, mine and establish permanent settlements. The discovery of gold in California in 1848 unleashed hordes of adventurers who, after booking passage on ships, sailed around Cape Horn to seek their fortunes in the gold fields. Other settlers were traveling west by wagon train. Some found their way to the Oregon Territories to homestead free government land. By 1850, gold miners were panning for gold in Oregon's Rogue River, leading to one of the last Indian wars and Oregon's own "trail of tears" as Native Americans were removed from their ancestral lands and herded onto distant reservations. This event would be one of the main factors in fomenting more hostile feelings and eventually warfare between the European settlers and the Native People.

Gold was found at Whiskey Run Creek, at the north end of today's Bandon Dunes Golf Resort, two years later. An account in *The Coos and Coquille: A Northwest Coast Historical Anthropology* tells how that watercourse got its name:

> Whiskey Run…derives its name from a very ludicrous circumstance. A miner from Empire City one day, bringing with him half a barrel of Whiskey, having placed this in a conspicuous position, and probably having imbibed as much to come up and have a drink, but "all hands" refused. Many of them knew that if they tasted Whiskey, good-bye to any more work for that day…"Whiskey! Run ye devils; whiskey, run;" but "Look here!" and he pulled the faucet out of the bung, and let the whiskey run out onto the dry sand. Now, no honest, industrious hard working black-sand miner, or in fact any other respectable man, could stand for that…Away goes the pan…away they flew to save the precious fluid.

Black sand found at the Whiskey Run Beach contained the gold. Miners flocked to the bluffs overlooking the creek, and the site quickly turned into a mining camp. The camp, in turn, quickly grew into the gold rush town of Randolph. In no time, the town grew to about 1,000 residents. Within a year, winter storms had washed away the rich black sand that held the gold, and the town disappeared as quickly as it had arrived. A few residents lingered on, tearing up the wood boarded structures and burning them for fuel. Nature quickly took over, and the area became covered with gorse and beach grass.

Later in the early 1860s, gold was also found in Cut Creek, just south of Whiskey Run Creek. Cabins for miners and a cookhouse were constructed on nearby dunes for use by Chinese and European immigrant miners. A plank road over the dune fields was built to provide all-weather access to the mouth of Cut Creek. The exploitation of this valuable resource—monetary gold—was short-lived at both creek locations. Today the lands adjacent to Whiskey River Creek and Cut Creek continue to generate wealth, but the coinage is in greens fees and other credit card charges at a golf resort.

Conflict over resource exploitation and different cultural perspectives ultimately resulted in full-scale warfare between the two cultures—Native People and the settlers. It was an unwinnable conflict for the Native People. Disease had already decimated the indigenous population, probably to the extent that up to ninety percent of some villages died from diseases introduced by the Europeans.

Settlement continued during the ongoing Indian conflicts and warfare. An extensive forested watershed on what later became the resort property fed Fahys Lake. Around 1853–54, two local residents named Stacey and Fundy dammed Fahy Creek as it flowed out of Fahys Lake. There they built the first sawmill in Coos County. A year later, Edward Fahy, an Irish immigrant, purchased the mill and the surrounding forest and dune lands. Logging of first growth timber commenced, resulting in the establishment of a local town center. By the 1890s, the timber was gone, ranching supplanted logging and continued until the late 1920s or early 1930s. By then Fahyville was a distant memory. In the 1950s, the Fahy Ranch passed out of Fahy family ownership.

For forty years, the ranch land lay fallow, resting, biding time for a reawakening. Farther south, the coastal settlement of Bandon continued to thrive on the area's fishing and timber industries.

A COMMUNITY IN TRANSITION

Bandon—or Bandon-by-the-Sea, as the city is sometimes called—is a small coastal community in southern Oregon, about 100 miles north of the California border. In 2007, the population of Bandon was slightly over 3000 people. Until the 1980s, Bandon had a viable timber and fishing economy. A logger required no more than a high school education, sometimes not even that. Young men dropped out of school to work in the woods. Back then, a logger made $30,000–$35,000 a year, enough to support a middle-class family. Skilled loggers made nearly double. Although the work was physically demanding and dangerous, life was good for loggers on the Oregon South Coast. By 1985, the local economy was in decline. Affordable timber stumpage was in short supply. Attitudes had changed about the forest industries; the mills in Coos Bay south to Bandon were closing, and good paying jobs for middle-class family men were a thing of the past. Commercial fishing was also in decline.

By 1994, all the mills in the surrounding area were shut down. Rogge Mill, near Bandon, was the last to go and signaled the end of the good times for the men who worked in the woods. As jobs in the natural resource industries dried up, unemployment grew, and there was an exodus of residents.

However, another change in the resident population was about to occur. The community underwent a transition as retirees from California discovered and moved to Bandon. A Californian, having bought a house thirty years ago for $40,000 to $60,000, could now sell it for several hundred thousand dollars. Some moved to Bandon, bought a house for half the value of their previous house and banked a substantial sum for retirement. These new residents became known as the "Last Pioneers" or the "Silver Economy."

These senior citizens liked the small town ambiance. It was laidback and hassle-free. Ex-Californians were pleased; there was no sales tax. There were beaches to comb, sport fishing and hunting were both good, and the local property taxes were very low. No referendum to raise local taxes has ever passed in Bandon.

Highway 101, Oregon's scenic coastal highway, runs through the town center like a main street with an assortment of retail and commercial businesses scattered along the roadside. It is a natural stop for tourists heading north from California or south from British Columbia or Washington State.

Before the rumor of a golf resort began circulating around Bandon, this coastal community had been a destination of sorts for Oregonians seeking an inexpensive weekend or holiday at the coast. Visitors came from up and down the Willamette Valley. After checking into a local motel, the visitor could drive over to Old Town and browse the shops, rent crab pots, drive over to the South Jetty and watch the waves roll in, walk along the beach or go beachcombing. In the evening, you could watch the sunset at Face Rock, or in the morning watch the fog as it lifted to reveal groups of sea stacks just off shore. At any time, an excellent meal of fresh seafood was available at one of the local restaurants.

There wasn't much nightlife twenty years ago. There was no movie theater, bowling alley or pool hall. Fraser's, a family restaurant by day, had a back room called the Quarter Deck. There you could get a nightcap, play pool or feed a poker slot machine. Things were about to change as word trickled out that a destination resort was being planned north of the town. Rumor and gossip floated around the community; reaction was mixed. Many local residents enthusiastically supported the proposal. Others, including many Last Pioneers, favored no change.

At first, most people thought Mike Keiser "was hare-brained." Who would ever want to come to Bandon to play golf? Locals remembered Duke Watson and a group of out-of-town investors who had similar thoughts some years before. That had come to nothing. The locals thought Mike would be gone in three or four years, richer in wisdom and poorer in cash.

Like other small communities along the Oregon coast, lack of customers or bad business practices occasionally forced local businesses in Bandon to close. In 2000, the Bandon Cheese Factory, which had been a must-tour for tourists, shut down, as did Fraser's.

Initial rumors about the resort swirled about, raising expectations in the business community. Many of Oregon's destination golf resorts include timeshare condominiums and private residences, and, to many of the local shopkeepers, this meant more business. The idea was that, once a resort opened, as the number of golf courses grew, golfers and guests from the resort would find their way into town to browse, shop and dine.

Bandon has had several restaurants over the years. In 1991, when we first started to work on the project, the Sea Star Bistro was a standout dining spot. But all good things come to an end and, in 1995, the Jenningses (owners and operators) sold the place and moved on. Other restaurants opened and closed over time, including Michaels and the Wild Rose. In time, the resort influenced the decision of two individuals to open a new restaurant.

Jeremy Buck and Lian Schmidt were culinary professionals. After looking at numerous locations in Oregon's major metropolitan areas and the North Coast, they settled on Bandon. Past news reports about the planned resort had made an impression on both of them. On reflection, Jeremy would say, "We'd been on a path our whole adult lives working toward having our own restaurant" and, due to the presence of Bandon Dunes, they opened the Alloro Wine Bar & Restaurant. In the process, Jeremy and Lian have reprised the art of good dining also available at many of the other local restaurants.

In the early years of the resort's operation, many in the community harbored opinions and mindsets that were deeply opposed to golf course development. Over time, the presence of a destination resort near Bandon brought national attention to the city, changing many minds, but not all.

OPPOSING MINDSETS

The Presidential election of 2012 resulted in something of a standoff between the Democratic and Republican parties. The day after the election, each side felt it had a "mandate" supporting its policies and positions. Each party had made promises to its political constituencies that were diametrically opposed to the other side.

In recent years, these political mindsets had become intractable. Each party espoused opposing beliefs about the necessity or the level of needed government regulation. For years, this had been a central argument: one side believed government regulation was often necessary for the general welfare of the nation; the other side believed government regulation too often constrained economic progress and job growth. The latter advocates the view that business does best with little or no regulation, federal or otherwise.

In 1991, Mike Keiser faced a similar predicament—he had an idea and wanted to build a golf resort. This was a man who had previously built a golf course in the Midwest with little or no regulatory interference from the government; the local jurisdiction "green-lighted" his plans. He now faced a regulatory environment that imposed high land use standards.

The State of Oregon had, and still has, a strict land use regulatory climate. One generally favorable book about Oregon's statewide land use program is appropriately entitled *The Regulated Landscape*. The guiding principle is "a place for everything and everything in its place." Oregon has put in place a comprehensive set of statutes, state administrative rules, local comprehensive plans, and zoning regulations to strike a balance between protection of farmland, forestland, and natural resources on the one hand and encouraging compact, efficient, and economically healthy urban development on the other.

Nice concept, but it comes with a complement of pertinent clichés, including, but not limited to:

- The devil is in the details.
- There's many a slip between the cup and the lip.
- We're from the government and we're here to help you.
- One person's balance is another person's Leaning Tower of Pisa.

The land Mike bought was zoned exclusively for forest and agricultural use. Here was the crux of our first obstacle: he needed a zone change.

A self-made businessman with an old-fashioned entrepreneurial spirit, he was not deterred. His mindset was basic and simple: I own the land, and I should be able to do whatever I want with it, within reason—my reasons.

This attitude is typically American. How many times have you heard the phrase, "You can't tell me what to do with my land"? Where did this viewpoint come from? One has to go back to early American history to understand the reason many Americans embrace this viewpoint.

In his book, *The Geography of Nowhere*, James Howard Kunstler provides an excellent explanation for why Americans hold this viewpoint as almost sacred. The first colonists discovered, to their amazement and joy, that land was plentiful in the New World. If you wanted land, all you had to do was move out into the "wilderness," claim it, clear it and defend it. It also looked like there were endless supplies of buffalo and passenger pigeons.

The Revolutionary War and the Constitution that followed gave Americans freedom in spirit and in reality. In forming their new independent nation, they gained rights that did not exist in the Old World.

First, they gained expanded rights in real property, freed from many common-law rules held over from feudal times that had been explicitly protected by vague but potentially broad due process and takings. These new rights were now safeguarded in their new written Constitution.

Second, the social notion of landowners being stewards of the land with a sense of public responsibility was severely diminished. Kunstler believes this new attitude asserted a new fundamental principle of American land law that defined and held that land is a commodity and, as such, can be bought and sold for profit. Historically, in the West, private land owner-ship and personal control by the landowner were hallmarks of personal freedom as America expanded westward. The range wars in the West were testaments to this attitude. This was in contrast to the Old World view that had attached community values, like stewardship, to the land. The idea of stewardship played an important role in putting together a master plan for the golf resort.

Initially, as America grew and flourished, there was little or no regu-lation of what one could do with one's land. As the country continued to develop, the idea of regulating various business activities, including land development, resulted in the adoption of various forms of legislative statutes and administrative rules. Oregon, in the early 1970s, adopted a comprehensive set of land use statutes and regulations.

Chapter Six

Working with Government

*Senate Bill 100 goes beyond requiring local governments to
plan and beyond state planning for areas of statewide concern;
it establishes a significant role for state government in
planning and regulating land use throughout the state.*
—Gerrit Knaap, Arthur C. Nelson, *The Regulated Landscape, 1992*

SENATE BILL 100

H oward was knowledgeable about Oregon's land use regulatory system. While living and working in Portland twenty years previous, he had been an active supporter of the legislation that created the regulatory climate that applied to proposed destination resorts. Now he had to work within a regulatory system he had embraced and respected.

Urban development begun in the post-war industrial period up until the 1960s had led to extensive suburban growth and sprawl in the Willamette Valley. Environmental groups—including 1000 Friends of Oregon, formed in 1975—were concerned about the loss of prime agricultural lands as more and more subdivisions were built on farmland. Things were viewed as "out of control."

A diverse collection of interest groups came to view suburban sub-divisions in the Willamette Valley as a creeping form of environmental devastation. They organized and lobbied the state legislature to reconsider and revise an earlier piece of legislation, Senate Bill 10.

Passed in 1969, this legislation had established ten broad statewide land use planning goals and required cities and counties to prepare comprehensive land use plans and zoning ordinances that complied with the mandated goals. The problem with Senate Bill 10 was that there were no standards or criteria for coordinating and assessing local plans on growth and development. The legislation also lacked enforcement mechanisms.

In 1973, the state legislature, in response to heavy lobbying, passed Senate Bill 100. This bill was a regulatory game changer. It expanded the reach of Senate Bill 10 and replaced its weaknesses with far-reaching substantive and procedural strengths. It created a new statewide land use decision-making system that, over time, gave the state strong centralized control over land use planning at the local jurisdictional levels—municipal, metropolitan and county.

The new statute called for establishment of what the state's courts came to call "Oregon's Land Use Constitution," a series of statewide planning goals intended to reverse current development trends. In addition, the law required all local jurisdictions to prepare new comprehensive plans in accordance with these state goals. The Oregon legislature created a state commission, the Land Conservation and Development Commission (LCDC), to oversee implementation of the new law.

To assist the commission, an administrative and technical arm—the Department of Land Conservation and Development (DLCD)—was created. The department's mission was not to make or interpret state land use policy itself, but to assist the unpaid LCDC as it fleshed out the goals, and to promulgate administrative rules and ordinances that would eventually underpin and provide enforcement mechanisms for the new law.

Over time, the original set of twenty broad and often vague state land use goals adopted in the mid-1970s were elaborated, overlain, and often obfuscated by interpretations, amendments, and elaborations, expressed in a regulatory sprawl of administrative rules, court decisions, new statutes, and agency rulings. And, over time—as with many local, state, and federal regulatory schemes—the professional half of the state's citizen-professional partnership came to be viewed by many observers as the dominant partner on policy as well as implementation.

In order to demonstrate that their plans and ordinances complied with state land use goals, counties, cities and metropolitan areas also had to develop defensible long-term population projections and conduct inventories of natural resources, urban lands available to meet projected needs for infrastructure, utilities, housing, industry, retail, and other urban uses. Then they had to adopt strict plan and zoning map designations to protect farmland, forestland, and other resource lands in rural areas while assuring that lands inside urban growth boundaries were available and adequate to meet projected needs for urban areas.

At the heart of the program was the concept of Urban Growth Boundaries (UGBs). The goals required cities and counties to establish UGBs, approved by LCDC, and sized and shaped to assure that each city and metro area had sufficient land to meet urban needs for twenty years. This was crucial to the land use bargain that brought homebuilders, local governments, farmers, and others into the coalition behind Senate Bill 100. Only with adequate, but not excessive, space for urban growth reasonably assured could the state be expected to require strict protection for agricultural and forest lands outside of those boundaries.

Not surprisingly, what in the past had been a fairly simple process to obtain planning and building permits became a more complicated affair. Moreover, some important uses inevitably got short shrift under the new land use constitution.

One such use was destination resorts located on rural lands. Oregon already had a few very successful state-of-the-art destination resorts. Sunriver, Inn of the Seventh Mountain, Bachelor Butte—all in Central Oregon's Deschutes County—and Salishan, on the Oregon Coast, south of Lincoln City, were all established in the decade preceding the adoption of Senate Bill 100. All were developed on large rural tracts with a mixture of overnight resort lodging, nice restaurants, gift shops, high-end recreational amenities—golf courses, tennis courts, swimming pools, etc.—and, crucially, permanent homes. All of these existing resorts had been developed with considerable sensitivity to their settings, including streams, beaches, wetlands, and open spaces.

Last, but certainly not least, all of these resorts were economically successful, both for their owners and for the rural counties where they were developed.

Destination resorts were popular with rural counties suffering from economic dislocations. They brought skiers, golfers, fly fishermen, hikers, and other urbanites with full pockets—some to play, and some to stay. As mills were dismantled, fishing fleets depleted, small farms consolidated, and young people drawn to the big cities, Oregon's rural areas looked to tourism, second homes, and active retirement as replacement drivers for their economies. Destination resorts were a bright gleam of hope in an overcast rural Oregon countryside.

Unfortunately, under the new regimen, the only way that additional destination resorts could be approved was through a complex, arduous, and usually futile effort to secure what was known as a "reasons exception" to the statewide goals' general prohibition of urban types and levels of housing. Difficult to start with, the reasons exception option was steadily constricted over the years by a steady trickle of state administrative and court rules and rulings. More than forty years after the adoption of Senate Bill 100, only one destination resort has ever been developed under a reasons exception: that would be Bandon Dunes, opened almost a quarter-century later, after nearly a decade spent in preparation and processing its application.

In the 1980s, Oregon's state legislature amended SB 100 to create a special set of permitting standards and procedures for what became known as "statutory destination resorts." Several resorts were permitted under this statute, but its one-size-fits-all locational requirements simply did not work for rural counties with very limited areas suitable for such resorts. One such county was Coos County, with its relatively short strip of private rural coastland between Highway 101 and the beach.

The 1980s were not good to rural Oregon. By 1990, Coos County was hurting. Its traditional economic drivers were on the ropes. It had a whole shelf of state-approved inventories, comprehensive plans, and zoning regulations—with accompanying maps, including economic development programs calling out tourism and destination resorts as keys to the county's future. But it had no destination resorts and no prospects for any in the foreseeable future.

COOS COUNTY

Local government officials and citizens were exceedingly skeptical in the early 1990s when they first heard about a proposed golf resort in the gorse scrublands north of Bandon. Everyone thought Mike Keiser was just another speculative developer with big ideas and feet well off the ground. The Coos County planning director considered the applicant and his representative—Mike Keiser and Howard McKee, and the consultant team another bunch of pie-in-the-sky guys. In one sense, he was right. We all had a lot to learn. But, in another, boy, was he wrong. In the coming months and years, Howard and his consultant team demonstrated, through their actions and submittals to the county, how an in-depth site inventory and analysis laid the foundation for a balanced program of site development.

Bill Grile had become planning director in 1979. At that time, there was little structure to planning in the county. Bill brought strong leadership to the planning department and was active in bringing new industries, companies and other development to the county. He wanted to replace the lost logging and fishing jobs and improve the local economy. When he met Howard, he hoped Howard was for real. Once Howard convinced Bill that Mike had the financial resources and wherewithal to build a destination resort, Bill's concerns evaporated, and we got off to a good start with the county.

In 1995, after sixteen years as the planning director, Bill resigned to become the city manager for Coos Bay, Oregon. This might have been a problem, but the new planning director—Patty Evernden—and Howard quickly established a working relationship.

THE NEED FOR AN EXCEPTION

The resort property was within three miles of cranberry bogs. This fact created a big-time land use problem for Howard and Al Johnson, our land use attorney. State destination resort statutes did not permit a destination resort, golf or otherwise, near what was a "high-value" crop area. In compliance with state land use goals, the property was designated for farm and forest use on the county's comprehensive plan and zoning maps, prohibiting the lodging, restaurants, and other elements of the proposed golf resort.

After researching the legal issues, Al determined a "reasons exception" was the only way to get the plan and zoning amendments and associated development permits required to allow the project to go forward. The county supported this approach and discussions with the Development and Land Conservation Department confirmed this was a viable option.

A series of lengthy meetings with DLCD staff at DLCD headquarters in the state capitol laid the conceptual groundwork. In those meetings and follow-up correspondence, Al and Howard confirmed that the state legislature, in enacting the destination resort statute, had recognized that all rural Oregon counties need destination resorts as a way of promoting local economic growth. They also confirmed that Coos County probably had no way to meet this legislatively-recognized economic need because of the locational restrictions built into the statute.

This would become one of the two key "reasons" for our reasons exception. It was one of two kinds of "regulatory-failure" arguments at the heart of our case. The other, amply documented by our inventories and graphics, was that the default regime of farm and forest zoning was not only failing to achieve the purposes of many statewide land use goals, it was actually defeating those purposes by aggravating the effects of previous human activities. Invasive beach grass and gorse were taking over open sand areas, eliminating important habitat for threatened and endangered plants and animals. Gorse and abandoned marginal tree farms were economically nonproductive fire hazards in an area that had seen catastrophic fires such as the one that destroyed the City of Bandon in 1936. Golf courses and associated development, properly implemented, could curb and even reverse many of these trends.

Al would use these key points in developing his legal argument and rationale for our land use application, and we would continue to develop the factual base to support him. There were other regulatory issues, but pursuing the reasons exception approach took five years of hard work.

The meetings with the DLCD staff also solved another problem Howard had encountered when contacting other state agencies that ultimately had regulatory authority over development of the resort. None of them wanted to participate in the planning process. Al knew an assistant director, Greg Wolfe, who advised him and Howard to contact Anne Squier, a charter member of the LCDC when it adopted the original set of land use goals back in 1974 and 1975 and, in the next few years, while Al was an LCDC hearings officer. Anne was now working in the governor's Salem office. Al and Greg thought Anne would be a good coordinator among the various state regulatory agencies that had input into the review process.

Al and Howard took this suggestion to heart. Three weeks later, Al and others—including Steve Oulman, a DLCD staffer—met with Anne. This meeting resolved Howard's frustration on how to engage with state regulatory agencies. Shortly afterwards, a pre-application conference was held to brief and solicit advice on our application process from a number of these state agencies. At this point, Al and Howard were excited, their spirits buoyed. Just maybe an approval was possible.

OREGON STATE PARKS

We made a special effort to collaborate with our neighbor, the Oregon Parks and Recreation Department aka Oregon State Parks. The proposed resort property was adjacent to the 1266-acre Bullards Beach State Park. This was good and bad. The good news was that most of the park's 1,000 acres was undeveloped. The bad news was that portions of the state park adjacent to our property had been classified either as a primary or secondary protection area. These "protection areas" abutted the proposed resort, and state officials were concerned about potential impacts on their property. It was a valid concern because a common boundary line traversed a sensitive duneland setting; Nature doesn't respect a man-made survey line. As we learned more about the duneland, it became alarmingly apparent the ecological setting was unstable, fragile and under attack by noxious plants.

Sand dune formations are not stable; subjected to ocean winds, they shift and reform different shapes over time. European settlement had introduced two exotic plants into the coastal ecology here: gorse and European beachgrass. The latter became an advancing carpet, serving to conditionally stabilize the shifting sand. Man's intervention had altered the natural dynamics of plant community succession. We would learn more details about this threat to the landscape during our analysis of the natural resource inventory data. But first we had to organize and accomplish the inventory work.

A master plan for Bullards Beach State Park was done in 1985. The plan was based on a comprehensive site inventory of the geologic features and hazards, soil conditions, water features and hazards, vegetation, wildlife habitat, scenic amenity value and historical and archaeological features and values. Using this database, the department has produced a development and park management plan.

Howard, sensitive to the State Park concerns, scheduled a meeting with their representatives to discuss a mutually beneficial approach to our land planning activities. In early 1992, Mike and Howard signed a memorandum of understanding with State Parks. We agreed to use their recreation and resource goals and methodology in conjunction with our inventory and analyses. The agreement acknowledged the importance of site planning based on an ecological approach. Natural functions, like drainage, vegetation succession and associated natural resource amenities and values, do not recognize a surveyed property line.

The Nature Conservancy, an Oregon environmental organization, in association with the Oregon Natural Heritage Program, had given State Parks site reports, maps and printouts that provided additional quantitative and qualitative data on significant natural features found at Bullards Beach State Park. Later, during the resort's analysis of the natural resource inventory data, we retained the services of the Conservancy to evaluate the habitat and value of coastal lakes on the resort property and to comment on other natural features regarding the feasibility of preserving these resources in our master plan.

Howard's strategy at this point was to gain support from State Parks officials. We did not want to face opposition from them at a public hearing. Objections from State Parks might have galvanized more serious opposition to the proposal. Fortunately, that didn't occur.

Now we had to formulate a strategy to deal with the general public. The local newspapers—*The Bandon Western World* and *The Coos Bay World*—found they had a hot topic to cover, reporting local citizen concerns, pro and con. A group of residents from Weiss Estates, a rural subdivision on the shores of Fahys Lake, soon became actively opposed to the project.

Chapter Seven

Concerns and Expectations

All of our experience is full of anticipations,
we love what we might be.
—Michael Murphy, *Golf in the Kingdom, 1972*

BAD PRESS, GOOD PRESS

"Destination resort plans unveiled" was the lead story in the *Western World* on Wednesday, November 15, 1995. The article officially informed local residents of a planned destination resort on more than 1200 acres of land just north of Bandon. The plans had been revealed at a meeting hosted by the local Chamber of Commerce. Howard had been scheduled to talk before this group. However, he was out of the country, so I took his place.

I presented preliminary drawings and briefed a full house of concerned citizens about the plan concept, phasing, and the construction schedule for the project. Bob Johnson had accompanied me to the meeting, and when I realized I was having a difficult time hearing questions (I needed hearing aids), I asked Bob to help me out. So he took the stage with me.

Addressing the audience in my opening remarks, I said: "I believe the effort that has been put into the planning process will, indeed, distinguish this project," and "that we, the consultant team, have a lot of faith in the process. We know that the land use process in the state of Oregon is very tedious and difficult, with high standards to meet. We also recognize that there will be opposition to the project. There will be concerns and many of those will be legitimate. But the team and the owner plan to respond to those concerns through the process." Later, in response to a question from the audience, I said, "Ultimately, if this is a project that is to be built, it will; if it's not, it won't. We won't ask you for your support, we hope to earn it."

The words I used reflected the approach and commitment Howard, I and everyone on the consultant team took in identifying and responding to any and all concerns that were expressed by the local citizenry. We were especially attuned to concerns from adjacent residents who lived in the Weiss Estates subdivision. However, as time passed, the local newspapers were filled with letters to the editor, lambasting the proposal. Howard considered most of these letters were "soft complaints." Many were emotionally- and not factually-based, and it was difficult to adequately respond to them. These newspaper accounts were useful: they gave us another source of information about local concerns.

Reading the "letters to the editor" was sometimes humorous. One writer wrote: "Let's tee off..." The letter referenced the statewide planning goals with statements like, "you and me, can find the number one hole in land use proposals that we deem unnecessary and unacceptable." In another instance, the author stated, "I will be taking a swing at Goal 8 Recreational Needs with a pitching wedge in a future edition." This sense of humor was uplifting, even though people had serious concerns.

Local concerns ranged from 1) the provision of "luxury homes" that would be priced out of the range of local residents; 2) a loss of water quality in lakes and streams on resort property; 3) a potentially polluted watershed: since golf course maintenance crews typically use chemical pesticides and fertilizers on fairways and greens, this was viewed as an adverse impact to the local groundwater system; 4) adverse impacts on wildlife; and 5) although the project could boost the local economy with new jobs, many felt most of these jobs would be service jobs with low pay.

There were other, more positive responses to the proposal. One letter-writer was critical of an opponent's letter because they characterized the land as virgin. They pointed out that the land was the old Fahy Ranch, and that, at one time, it had been a mining area and that a major part of the property was covered with gorse. The author also pointed out that having 300 new homes would increase the local tax base. Anyone living in Bandon knows the only thing worse than a destination resort is an increase in local taxes. However, many supporters saw a destination resort with guests and residents as an economic boon for the local economy. They thought it would replace lost logging and fishing industry jobs.

Even after extensive meetings and presentations about the benefits associated with the proposed destination resort, we faced continued opposition. In Oregon, opponents sometimes keep contesting a project just to delay it. This can be an effective strategy if the applicant has limited financial resources. In this instance, Mike had an unshakable belief in his vision and deep pockets to pursue it.

The promise of a destination resort brought forth expectations among the local populace. There was a general feeling that the city was on the cusp of better times. Many felt the forthcoming years would see a booming economy once again, based on the belief that thousands of golfers, retirees and seasonal tourists would fill local restaurants and shops.

According to Matt Winkel, the city manager, the local residents held two basic opinions. Some thought and liked the fact that the master plan included private homes. This would increase the tax base for the county. Others felt this project would never happen. Who would want to come to a small coastal community to play golf?

At the time, the city was experiencing strong interest in new home and second home construction along Beach Loop Drive, where most of the new homes had been built. Low interest and accessible credit fueled new construction on ocean view sites. As usual, land speculation followed on the coat tails of the resort proposal.

Over the next decade, local residential development was in high gear. Several large-scale projects—including the Colony; Bandon Commons, a subdivision by David L. Davis; and the Sea Bird project—sprang up to provide new lots and condominiums for the local real estate market. It was all fantasy and, during the height of the 2007–2008 recession, all sales for new homes and condominiums stopped. There were no buyers. A local version of default and foreclosure followed the national trend.

LAND SPECULATION

Development breeds other development and land speculation. There was a related concern that the resort would drive up land prices, thereby adversely affecting the expansion of cranberry bogs in the future. The latter never happened. Some locals believed property values would go up. Values did. A few others believed this was a good time to buy up forest and farmland, hold it and perhaps develop the land into rural subdivisions sometime in the future. That happened.

The best example is a land holding of about 200 acres that was assembled in 2006–2007, immediately adjacent to the resort. A California investor acquired two land parcels for about $4.5 million. Directly accessible off the same paved road leading to the resort entrance, this was a desirable location for a future rural subdivision.

To determine the real impact on property values, I looked at the county tax assessment rolls from 2001 to 2006. During that five-year period, land values in many instances doubled. If you bought early, your land increased in value, at least on paper. If you bought in 2006 and still owned it, your land was now worth less than what you paid for it. So the initial criticism directed at Bandon Dunes about land speculation was correct.

Chapter Eight

Master Planning

Plans are nothing; planning is everything.
—Dwight D. Eisenhower

DISCOVERING THE SITE

Walking among the sand dunes is hard work. The loose sand clings to your shoes and pulls you down into the earth; it reminds you that you are part of the physical world. Constant wind action along the Oregon coast dunes continually alters the terrain. It is not uniform; the terrain rolls up and down in sweeping rises and valleys. One walks up and sees the horizon and ocean, and then one walks down, where one's perspective is limited to a tunnel-like view of the world. The plants at your feet become noticeable.

The sand dunes found at the resort are a remarkable natural treasure. They are elemental in nature—forms shaped by the wind, ever changing. They resemble waves of sculptured forms; they are pleasing to the eye. Walking in and out of sand troughs changes your perspective from micro to macro and back to the micro view. The wind is ever present. It may subside for a day or two, but it always returns. Summer winds come out of the northwest; winter winds come out of the southwest and become a major factor in golf play. As the wind blows, clumps of beach grass sway in the breeze, becoming a visual symphony. It's picture perfect.

But you need to be alert. You need to step carefully to avoid damaging delicate duneland plants, like the silvery phacelia. The ecological setting is fragile.

This is not a place to hurry. The wind may push and deflect you from your path. On a hot, sunny day, a breeze will cool you down, and the warmth of the sun will caress your face. Here you are in direct contact with nature. Rain, a seasonal visitor, is another natural experience at Bandon Dunes. All of these experiences are sensory and sensual. These are not intellectual experiences.

Fig. 5: Sand Dunes

When we started the project, we stayed in Bandon at the Harbor View Motel. Perched on a bluff overlooking Old Town, it was our base of operations for several years. After eight or ten hours of trudging through the sand dunes or dense forest, we would retire to the motel and soak our sore legs in the motel's hot tub room. Frequently, a bottle of scotch, only for medicinal purposes, eased our discomfort and put us in a very relaxed state. These were bonding times among the team members.

The next day, rising at six o'clock or earlier, we would eat a hearty breakfast and go back to work. Day after day, we explored the site, discovering features that provoked new ideas that were discussed over a late dinner. Every day in the field confirmed that there were special qualities present and worthy of preservation.

The resort property was rich in natural resources: there were sand dunes, evergreen woodlands, coastal lakes, streams and wetlands—all intermingled together, forming a tapestry of incredible diversity and contrast. A prominent wooded ridge divided the site into two distinctively different halves: windward, the ground was all sand, with little organic material; leeward, a dense conifer forest grew, embracing three coastal lakes. A sunken interdunal valley, sandwiched in between the marine terrace and sand dunes, hid an extensive wetland that hugged the base of a precipitation ridge. This ridge, the eastern edge of the duneland, dropped fifty to sixty feet down to the wetland. Beyond, stands of stunted Shore Pine trees gave cover to a mosaic of seasonal wetlands scattered throughout the valley. In contrast, groups of Shore Pines on the marine terrace above the beach were sheared along the edge of their windward side. There, gorse had proliferated into masses that were impenetrable to foot traffic. The thorny spines on this plant were like mini daggers.

Heavy construction equipment—a bulldozer and backhoes—was needed to remove the gorse during the construction of the golf courses. The spoils were either buried or burned on site. Wherever the fragile soil was disturbed, either by construction or during selective logging operations, gorse would inevitably establish new plants. Without some form of intervention and abatement, the advancing gorse and other exotic vegetation would overwhelm the native plant community.

The eastern side of the ridge had an established conifer forest consisting primarily of Douglas fir, Sitka spruce and native cedar trees. This woodland was so dense that Howard had decided to initiate selective logging in order to allow better foot and visual access. This effort occurred in the late fall, and the consultant team learned an important lesson: the predominant Douglas fir trees grew in a thin layer of organic soil over a sand base. Their roots typically spread out horizontally and grew together. Once we removed a few trees from the stand, the resulting opening in the forest canopy became a problem. Strong winds dipped into the opening, causing havoc. The winter storm winds along the Oregon coast can approach 100 miles per hour, and inland winds can exceed eighty miles per hour. The remaining trees on the edge of the opening had only half a root system. With only partial anchorage in the ground, the result was "blow down and wind throw." It's the classic domino effect: knock one over and it will take down others. Our use of selective logging wasn't the best choice at the time. On the Oregon coast, if you decide to remove trees in a stand, leave a very, very small hole in the canopy. In a large stand, the cleared area should not exceed ten percent. Once construction began, we determined, in special situations, it was better to take the whole stand rather than leave a partial stand with weakened roots. If we wanted trees for landscape purposes, we planted new trees.

Howard and I spent months walking the property and, through an osmosis-like process, became conscious of the *genius loci*—the spirit of the place. This pervading mood found at site had an intangible quality that was difficult to put into words. Unlike soil types, vegetation type, landform and other physical characteristics that could be described and mapped as part of a site inventory process, this site attribute could not be documented objectively or put on paper. It was experiential; you had to be on the land and feel it. It raised a fundamental question: how do you document the fact that a particular piece of ground has a spiritual context and a value(s) that should be left intact? That is not to say you can't develop the land, but respecting the "spirit of the place" became extremely important in preparing the master plan. Our respect for the *genius loci* became a "touchstone."

As Howard and I formulated alternative master plan schemes, this sense of protecting the spirit of the place was our standard of measure. We asked ourselves whether or not we were enhancing the site or taking something away that shouldn't be lost. After the resort opened, resort managers asked a similar question: Will this decision enhance the resort golf brand, or will it diminish it? The priority given to these questions and the answers contribute to the success of the resort and, perhaps, the sense of uniqueness associated with Bandon Dunes.

As the consultant team grew in members, Howard decided we needed a place to assemble and meet together on-site. The previous owners had left an old, dilapidated doublewide trailer on the west shore of Round Lake. Entering the building the first time, we found the floor littered with trash. After cleaning out all the debris, and applying a coat of white paint to the walls, the place was quickly converted into a working environment—our first design center. The building was crude, space was tight, but there was a working kitchen with a stove and refrigerator. Stocked with beer and wine and the obligatory coffee urn, consultants could meet, plan and warm up with a cup of coffee after working outside in the rain. An adjacent room held a long conference table. We installed pin-up board walls, allowing us to review drawings and other graphic materials. This room became our "war room."

Besides variety in topographic features, flora, and ocean views, the property was home to three coastal lakes: Chrome, Round and Fahy. Two were natural; Chrome Lake was man-made. During World War II, chromium mining along one of the streams had resulted in this water feature. Initially, we thought the lake was only a couple of acres in size, smaller than Round Lake. However, an exploration of the lake's perimeter revealed a wooded peninsula that hid a narrow expanse of open water and marshland that continued for hundreds of feet upstream.

The outflow from Chrome Lake forms Cut Creek. This stream meanders along the south edge of the upland marine terrace. Sand dunes line the opposite creek bank. The creek eventually becomes an emergent freshwater wetland, a delta formed by braided streams that twist and flow through a mixture of willow, gorse and wetland grasses. In the middle of the delta, a patch of high ground serves as a reminder that miners had once worked this creek, looking for gold. Years later, a golf course architect would suggest building a golf green there.

Fahys Lake, the largest of the three coastal lakes, nestles up against the east side of the central ridge. It has an elongated L-shape. Except for a few visible lakefront homes in the Weiss Estates subdivision, the shoreline is heavily wooded. The lake is the potable water supply for residents of Weiss Estates. This fact was one of their major concerns.

SITE INVENTORY AND ANALYSES

When completed, the natural resources inventory gave us a comprehensive database. Much of the information was interpreted and documented in graphic form on maps. Following general land use suitability analysis methods authored by Ian McHarg in his 1969 book, *Design with Nature*, critical information on site conditions—slope, relief, hydrology, prominent visual features and other important site attributes—were mapped and then compared or "sieved" to see what areas of the site were most suitable for recreation, conservation or building development (residential, lodging, etc.). From this exercise, we were able to determine opportunity sites suitable, and problem or hazard zones unsuitable, for specific land uses. At this point, I assembled and prepared a briefing report containing all our inventory database and analysis information. This document was used as part of our community outreach and public relations program.

Professionally pragmatic—that was Howard. The analysis work had to have relevancy. He is on record as saying, "We had no cards," to trade or use for leverage when we began the master planning and land use permitting process. That's why we took special pains to see what was there, to document it and to understand its relevancy to the overall process. The site inventory database became our "cards to play" when we got to the public hearings stage. Our master plan was built on a rationale of facts and analyses we could use to refute argumentative commentary from opponents.

Our database provided us with a basis for defining sensitive environmental areas that would become the conservation set-asides. Removing these areas from consideration for "development" meant we could characterize the project as responsive to environmental issues. By adhering to all of the required setbacks from existing watercourses, avoiding impacts to existing wetlands and maintaining about eighty percent of the land in open space, we were able to preserve almost all of the valuable natural resources on the property. In situations where the wetlands were seasonal and scattered intermittently in forested areas, we classified them as mosaic wetland areas in order to protect these aquatic habitats.

Our inventory of flora revealed the presence of silvery phacelia, a native plant that establishes colonies in open sand dune habitat. This small, delicate plant was also found intermingled with European beachgrass, sometimes hardly visible among tufts of beachgrass. Fortunately for us, it was not federally listed, but the State of Oregon listed it as a threatened species on public lands. This meant we could remove plants on resort property while the public agencies faced restrictions on their properties. However, we decided it was in our best interest to preserve as many plants as possible and to include habitat restoration where opportunities at the resort presented themselves.

Phacelia plants tend to emerge voluntarily where there is disturbed, open sand. Once established, the plant spreads by underground runners, forming a mat like carpet. Eventually, it can become a colony or "mother" plant,

Fig. 6: Silvery Phacelia

appearing as a raised dome—a very distinctive feature in the dunes. Rising above the sand, a mature plant may be a two-feet high mound sometimes as much as five or six feet in diameter. If it dies, only a scattered array of debris remains.

Open sand habitat on either side of the common property line between the resort and the adjacent state park is primary phacelia habitat. When I first set foot in the dunes, I noticed the silvery phacelia plants also grew among the local beachgrass. The deep-rooted, tall beachgrass has and continues to overrun and threaten the phacelia plant population on both properties with extinction. Is this important? Absolutely! The remaining plants found here constitute the largest remaining group along the west coast of the United States. Our review of scientific literature by the U.S. Fish and Wildlife Service and other literature sources confirmed that, among a total of thirty-three known sites along the West Coast, the resort property hosted the largest remaining population on the planet.

I also found out that early explorers and pioneers had observed and noted the presence of prairie type grasses and occasional stands of trees along the Oregon coastline. A hundred and fifty years ago, there was much more open sand. However, grazing and cultivation activities by pioneers destabilized sand and the natural plant communities.

Two historical events foreshadowed the ecological conditions that we found in the duneland. The first event occurred in the early 1900s, when the Army Corps of Engineers planted European beachgrass along the Oregon coast. They wanted to stabilize the foredune and the shifting sand associated with the inland edge of the beach zone. The stabilization program was successful. But south of Cut Creek, the beachgrass began moving inland, eventually forming a deflation plain and seasonal wetlands.

A review of historical aerial photographs taken in 1939, 1964, 1977, 1989 and 1994 allowed me to compare the progressive loss of open sand areas and the changes in associated vegetation patterns. These photographs clearly showed a startling reduction of open sand areas and a significant increase in ground and canopy cover.

The second historical event concerns gorse. When Lord Bennett founded the City of Bandon in the 1880s, he introduced gorse, a native plant from Scotland. He liked yellow flowers. They reminded him of Scotland, where he had enjoyed them at Easter time.

By the 1990s, both of these exotic plants had overrun the dune lands, conditionally stabilizing what had once been an un-stabilized open sand habitat. Once the ecology had become conditionally stable, the stage was set for the spread of another plant: the Coastal Shore Pine. This is nature's way; it is called plant succession.

Pioneer plants or introduced plants emerge first. They are the colonizers. They change environmental conditions, thereby giving other plant species the opportunity to establish a presence. By 1993, there was an established Shore Pine duneland forest, primarily on state park land adjacent to the resort property. Today, the pine stands continue to advance, year by year, toward the remaining open sand habitat on both state park and resort land. Unless checked by an effective exotic plant removal and abatement program, the remaining open sand environment could be gone in fifty years.

NATIVE PEOPLE

Early during our site investigations, Howard and I knew we were going to intervene in a cultural landscape. We weren't the first to do so.

Before the first bulldozer blade cut into the ground and shaped a fairway or golf hole, the first inhabitants had already intervened and shaped their environment. The Native People didn't have a bulldozer, but they had fire. With fire they burned the understory of the forest to make hunting for game easier or fired grassland to revitalize the soil and renew plant communities. At Whiskey Run Terrace, they managed the area to encourage the growth of Camas plants. There along the bluffs and marine terrace, encampments sprang up in the summer. These were festive occasions attended by local bands, tribes and other groups from more distant interior lands to the east. These were occasions to share food, socialize, gamble and trade. They were also an opportunity to make working arrangements or treaties that allowed mutual access to one and another's fishing or hunting grounds. One of the main attractions was the presence of the Camas plants. Dug up and steamed in pits, they were a prized menu item. When the Native People lived here, the land extending away from the bluffs was treeless. The marine terrace was an open, grassed meadow. Red Fescue grass, Camas and other native vegetation blanketed the ground. For thousands of years, the land was used for gathering and celebrations. That changed as Europeans migrated and settled in and around the Coquille watershed.

Settlement introduced both cultural and economic changes to the landscape. Realizing that the Native People had a strong attachment to the local landscape, Howard knew the planning process needed to recognize and respect how tribal leaders and members viewed proposed changes to the landscape.

Our site investigations had documented how the past one hundred years of history had seen a shift in human values and use of local natural resources from culturally supportive to intensive economic use. Previously, the Native People exercised a purposeful use of the land in ways that were respectful and in harmony with the landscape. The newcomers began to exploit the natural resources. Settlement brought saw mills and clear-cutting of forestland. The Fescue meadows became pastureland for cattle. The native grasslands were fragile and ranching disturbed the stability of the sandy soils. Eventually the cattle were gone, and the land fell into disuse and degradation soon followed. Sand buggies and motorized trail bikes left new patterns and trails in the sand.

Howard was keenly aware of the fact that planning for the proposed resort needed to be seen as working in ways compatible with the landscape rather than disingenuous and harmful to the local community.

Construction of the Bandon Dunes resort and golf courses changed what was previously there, especially along Whiskey Run Terrace. Most of the Shore Pines and gorse are gone. As the golf courses were built, a grass carpet containing native Fescue stabilized what had been a degraded landscape. A few remnant trees and hedgerow-like clumps of gorse remain scattered among the golf courses. They added structure and beauty to the layout. Unexpectedly, the new landscape appeared similar to the pre-settlement era.

Don Ivy, the resources coordinator for the Coquille-Coos Tribe, visited the resort a few years after its opening. Looking around, he thought to himself, 'A different cultural context is in place, but how ironic: the resort guests are using the land again for festive gatherings and recreation activities.' On a basic human level, the purposefulness of the landscape had returned to how it had been used hundreds and thousands of years before golf even existed.

On June 28, 1989, Congress passed Public Law 101-42, the *Coquille Restoration Act*. This act re-established and restored the Coquille Indian Tribe as a sovereign government. It gave the tribe and tribal members the right to participate in federal Indian programs and services. It also gave the tribe "the authority to manage and administer political and legal jurisdiction over its lands, business and community members." The tribe no longer owned any land on the Whiskey Run Terrace, but they had a "history" associated with the land. Howard knew he needed to talk and work with the tribe. He didn't have long to wait.

When you buy property you get a title report. The report mentioned a possible allotment—the Ned Allotment—on the Fahy property. Howard was concerned about this, and so he called the Coquille Tribal office in Coos Bay because one of the Ned descendents worked for the tribe.

Officials at the Tribal office had heard about Mike's purchase of the property, and they wanted to know what the plan was. Calls were made, arrangements made, and a week later Don Ivy, Howard and Bob Johnson found themselves crashing through dense underbrush, looking for a long-lost cemetery. A review of the records on file at the Tribal office suggested there was an allotment cemetery somewhere in the area. The trio searched for several hours but did not find a cemetery. They did, however, find the remains of what could have been Ned's old house. Later, the cemetery was discovered on an adjacent property. This informal excursion would grow into a lasting relationship with the Coquille Tribe.

As mentioned earlier, the tribe was very concerned about construction along the ocean bluffs and the marine terrace. They wanted assurances that construction workers would be as concerned as they were about potential harm to native artifacts. The tribe requested a meeting to clarify what the resort would do if any artifacts or human remains were uncovered during construction work. A worker on a bulldozer can't see what is in front of the dozer's blade.

You could walk around the site and kick at a stone that was in your path. If you stopped and picked it up, sometimes you'd discover you were looking at firestone. These are cultural artifacts the Native People left behind. It was common knowledge among locals that you could find arrowheads on the bluffs as wind erosion continually exposed what was immediately beneath the surface.

At a meeting, Howard learned the tribe had mapped archaeological sites of importance on the resort property, and he was given a copy of the map. He responded immediately, and an archaeological assessment of a section of the coastline, known as the Five Mile Point/Whiskey Run Area, was undertaken and completed on May 10, 1996.

As the construction for the first golf course moved forward, an agreement between Bandon Dunes and the Coquille Tribe was forged that mandated immediate notification and cessation of construction activities if and when any archaeological artifacts or remains were unearthed. Later, as construction on the first golf course began, earth grading and shaping along the ocean bluffs exposed Native American artifacts. This became a "red flag event."

The bluffs have sparse vegetative cover, and the surface is fragile. Besides the winter storm winds, the fragile sand surface is further eroded by seasonal rain storms. Nature was an active participant in uncovering native artifacts, too.

The solution to this problem proved remarkably simple. Construction of the coastal golf holes required importing additional sand that met the architect's specifications. By building up an additional layer of sand, applying seed for turf and later growing in the turf, the construction of these golf holes effectively "encapsulated" any artifacts that might be present. Continued turf management and maintenance resulted in long-term, permanent preservation and protection for any buried artifacts along the bluff.

From the tribe's perspective, Bandon Dunes has restored the environmental consciousness previously accorded to the landscape by the Native People, while also reestablishing a compatible and harmonious relationship between human use and natural resource values present at the Whiskey Run Terrace. This is profound. The act of planning and achieving the Bandon Dunes Golf Resort also produced "a cultural bridge" that connected two divergent worldviews.

VIDEO TIME

As we began interacting with people who had oversight and review authority, Howard realized we needed a way to educate them about site conditions and our preliminary conceptual thoughts. He was frustrated because, generally, no one wanted to engage with us in the process. He and I mulled this problem over; how could we remedy this situation?

As part of the site planning work, I had been preparing preliminary sketch plans of various alternative conceptual approaches. These drawings transferred the ideas from our heads to paper and allowed us to communicate better with others. Such drawings are good props to review with other professionals, but sometimes they don't work with lay people because they are abstract representations. And some people just can't read two-dimensional plans.

You can use three-dimensional sketches, but some people also think they are artificial. They think they are made up and don't represent the real thing. If you can present these sketches personally, you can amplify what you are trying to do and clarify questions. We considered making a slide show. Both of us had used photographic slide presentations in the past, but taking a slide show on the road was impractical. We didn't have time to do a "dog-and-pony" show for each agency or group.

Sensing Howard's continuing frustration, I suggested we make and distribute a video. What is simpler than sending out a VHS cassette (remember this was about 1993)? Howard liked the idea. Now I had to make a video. Making the video was a personal mini-adventure, as I'd never made a movie before. First I needed a camcorder, so I went out and bought one. Not sure about what all I would need, I also bought telephoto zoom and wide-angle lenses. That turned out to be a good decision. Then I went down to the resort and began filming. After shooting ground level footage, I decided some aerial footage might be useful, so I rented a helicopter from a local logging company. Good thing I bought the extra lens. The ability to capture wide-angle shots and to zoom in from the air was a godsend.

Back in Portland, I gathered up all the shot footage. I then previewed and noted tape segments that could be used to illustrate key development concepts in our master planning approach. Howard and I then screened the footage. After we decided on the segments we wanted, I contacted MIRA, a video production company in Portland. A couple of days later, I met in their offices, signed a contract and left them our original Hi8 tapes so they could make copies for an editing session.

A week later, I was seated in an editing suite together with a video producer. We began by having a technician bring up the selected tape segments on a large TV screen. We then reviewed the tapes and edited them, following a basic script Howard and I had written up earlier. After putting together a initial tape, I took a copy back to my office and reviewed it with Howard. We made a couple of minor adjustments, but the visual story was pretty much there. The visual images were good, but we felt we needed some audio highlights. Howard took the lead and drafted a script. We reviewed it together and polished it.

I returned to the video production offices, the producer brought in a "voice"—Mark Ellis—and Mark did a voice-over reading of our script. Last but not least, the producer added graphic notes we'd prepared on selected images and a background music track. A week later, we had a finished product.

By doing the filming and scripting the video ourselves, we saved lots of time. Plus we completed it on our schedule instead of having to have others come to the site, shoot the film and then endure endless meetings until we all agreed on the film theme and composition. Besides reducing the complexity by not outsourcing the work, there was also a substantial savings in cost: we probably spent half of what it would have cost to have a media company do the work.

The seventeen-minute video, entitled *Coastal Dunelands at Bandon*, documented what the property looked like in 1992, before development. It described problems, threats and development opportunities at the site, and ended with a theme that embraced a mixed conservation and recreation planning approach. We probably ordered fifty copies and sent a copy to every regulatory agency that had review authority over the project and others we felt couldn't or wouldn't take the time to visit the site. This ended up being a great way of introducing the project and our preliminary concepts to a wide range of people. However, we still faced a real challenge: how were we going to change bureaucratic attitudes and mindsets, some of which opposed the proposal from the onset?

CONCEPT PLANNING

After completing the site analysis, I prepared four alternative concept plans for development. Each illustrated variations as to how the resort property could be divided into three primary activity use areas: 1) natural resource conservation, 2) golf course/residential and 3) the resort village center. These concept studies were then reduced to three alternative concept plan schemes.

These schemes were circulated and discussed with local citizens and state agencies. After extensive private and public reviews and team discussions, Howard and I came up with a preferred master plan direction. This reflected our best response to Mike's desires, citizens' concerns and environmental issues.

Concurrently, our land use attorney prepared a preliminary goal exception statement, recommended zoning changes to the county code and land use findings regarding compliance with state regulatory statutes.

We also initiated technical studies to investigate alternative wastewater treatment methods in lieu of septic tanks and drain fields, as existing soil conditions did not permit this method of disposal. Explorations were also under way to locate and test drill for sub-surface water sources. The resort needed its own independent water sources for both potable and irrigation water use.

The preferred concept for the master plan evolved into a balanced, integrated land use approach that would allow conservation uses to co-exist with recreational use and other resort facilities. This concept emerged as a direct response to the landscape's *genius loci*.

This initial work brought forth a clear realization about the relationship of the buildings to the site. We had recognized the spirit of the place; now we needed to preserve this special landscape quality. This realization gave birth to one of our first site development guidelines and architectural design. The buildings needed to be subservient to the landscape. Not every building solution is as successful as it might have been. But for the most part, comments by guests have confirmed that the scenic values and natural beauty of the site that we found in the beginning are still there.

Mike was now anxious to begin golf course construction. During the preparation of the development concept plans in March 1993, he had identified and designated the boundaries for the first golf course. As we studied and developed alternative locations for other future golf course development, Mike wanted to know if it was possible to site a golf course on state park land.

Among the four alternative concept plans, I studied the idea of locating portions of an eighteen-hole golf course on adjacent state park land. To implement this idea, Mike would have needed to purchase or lease a small portion of Bullards Beach State Park. To find out if this was feasible, Howard met with State Park officials and presented a sketch idea as illustrated by the sketch plan below. The State Park planners liked the concept of adding new recreation uses into the state park.

Howard characterized the scheme with a view towards creating a "mega park" with cross easements or a land exchange to rationalize the boundaries to the mutual benefit of both parties. At the time, the Oregon State Parks had little public funding by the state government, and they were interested in exploring public–private partnerships.

Unfortunately, a partnership was not possible. The land that became Bullards Beach State Park was gifted land, and a restrictive clause in the land deed prohibited any future sale, lease or transfer for private use of what was now public land.

Continuing discussions with State Parks officials had a telling effect on the final master plan. The high ridge on the southern half of the resort had magnificent views of the ocean. However, development on this ridgeline would be visible from the state park. Therefore, in order to gain support for the project from the Oregon Parks and Recreation Department (OPRD), the ridge top became off-limits to building development. At that point, State Park officials became committed supporters of the proposal. Their support throughout the public review process was crucial. Had State Parks opposed the proposal, they and other opponents could have formed a major coalition against the resort.

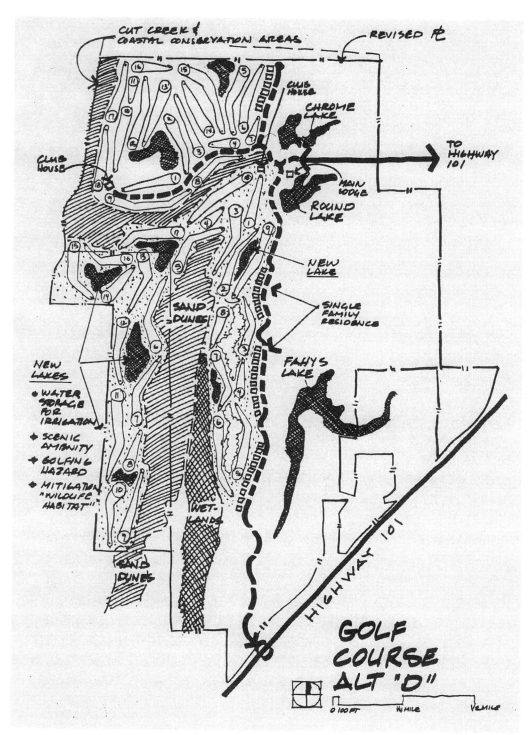

Fig 7: Golf on Resort and State Park Lands

SITING THE FIRST CLUBHOUSE AND LODGE

At Bandon Dunes, the main lodge and clubhouse are in one structure, and the structure does not overlook the ocean bluff. Many owners, other than Mike Keiser, and architects might have sited this building as close to the ocean as possible. The bluff is eighty feet above the beach and delta at the mouth of Cut Creek. The view is outstanding—it was a natural location for a building, and it was an early consideration.

However, David Kidd, the architect for the first course, had a different idea in mind. While analyzing the classic British courses, he had sought a common theme for organizing golf courses and their relationship to a clubhouse. In replaying the evolution of golf in his mind, he remembered two key facts. First, the coastlands were developed around harbors and their villages, since fishing was the primary industry. Second, the linking lands between the sea and the agricultural fields were what became the golf links land. Players walking out from an inland village to the course played their rounds and returned to the village. On the way back, different players stopped at different pubs. The pubs became the de facto clubhouse(s).

To build the clubhouse on the bluff overlooking the ocean would have necessitated building a road to it. Neither David nor Howard and Mike wanted to see vehicles ferrying people and supplies to and from the building. But, more importantly, the road would have invited potential construction of guest lodgings or even private housing along the north side of Cut Creek or near the ocean bluffs. This could and would have sullied the wonderful golf experience golfers and guests now enjoy at the resort.

Developers in America love to use golf courses as the central feature of what is really a real estate development scheme. These golf communities tend to be family-oriented as they offer other recreational activities, such as swimming facilities, tennis, horseback riding and other activities to attract families. Developers who follow this business model do so to make money and many succeed. Fortunately, Mike Keiser was not a real estate developer. Good design and common sense won the day for the location of the first lodge and clubhouse.

The main lodge and clubhouse were built in the shadow of the prominent ridgeline where it breaks to allow the passage of Cut Creek. A construction road would be built through the gap in the ridge. Later, I designed a curvilinear road that appears to have been on an elevated causeway or land bridge over water. Eventually, several buildings—including a Pro Shop for retail sales, a conference center building, a pub, and an administrative office building—were built, forming the Resort Village Center.

M ike Keiser liked flexible plans. Our application to Coos County had to include a master plan and a resort-zoning plan. And as we entered into discussions with the county and other regulatory agencies, a question arose over how much detail to provide in our submission. At the extreme, the regulators wanted specific detail about the building architecture; we wanted less. The master planning process was going to be tricky.

After rejecting the idea of locating the first lodge and clubhouse on the ocean bluffs, our attention shifted to the coastal lakes. Howard knew we were going to build a village to serve as the resort core. A site between Chrome and Round Lakes emerged as a perfect setting for a village center. David Kidd liked this location as it fit his historic Scottish model for a clubhouse. David wanted to locate the clubhouse and lodge next to the first fairway and eighteenth green, with the rest of the village buildings removed at a distance so the buildings did not impinge on the golf course environment. In November 1994, this design idea was committed to paper as a preliminary concept for the village center (see Fig. 8). The intent was to group several facilities in a core area, including a main lodge, residential lodges, and business conference and recreation centers. The surrounding lakeshores would be developed as informal parkland with outdoor pavilions and patios near the lakeshores. This lakeside-oriented village center plan became part of the Conservation, Recreation and Resort Development Concept Plan in our permit application to the county.

This early plan indicated a second eighteen-hole course that assumed an arrangement with State Parks that would have allowed golf course facilities to be built on public lands. As described earlier, this golf course layout proved unworkable due to a legal constraint. Some of the private residential areas shown on this plan were subsequently used for the layout of the Bandon Trails Golf Course.

By the spring of 1996, the master plan was finished. Al Johnson had completed his work, too. We had worked out a phasing plan that projected construction over a twenty-year period. Mike and KemperSports, the management company hired to operate the resort, had been getting positive comments about the resort, but we really didn't know what would happen when the resort opened for business. Uncertainty is always present, and unforeseen events always occur. As insurance in the future, the master plan had been crafted to allow flexibility as we transitioned from conceptual to detailed design. And future events would necessitate substantial revisions to the early resort master plan.

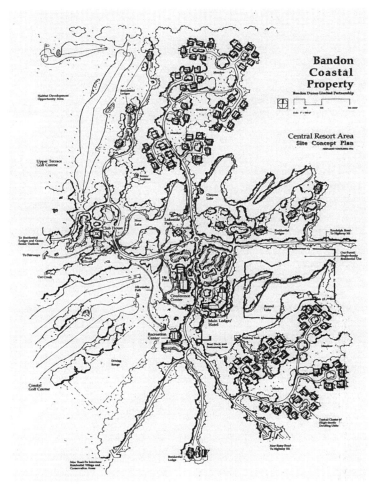

Fig. 8: Preliminary Resort Village Center Concept Plan, 1994

Chapter Nine

Towards Development Approval

One man sees the Burnin' bush Links as a beautiful thing,
the next sees it a menacin' monster.
—Michael Murphy, *Golf in the Kingdom, 1972*

PUBLIC HEARINGS, 1996

Finally it was time to get an answer to the question: Will the county approve or reject the application? After five years of site investigations, team workshops, public community meetings, neighborhood meetings with Weiss Estates residents, community leaders and officials, regulatory agencies and a variety of interest groups, including coastal environmentalists, Howard and his team were ready for the grand dog-and-pony show. In all Grand Adventures, there are high points; this was one of them. We'd turned in our submission, and the county proceeded to schedule a series of public hearings with the County Planning Commission and the County Board of Commissioners. We were primed to argue the merits of the proposal.

Three public hearings were held in May, June and July 1996, before county officials. The first hearing, on May 8th, was at the Coos County Annex Building in Coquille, Oregon, where team members, led by Howard, appeared before the Planning Commission. Howard went at this task like an orchestra conductor. He didn't want to leave anything to chance, so he had sent out a memo before the hearing, listing everybody's roles and responsibilities. Our presentations were scripted and rehearsed.

Al Johnson spoke first. He summarized the legal context for a destination resort application and explained the reasons exception process. Sitting in a front row chair next to Howard, I glanced over and saw Howard scribbling a few brief notes on the back of an envelope. Al finished and ended by introducing the team members present and Howard.

Howard stood up, walked to the front of a room packed full with people, and introduced himself: "My name is Howard McKee, and I am the resort architect for Bandon Dunes. I represent the owner, Mike Keiser." He then proceeded to tell an anxious audience who Mike was, and what Mike wanted to build on a piece of coastal land located about five miles north of Bandon. I was amazed at Howard's presence before the assembled group. Blessed with great charisma, a keen intellect and an eloquent gift of speech, he outlined the site planning concepts and process the team had used to develop the proposed master plan. He continued by identifying negative issues that the master plan addressed:

- Unregulated hunting and trespassing
- Off-road vehicle use that has led to erosion
- Loss of threatened flora—silvery phacelia
- Invasion of non-native flora—European beachgrass and gorse
- Loss of open sand dunes
- Of particular concern—the danger of coastal fires

He described how several alternative concept plans had been studied and evaluated, which then led to the formulation of the proposed master plan and an integrated land management strategy. He explained that Department of Land Conservation and Development staff had confirmed that the project met the state's definition of a destination resort, and that the resort would have to provide prescriptive facilities as defined by statute. In essence, the development program consisted of:

- Three golf courses and supporting facilities
- 150 overnight lodging accommodations
- Restaurant facilities for 100 people
- Public meeting facilities

The destination resort statute also gave the developer the right to provide private overnight facilities at a ratio of two dwelling units for each public lodging unit. Therefore, a total of 300 private residential units were included in the initial development program. The proposed private residential density at the resort would be one dwelling unit per four acres of resort land. By clustering these dwelling units, either as detached residences or small groupings of condominium structures, the intent was to design small village-like building clusters in wooded areas. This would provide privacy for the guests and homeowners. All of these structures would respect a minimum 100-foot setback along the resort boundaries. Howard also emphasized that we wanted to subordinate the architecture to the landscape setting in order to maintain the existing landscape character.

Howard knew there was also public concern about condominium development in destination resorts, so he went on to speak about the current formula and rationale in the statutes. Typically, the primary reason a destination resort is built is to sell lots and residences. In Bend, Oregon, the ratio of private homes to public units at existing resorts had reached as high as twenty private dwelling units for each public lodging unit. This was viewed as very undesirable—that many private dwellings felt like a rural subdivision. The two-to-one ratio (based on ratios at the Salishan Resort near Lincoln City) became a density standard to restrict future resort subdivision development. Mike, unlike many resort developers, had no real interest in residential development at this point. He just wanted to build golf courses.

Howard continued highlighting the main features of our resort master plan:

- Low-key buildings, with a modest retreat atmosphere
- An emphasis on the natural landscape—downplaying the architecture
- Encourage walking and nature experiences
- Avoid structures that could be seen from the nearby state park
- Minimalist golf course design
- Minimum use of irrigation water and chemicals
- Water reclamation where all wastewater is purified and recycled

Howard concluded his presentation by emphasizing the team's concerns about respecting the natural resources of the site, the recognition of the potential coastal fire hazard present in the area, and the fact that the team wanted to continue interacting with neighboring residents and environmental groups to resolve concerns and issues about the project.

We had put together a slide show to graphically illustrate our master planning process. A projection screen was pulled down, and I flipped through a series of slides that highlighted our site inventory, the analysis process and early plan alternatives. Other team members then took the stage to provide additional technical information, after which the public got a chance to voice their opinions and ask questions. We had heard most of these concerns and issues, but now we got the opportunity to respond and argue the merits of our case.

Over the next two hours, members of the audience stood up and gave their support; others stood up and vehemently stated their opposition to the proposal. Among the citizens who opposed the project, there was informed individual, Steven Brown. Quite knowledgeable about Oregon land use law, regulations and procedures, he objected to the proposal because he believed the applicant's arguments did not meet nor satisfy many of the state land use goals. He also disputed the applicant's argument that the project would bring more jobs to the community. He agreed there would be additional jobs, but he believed the jobs would be minimum wage jobs. In addition, Steven believed these local jobs would be seasonal, and that they would place additional demands on the school system.

But the majority of those who spoke supported the project. One supporter stood out: Bill Grile, the Coos Bay City Manager, who had been the Coos County Planning Director at the onset of the applicant's conversations in 1991, had high praise for the consultant team and its planning approach. In a subsequent public hearing with the Coos County Board of Commissioners, Bill characterized the proposal as a "gift." He felt no market research consultant would ever recommend a project of this type at this location because of its remoteness to any established metropolitan center.

Other professionals echoed this sentiment as well. Still, locals could be overheard in restaurants, eating breakfast or nursing a cup of coffee: "What is Keiser thinking? No one will play golf here."

The Planning Commission approved the Bandon Dunes destination resort application, subject to five conditions:

- A road agreement between the Oregon Department of Transportation (ODOT), Coos County and the applicants would be implemented as requested by ODOT.
- All construction approval to be subject to review by the county.
- The applicants would file a waiver of liability claim form regarding farm use on adjoining property; this would prevent future home owners from opposing existing farm practices in the future.
- The applicant was to file periodic turf reports to the county regarding pest control and fertilizer use.
- Guidelines included in the May 8, 1996 memo to the planning commission, by the applicant's attorneys, to apply to the approval.

The stage was now set for another hearing on June 5th. This hearing was before the Coos County Board of Commissioners. They had the authority to review and approve or reverse the approval by the Planning Commission.

Again Al and Howard spoke, reiterating the rationale for the project. Howard and the consultant team tailored their words to address some of the concerns that had been raised in the previous meeting. The resort would have a structured water management program to recycle and reuse gray water for golf course irrigation. We gave examples of how the buildings could be designed to fit into the landscape. We provided more detail on how and where the conservation and habitat restoration projects would be integrated into the project. And I explained our intent to restore natural areas disturbed during construction with native plant materials. Board members were interested in the legal language of the supporting land use findings, goal exception statements and proposed Bandon Dunes Resort (BDR) zoning regulations. A lot of time was spent during this hearing clarifying wording and answering questions from the commissioners.

Mike had already selected a golf course architect to design the first course. He had hired David McLay Kidd, a young Scotsman. David and his father, Jimmy Kidd, had come to attend the hearing at Howard's request. Jimmy was a turf specialist, but in truth Mike had hired them as a package. David was untested while Jimmy had years of experience working on linksland golf courses. David and Jimmy took turns describing the differences between Scottish links courses and typical American courses. Speaking in their heavy Scottish brogue, they added a bit of color to the proceedings. Of course, opponents attending the hearing were not impressed.

Howard was worried that representatives of Weiss Estates subdivision would again bring up the issues they had raised at the Planning Commission hearing. He was right. Steven Brown was in attendance. Testifying against the proposal, his was a passionate voice. He asked questions about alternative locations for the development. He also believed the local housing market would be impacted, and asked why this had not been addressed. He asked why no cost benefit analysis had been submitted. He suggested the land was better suited for agricultural land use, like cranberry bogs. In essence, he objected to the idea of a golf resort at this location on principle. He firmly believed, on principle, that the property was inappropriate for golf development.

Steven and others were opposed to the proposal principally because the property was resource land; it was zoned as forest and/or agricultural land. If up-zoned for a higher use (some would say best use), the action was irretrievable: it could never be returned to its natural or undeveloped state. It was lost forever. There were others who shared this view. Among them were the Leisys (Michael and Lynne), homeowners in Weiss Estates. The last thing in the world they wanted was to see a golf course or resort condominiums across the lake from their home. Howard and I had met with the Leisys and some of their neighbors in the past to discuss the project. As hosts, they were gracious, but they and their neighbors were concerned that fertilizer and pesticide use on the golf courses could pollute their potable water supply—Fahys Lake.

Again, supporters voiced their approval as they mainly felt the project would provide needed jobs to a local economy that had been devastated due to the loss of employment in timber and fishing industries over the past five years.

The meeting came to a close after two proposed ordinances were read into the proceedings and the public record. Since these needed to be considered by the commissioners, the hearing was continued until the following month in order to allow the commissioners and the public to review the documents and testimony that had been put into the public record.

The third public hearing was held on July 11th, and it was a contentious affair. We had further refined and revised the resort master plan and supporting documents that addressed past concerns voiced by opponents. These were read into the record, together with more submissions from opponents and supporters of the project. A local conservation group, the Oregon Shores Conservation Coalition, had submitted a letter of objection, one of the few organized conservation groups to do so.

During the hearing, two of the commissioners made remarks that many in attendance thought represented a bias towards support of the application. Jim Whitty, a golfer himself, felt the proposed location was the only suitable site for a destination golf resort in Coos County. Another commissioner, Gordon Ross, stated: "For ten years we've been told by the state that we have to diversify [economic activity in the county]." He continued, "Why is it that we need some kind of analysis when we go forward on anything?"

These kinds of statements angered many of the opponents. They felt the commissioners had already made up their minds on the application. When public comments were invited, Michael Leisy rose and spoke. He again outlined and emphasized concerns held by Weiss Estates residents. Towards the end of his testimony, he said, "You've already obviously made up your minds without hearing testimony. I think this hearing is a farce." He then added, "Supposedly this is for public input; we've been ridiculed, and no one has been listening."

Gordon Ross took extreme exception to these words. He jumped up from his seat, got red in the face, clenched his fists and started to come around the table separating him from Michael. Quickly, Al Johnson intervened. The two men never physically met, but this outburst clearly characterized the polarized views held by proponents and opponents.

Al Johnson was uneasy. The land use hearings process in Oregon is subject to legal procedures and practices. Either party to a decision can appeal the decision to the Land Use Board of Appeals (LUBA). Both oral and written testimony are important, as well as behavior. There were many in the Bandon community who believed the Planning Commission had been in favor of an approval before the hearings began. The type of behavior exhibited by the commissioners only served to foster the impression, as many people had felt, "it was already a done deal."

Gordon Ross stomped out of the meeting, only to return a few minutes later. He then stated: "I'll tell you what's a farce: our county's land use system. If a person buys land he ought to be able to do something with it. I've been opposed to our land use system since I've been a commissioner, and people (opponents) use the system to bankrupt people." What he said is sometimes true, as opponents to a proposed land use zone change in Oregon can use the process and the appeal process to delay a project in hopes the developer will run out of money, or the delay will make the cost prohibitive at some point.

Gordon, still angry, added more fuel to the fire by telling Michael, "You're disgusting, absolutely disgusting." Someone from the audience shouted back, "So are you." Later, when tempers had cooled, Gordon Ross approached Michael Leisy and apologized for his words. Gordon added, "I'm not proud of myself, I'm ashamed of myself." Others in attendance offered comments, such as: "I have never seen this kind of rude, unprofessional, unsolicited comments" [sic] and "As a woman, I'm disappointed in how this hearing is being conducted." Many opponents felt that approving the application would be like "opening Pandora's box" of troubles. In general, more local people seemed to support the project than opposed it. Order was restored, and the meeting continued.

Al Johnson, troubled about what had happened, focused on damage control. In his concluding remarks, he emphasized that the project had been tailored in response to local concerns and objections. Not all the concerns had been satisfied, but the application had been customized with regard to state land use rules and regulations. He emphasized that the process had been rigorous and comprehensive, and he ended his comments by asking the commission to "make your decision on what has been presented, not on personal opinions." He didn't want the opponents to use a bias argument on which to base an appeal to LUBA.

All in all, it had been a stimulating three hours. Commissioner Ross, still irked by what had transpired, had the last word. He viewed the proposed golf resort as "the highest and best use" for the property. But he added that his decision would be a "legal one," based on what he had seen and heard during the hearings.

Steven Brown, on the other hand, felt that another "value system" should apply to the application. He had testified earlier that: "I have had a lot of people ask me, 'what's the big deal, it's just a gorse wasteland.' Well, it's not a gorse wasteland. My question is, is this the most appropriate place to do this? I have to be honest about my feelings, and my feelings are that I used to go there a lot and it's beautiful. A healthy environment is one of the things that attract people to this area. If a Scottish links golf course and a destination resort is such a tremendous draw, then the question is, is this the best spot for it? Where is the best site to have this [development] with the least environmental impact? I don't think economically, environmentally or socially that building this [resort at this location] is good for Bandon." Steven saw the proposed golf resort as "Burnin'Bush Links" and clearly perceived Bandon Dunes as the "menacin' monster." He could never be persuaded that any good could come from building a golf resort at the proposed location.

The hearing had been absorbing and an emotional drain on everyone. To the dismay of everyone in the room, the commissioners concluded the meeting with no action or vote on the Bandon Dunes proposal. Again the record was kept open for additional comments. The matter was continued for another month, at which time they would vote on the application. Steven Brown, convinced that the board would approve the proposal, stated that he and others were considering filing an appeal to the state Land Use Board of Appeals.

On July 31, 1996, the Coos County Board of Commissioners met and approved the application. Principal objections came from Weiss Estates residents, who believed they would be directly impacted by the proposal; local residents, who felt there were already enough golf courses on the South Coast; and the Oregon Shores Conservation Coalition, which had sent a letter to the Coos County Planning Department, stating there were many adverse environmental impacts that hadn't been adequately addressed.

Fortunately for us, opponents consisted mostly of local residents. Had there been more organized opposition from environmental groups or multiple regulatory agencies together with local opposition, the outcome might have been different.

On reflection, Al Johnson thought the approval was only possible because "we, in essence, had a perfect client, a perfect setting, and we had a situation where we could more or less guarantee the state's bureaucrats that they wouldn't have to apply our precedent to anybody else."

THE HANDBOOK AFFAIR

O n at least one occasion, that opposition set off our "unflappable" attorney, Al Johnson. Participants can enter pertinent information into the public record once a public hearing begins, if the record is kept open. The morning after the first County Planning Commission hearing on the Bandon Dunes application, a representative of the Department of Land Conservation and Development (DLCD) entered a Thursday-morning-surprise into the public record by dropping it off at the County Planning Department, with no notice or copy to the applicant. This very-official-looking document was entitled *Destination Resort Handbook, A Guide to Statewide Planning Goal 8's Procedures and Requirements for Siting Destination Resort.* Its cover looked much like a familiar document, with the same title, that we had been relying on as the basis for our understandings with DLCD staff in the years devoted to preparing our application. With one difference: in place of "1989," the cover read, " Revised, August, 1995."

Inside, there were other differences, bearing directly on our application and directly undermining some of the basic premises of our reasons exception application and propounding a much more restrictive view of how a reasons exception could be used to address the legislatively-recognized need for destination resorts.

When he learned about the revised handbook, our unflappable land use lawyer flapped. He also squawked. A few hours and 200 miles later, Al was perched in the office of Dick Benner, DLCD Director, asking, "What the Hell is going on here?" and expressing outrage at what he saw as rogue behavior by Benner's subordinates, both in the way that the document was created and in the way it was submitted. He pointed out that no one at DLCD had ever mentioned to the county or to the applicant that this revision was in the works, either in meetings or in the agency's comments on the application; and that the agency had not followed open notice and comment rulemaking procedures as required by state law.

As Al recalls it, Benner seemed nonplussed. He denied knowing anything about the revision and confirmed that it had never been through rulemaking or otherwise approved by the Land Conservation and Development Commission. Skeptical, Al contacted one of the commissioners, a fellow land use lawyer and former associate in Al's law firm, Steve Pfeiffer, who told him that he, for one, hadn't heard anything about such a revised handbook. Al then called another lawyer, who was working on a proposed destination resort exception for a site near Smith Rock in Central Oregon. The lawyer, whose project eventually joined the list of unsuccessful reasons exception applications, knew nothing about it.

What to make of this? The handbook was not an administrative rule. It had no statutory power. But as an official-looking DLCD publication, it could and would be viewed by local planners, decision makers, and citizen decision makers as the agency's authoritative interpretation of legislative policy. That, Al believes to this day, was the clear intent of what he still views as rogue behavior by still-unidentified opponents of the project within the Department.

Dick Benner is a land use lawyer himself and knows the law, including the laws that govern state land use policymaking and interpretation. Soon after Al showed up at his office, the handbook was quietly withdrawn. It was never submitted for Commission approval or for adoption as an interpretive rule. Its authorship and the manner of its creation and distribution remain unknown to this day.

The changes in the handbook language were few, subtle and, in Al's mind, potentially lethal to our project. The revised language inserted at the end of the handbook stated:

> "In counties that have not adopted a Goal 8 program for resort siting, the exception process is available, but also difficult. Resort developers should keep in mind that without the county-wide assessment through a Goal 8 process, showing the need for a large-scale development outside an urban growth boundary is difficult. Where counties have not carried out a Goal 8 program, there is no benefit from the legislature finding of need for resorts in rural areas."

In our case, Coos County had not carried out a Goal 8 program. Applied to the county, the guideline suggested the county had no basis to claim and benefit from a previous right to have a resort. The 1989 DLCD Handbook had explicitly stated:

> "The character of the proposed development is critical in meeting the exceptions test. The key tests in the exception process are reasons and alternatives. Goal 8 effectively says that there is a need for destination resorts in the state and that resorts can only reasonably be located in rural areas."

Many years later, I was told that "Staff" felt that the new 1995 handbook reflected the department's current understanding and interpretation of the Goal 8 law given current use. The department had always had internal discussions and evaluations on what the law and administrative rules were intended to do and how they should be applied. However, "Staff" felt that a revision was not an explicit regulation or policy change that was directed from the legislature or the Land Conservation and Development Commission. "Staff" thought of the 1995-revised handbook simply as advice to Coos County officials and the planning staff.

Al still doesn't buy any of it. He says that staff knows the goal-making and rulemaking statutes were put there specifically to prevent "Staff" from making surprise, behind-the-scenes changes in policies and interpretations of state land use goals. They know that the Commission and the legislature, not "Staff," are the only state entities authorized to make and change those interpretations. Putting all this together with the secrecy of the project and the manner in which it was quietly slipped into the post-hearing record, Al believes to this day that DLCD's "Thursday-morning-surprise" can only have been an intentional end-run of those laws.

The DLCD and 1000 Friends of Oregon invested lots of time in opposition to the Bandon Dunes application for a destination resort. Why expend this much energy? The answer to this question requires an understanding of the early political history of Oregon's land use system. The state's land use program, at its inception, was seen as an "aspiration" by many of its founders. There was an expectation that the program would have a high level of achievement. The policymakers and certain individuals who created the program wanted it to be product-oriented instead of process-oriented.

Conceptually, the program had to deal with two layers of government: state and local. The state's interests were broad in nature and dealt with policy and mandates, while the local interests (county and municipal) were supposed to deal with implementation and enforcement. This presupposed a continuum—the state's interests would go so far and the local interests would continue the program. This separation of broad policymaking and local implementation would have flexibility and some degree of discretion if left to counties and municipal governments to approve projects and improvements that fit the local circumstance and need.

In the beginning, some of the DLCD executive directors and staff viewed their mission and mandate in broad terms and saw the local government units as partners in the program. However, over time, the system began to morph. The personalities at the DLCD became more intertwined and much more engaged in administrative rulemaking. They started formulating rules geared toward implementing the broadly stated goals of the state legislature and the oversight commission, the LCDC. And those rules became increasingly narrow in scope and definition. By the late 1980s, these administrative rules established specific requirements for local governments.

A decade later, rulemaking became the focus of the DLCD. The rules became directive in tone: 'you shall do such and such.' Where there had been flexibility, the approach now was regulatory and prescriptive. A good example was a rule passed in the mid-1990s that stated a habitable structure (residence) could not be built on a piece of agriculture zoned land unless the occupant made at least $40,000 in annual income from agriculture activities on the property. The intent was to restrict people from having a hobby farm in the country.

The relationship between state and local government, which was once viewed as a working partnership, no longer existed. Local officials, planning departments, planning commissions and county boards of commissioners were now viewed by agencies like the DLCD as entities to "direct" to achieve compliance for state-wide planning goals.

What methods did the DLCD use to achieve these ends? More specific rules and grant monies to counties and cities came with strings. State planning grants were available, but they could be denied or even rescinded if the DLCD felt the local governments didn't apply the appropriate rule, or when the department simply disagreed with a local decision. Grant contracts sometimes stipulated that the grant funds were contingent upon achieving stated goals and objectives envisioned by the department. This was the ideology: state agencies knew best what was good for local government.

Many local officials and others were frustrated with the current state of affairs. Could the system be reformed? Unfortunately, as more and more individuals got involved in the process, the process took on a Pogo-like mindset: "we have found the enemy, and it is us." The result today is that the rules won't be changed because the people who wrote the rules are still in charge.

Therefore, the fact that the DLCD attempted to enter a new handbook into the public record was not out of place for the way the department operated back then. The reality is that the DLCD has, in the past, been led by and controlled by strong-willed individuals with particular views about development and environmental protection. At times, the DLCD has led the LCDC commission in how to approach statewide land use planning issues. The revised handbook was never presented to the commission, principally because it would have required a public hearing and airing. Al Johnson's single objection during the 1996 public hearings would have been overshadowed by a multitude of objections from individuals, interest groups and local officials had a revised handbook been presented in 1995. Public exposure was the last thing the department wanted.

If challenged about a rationale for the revision, the department might have claimed all it wanted to do was bring more certainty to the process. But in submitting the revised handbook in the public record (during the Bandon Dunes hearings) and in reversing course on understandings that had guided the process up to then, they were only trying to use intimidation as a ploy with county officials. In the end it didn't work.

1000 FRIENDS

Earlier in the planning process, Howard had contacted 1000 Friends of Oregon. He knew this environmental organization would have an interest in the proposed resort. He also knew that 1000 Friends could become a formidable opponent if they chose to object to the proposal. Howard's invitation to discuss the project was turned aside by the organization.

Howard had been a founding member of the 1000 Friends. Now he found himself aligned against them. This was an organization that had been instrumental in reforming the state's land use planning system two decades previous. Howard never regretted his earlier support for 1000 Friends. Nevertheless, as he and Al discussed legal strategies and submittal requirements, occasionally he vented about how excessive legal procedures and precedents could be used to thwart a reasoned planning and design approach.

True to their nature, 1000 Friends of Oregon objected to the proposed destination resort. They entered into the approval process when a request by an affiliate group was made for their assistance. The request most likely came from the Weiss Estate neighborhood association or someone allied with the group.

1000 Friends assigned Chris Cook, one of their staff attorneys, to the case. The fundamental reason 1000 Friends and its affiliates opposed the resort land use application was because the proposed site was zoned as resource land with a forest and agriculture use designation.

We argued that the land could not support those uses, and that the land had been mismanaged in the past. In opposition, Chris argued: "Since the resource land is not, at a particular point in time, well-managed for resource purposes does not mean that it could not or should not be."

She also believed just because resource land is usually cheaper than land zoned for development and easy to develop to the "highest and best use" does not necessarily mean one should be allowed to do so. Once developed to a higher or better use, the land can never be returned to resource use. There is a principle associated with that last statement: up-zoning resource land is an irreversible action.

Steven Brown had made the point during the hearings. Today he still feels the resort, even given its success and the contributions it has made to the local economy and community, is still in the wrong place. To him, the resort or Fahy property, in an undeveloped state, was irreplaceable, priceless resource land that never should have been developed.

In retrospect, Chris felt the applicant's attorneys, Al Johnson and Corinne Sherton, had done an excellent job for their client. Bob Cortright, a DLCD staffer during these proceedings, reflecting on the land use decision, said: "Al Johnson made it [the process] work and showed it does work. Exceptions are not supposed to be easy, but [the resort] got through the process."

After reviewing the legal record of the public hearings and the applicant's submissions, 1000 Friends decided they could not win on appeal at the Land Use Board of Appeals. Chris never filed an appeal brief. Her view was that the reasons exception process was procedural, and that it didn't make any difference what you came up with as long as you asked and answered the right questions. Enough written material had been submitted by the applicant that supported their argument, and the law was sufficiently deferential to the decision maker's view of what the evidence showed. She would later say: "They did it right. They did what they needed done to justify it. They checked off every box."

There is, perhaps, another explanation to the story of why 1000 Friends never filed a brief for an appeal. This particular environmental organization is very protective of its win-loss record. Sometimes an organization will not appeal or will withdraw an appeal if they think they will lose because they don't want that case to become "case law" in the future. Existing case law always gives someone a basis to argue for or against something. It's a basic legal strategy, which an attorney uses by threatening a lawsuit by saying your argument is just a "theory"; there's no case law to support the argument.

With the appeal dropped, Howard and Mike could proceed with facility design. The focus was now on designing and constructing a resort complex that resembled and functioned like a small town—a village. And the original development program would expand as demand grew for more facilities over time.

THE SCHUMAN PROPERTY—GOOD AND BAD

Mike had had his eye on the 825 acres abutting the resort property to the north. He had tried to buy it a couple years earlier, but Schuman—the owner—wouldn't sell. Schuman was now on the brink of bankruptcy. Now he had to sell.

We were days away from the first public hearing, and the ground shifted when Mike bought the Schuman property. To Mike, this was a godsend. There was more room for more golf courses. He and David Kidd were ecstatic. Having the Schuman property meant David could revise and improve the design for the Bandon Dunes, the first golf course.

Mike's land purchase couldn't have come at a worse time. This godsend was a giant headache for Howard and me. As Mike began making plans for more golf courses, Howard and I re-examined the resort master plan.

Clearly the master plan needed revision since the southern resort entrance drive would no longer be the primary access off Highway 101.

We had to keep the land purchase a low profile event so it wouldn't raise new issues we couldn't address during the public hearings. Obviously, we would rethink and formulate a new design program for the future resort expansion. Our land use attorney made us aware of the fact we would need to go back to the county and make minor adjustments to our permit approval, assuming the county approved our current application.

So we proceeded with the planned hearings. We had already spent almost four years, and a further delay was unacceptable. At the same time, Howard directed me to immediately extend the natural resource inventory (using the same methodology) for the new property. So, as we prepared and participated in the 1996 public hearings, Howard and I were already thinking about revisions to the master plan.

More land precipitated a shift in the resort's center of gravity. It became obvious that the village center needed to be consolidated in conjunction with the first lodge and clubhouse building. We also changed the location of the main entrance road to the resort. It shifted from the southern entry to a northern entry, using the intersection of Randolph Road and Highway 101 as the primary resort entrance.

DEVELOPMENT APPROVAL

The moment was at hand. On August 21, 1996, the Coos County Planning Commission and Coos County Board of Commissioners approved the destination resort permit application for Bandon Dunes. All of our exhibits, including the *Bandon Coastal Dunes Conservation, Recreation and Resort Development Master Plan, Land Use Findings and Goal Exception Statement & BDR Zone*, had been compiled into a single document, entitled "FINAL DECISION"; this was the last step in the permitting approval process.

We had translated the development and building program into specific activities, buildings, and supporting infrastructure—roads, community water supply system, wastewater treatment plant, electrical power services and other facilities needed to construct a planned destination resort over a twenty-year time period. It was as complete a document as one could prepare, given what we knew at the time. Uncertainty is always present, and unforeseen events always occur. But the master plan had been crafted to allow flexibility for phased detail design.

We had received criticism about the lack of design detail on proposed facilities. How big would the building footprints be? What would the buildings look like? Who knew?

To address this issue and other concerns, a two-step approval process was incorporated into the final submittal documents. A strong case can be made that the type of design detail the public and some regulatory agencies originally sought was unwarranted in the preliminary stages of this project. If you develop a master plan based on only past project experiences and adherence to strict requirements, what happens when major change occurs? Not in our wildest dreams could any of us have contemplated the events of 9/11, the mortgage industry debacle, and the resulting stock market downturn in 2007–2008—all of which affected the schedule of design and construction at the resort. At Bandon Dunes, having the two-step review process resulted in better design decisions and a better resort.

Up to now, Howard's primary attention had been on securing the "prize"—the statutory permit approval. Mike's vision was closer to reality. Our mission had changed: now we had to design and build the infra-structure to support dream golf.

All Mike wanted to do was build the first golf course.

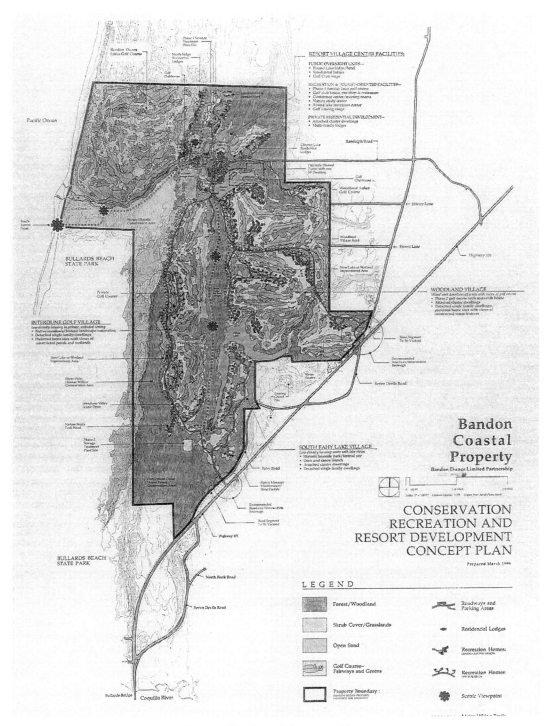

Fig. 9: Preferred Concept Plan

PART THREE

BUILD OUT

Excellence is the only market that isn't crowded.
—Scott Adams

Fig. 10: Main Lodge, Clubhouse and Arrival Area

Chapter Ten

Links Land

True links works in America.
—Mike Keiser, Chicago, Illinois

COURSE DESIGN

Many golf course owners sit on the sidelines while their architect designs and oversees the construction of the course. That wasn't Mike Keiser; he was engaged as an active partner with his architect. His philosophy about designing and building great links style courses began with a touch point: "Oceanside location, sand dunes and good architects." Mike's touch point continued as "we get to know the site, and plan the holes and the overall feeling. Each hole is built with reference to a Great Course. We're not duplicating a specific hole or course layout. Instead we try to evoke the spirit of links golf." Among the four eighteen-hole courses at the resort, this philosophical approach is best expressed in the design of the Old Macdonald course.

Mike was an English major in college. This meant he learned about the Great Works of Literature and the almost great works. Mike realized he could do the same with golf courses. Like others majoring in literature, he spent time deconstructing the great works to prove they were great. When Mike became seriously interested in golf, he made a list of the best golf courses in America, the British Isles and elsewhere. What he found was that "almost all are on the ocean, almost all are built on sand, and most interesting they're almost all old classic courses from a previous era." These courses became his models when he decided to build golf courses.

Mike loves to play golf. And his appreciation of the game is not so much about the game itself; it's really about appreciating the beauty of the landscape—"the walk is as good as the play." When you think about playing a round of golf, if you don't use a cart, you actually spend more time walking and looking around than hitting the ball.

Bandon Dunes put a spotlight on Scottish links style golf courses. However, it wasn't the first linksland style course in America; another one inspired Mike.

A maverick golf developer by the name of Dick Youngscap also loved links style courses. In the mid-1980s, Dick decided he wanted to build an authentic links golf course, and he chose a remote site in Mullen, Nebraska. But where was the water? There's no seaside property in Nebraska. How could you have a links course with no ocean view? This fact did not bother Dick. He didn't have any coastline and water, but he did have an awful lot of sand. There was sand as far as the eye could see in the north-central part of Nebraska known as the Sandhills. The area is a grass-stabilized prairie over pure sand that covers about one quarter of the state's landmass.

Dick's course was designed and built by Bill Coore and Ben Crenshaw. Naturally, Dick called the course Sand Hills, and it opened in 1995. Incidentally, Mike was one of the founding members.

Mike had been treading water for five years, but now he was ready to built his links style course at Bandon Dunes. He had hired David Kidd, and David made the most of this special opportunity.

BANDON DUNES, THE FIRST COURSE

Many nationally renowned golf course architects vied to get Mike Keiser's attention when it became known he wanted to build a golf course near Bandon. Instead, Mike chose an unknown. At the time, David, a young Scotsman, was director of golf design for Gleneagles Golf Development (GGD). He had been around golf courses his whole life and previously had worked in the field actually building golf holes while an intern with Southern Golf, an international golf construction and contracting company.

At Gleneagles he had spent most of his time doing reconnaissance work, visiting potential job sites. He also found time to design several master plans, but nothing ever got built. In retrospect, David considers the years he spent at GGD a postgraduate course.

Unless you are a famous professional golfer and decide to become a course designer, most golf course architects struggle in the trenches paying their dues for years. David was only twenty-seven years of age when he and his father, Jimmy, flew to America to visit the resort property at Bandon. So why did Mike hire a young golf course architect who was just starting out in the profession? David Kidd was available. Actually, Mike hired David and Jimmy Kidd (they were a package), and he could fire David if things didn't work out because there wasn't a contract.

The Kidds spent a week walking the property and getting a feel for the topographic features of the land. David had also spent time thinking about how he would approach the course design. In his mind he had deconstructed all the famous golf courses in the British Isles he had visited, and he had made a list of key points.

Jimmy began their presentation to Mike, but David took over and laid out his design approach, referring to a preliminary routing plan he had drawn up the night before. Mike liked what he saw and heard from David and Jimmy. They were given the OK to proceed.

David, like each of the other golf course architects, faced many challenges in designing and constructing his particular golf course. His biggest challenge was overcoming perceptions held by the American golf industry and golfers about links style play. There was lots of resistance. He had to work extremely hard to convince his critics that this style of golf would be acceptable to retail golfers. Most retail golfers, especially the ones Mike brought out during construction, had never seen a course like David was building; it was out of their comfort zone.

Thinking back, David feels fortunate that Mike persisted in his quest to realize his vision, while at the same time supporting his architect. This support was important, especially during construction, as David often found himself junior to a few of his critics. Often, he felt, others were trying to "Americanize my Scottish design ideas."

Except for Jim Haley, his shaper, none of the other people on the construction crew had ever built a golf course before as David hired local workers to do the job. Since they had no preconceived ideas about how to go about it and they also had no work skills relating to golf course construction, David had to educate the construction crew on how to build a golf course.

As they started to clear the site of vegetation, they discovered a major problem that irritated Mike to no end: the edge of the ocean bluff had an exposed reddish granular material known as red shot. Beneath this was a layer of volcanic ash about eight to nine inches deep. The material was impermeable to drainage.

To overcome this condition, an underground drainage system was installed. This resulted in a network of area drains, in low spots, throughout the course. These drains were connected via a system of pipes that carried surface runoff to two major discharge points. Without this drainage system, the course would have been soggy and wet in the winter. Installing this drainage system added about a million dollars to the overall construction costs to build the course.

Another cost was the need to provide irrigation. Summers are dry. Irrigation added another million dollars. Building the Bandon Dunes course came to $3.5 million. Mike had wanted to build the course for $1.2 million; that's what it cost to build Sand Hills. He was not happy.

David has gone on to build many more courses, but the opportunity to build the first course at the resort, in his words, "set a new benchmark in American golf course design." Ben Crenshaw put it another way: "David turned people's heads."

The advent of the Bandon Dunes Golf Resort changed the mindset of the American golf industry. What it really did was give American golf a different personality; golfers and golf writers began to think of golf in a different direction. When the pictures of the Bandon Dunes course first hit the news and magazine stands, they enhanced people's imaginations of what golf could be. They whetted a true golfer's appetite.

David also believes that Mike and he were extremely fortunate in their timing. The golf public was ready to accept the idea that target golf was not the only available choice. Golfers were ready to return to the origins and enjoyment of hitting a small object around ocean side pastureland—

namely, links land. This was an affirmation that golf is, as David has said, "a casual recreational activity that combines aspects of a sport with an outdoor experience in nature."

PACIFIC DUNES

Tom Doak was forty years old. Some days he thought, "Maybe I'll be a really good architect some day." That day arrived when Mike Keiser asked him to design the second course at the resort. "It was like a door opened for me."

He and Mike toured golf courses in Ireland before the first course was built. Mike had planned a trip with a group of friends, high school and college buddies, and one of them dropped out. Mike asked Tom to come along to fill out the group. It would also give both of them a chance to get to know each other better.

On this six-day trip, they did get to know each other better. In Ireland they put their heads together and talked about the distinctions pertaining to links golf. Mike was asking questions about why he liked this particular course or what design principle was behind a noted classic hole. They found they liked the same things.

Mike had even considered Tom as the architect for the Bandon Dunes course. He thought Tom was great, but Tom was controversial. Tom had published his *Confidential Guide to Golf* and irritated many people in the golf world. Mike thought if he used Tom, people wouldn't come to see what was at Bandon Dunes.

Tom was a classic golf course architect, and he was a minimalist. His philosophy was rooted in the belief that a good architect can find "natural" golf holes in the landscape. The site Mike gave him for the Pacific Dunes course had lots of undulations, angular topographic shapes and hummocks.

Visiting the resort while the first course was under construction, Tom peeped over a fence at the Schuman property and saw some fairly big sand dunes (where holes 2, 7 and 8 at Pacific are now). It was clear that this property was more attractive than the first golf course site because David's site was covered with pine trees and gorse.

When Tom started work on Pacific Dunes, he also had to remove gorse.

However, the site also had duneland topography where, with little modification, a golf hole awaited discovery. Consequently, Tom didn't have to disturb the natural topography as much as David had had to do on the first course; the Pacific site had more variety of vegetation, more open sand, and extensive areas of open sand blowouts. Tom remembers thinking: "we had a natural, very scenic site that was conducive to minimal disturbance." He and Jim Urbina, his associate and shaper, didn't have to remove as much gorse so they had the opportunity to insert golf holes into the natural landscape, and, at the same time, they were able to leave intact the general scenic character of the existing landscape. This produced a design that was completely different from David's course. Neither course was better than the other; they were two very different golfing experiences.

Some people, including Grant Rogers, the resort's director of instruction, say the Pacific course is magical. What makes it so? Except for the turf today, players on the 1st, 3rd, 4th, 5th, 7th, 10th, 11th, 13th and 14th holes see what the golf architects saw years ago. There's magic in, as Ben Crenshaw noted, the "vast array of holes that were available to Tom, and the manner in which he put the puzzle together!" The fact that the course was built on sand, by the sea, and its elevated height relative to the water presents golfers with wonderful, panoramic ocean views that enhance the magic.

When talking about Mike, Tom has said, "The amazing thing about Mike is that he keeps things simple. He only has one goal: 'build the best golf course possible on this piece of ground.' That was the architect's initial challenge. But, the thing about Mike is that he is fairly open-minded about what that means."

Many clients can have rigid definitions in their heads about how long the course should be; how difficult or easy it should be; or they have a lot of perquisites for what they're looking for. Sometimes they turn the architect loose, but later bring up lots of issues and details. It's like they have a list, and they want the architect to check off their boxes. Instead, Mike "looks for an impression of a hole, and how that resonated with him, not individual items."

One of the more interesting things about Tom was that he graduated from a landscape architecture program unlike many golf course designers who played professional golf or came to the profession with another background. And Tom operated completely differently from the way landscape architects are taught in school. Most of the time landscape architects approach a project by coming up with a plan that envisions what a final product will look like in twenty years.

Mike liked an incremental, trial and error approach: build something and see if it works; if it doesn't, then change it. And when it came to building Pacific Dunes and the other courses that followed, Tom believes Mike's attitude was: "Right now, we're building one golf course; the goal is to build it without making any tradeoffs for any other golf courses we might build in the future." Focusing completely on the task at hand instead of trying to consider what might be in the future: that's how Bandon Dunes ended up with five golf courses (not including Shorty's course) that have their own exceptional character. Together, they offer golfers the opportunity to experience golf beyond anything they could ever dream about at one location.

Most architects designing an oceanside course tend to focus on the holes that have the ocean views. Golfers like drama. To walk up over a rise and come face to face with the ocean is a grand experience. Hitting a drive across a huge gully to reach a green laid on a piece of land jutting out towards the sea stirs the emotions. At Pacific, Tom felt the inland ground was "more protected and scenic in a dramatic way. It was the most attractive part of the whole place."

During construction there was a period of preview play. People were so excited about the course design, and Tom remembers: "I thought, geez, we haven't even built the two holes [4th and 13th, right along the coast] people will remember best. I just knew the design could only get better."

And there were design issues to resolve. Because there was a variety of vegetation and a visual contrast between the inland and ocean side holes, the designers needed to create a contiguous environment; they needed to blend these differences into a holistic design. The course also had to look like it had always been there.

Construction also proved to be challenging. High school students had been used to construct the Bandon Dunes course, and they were also used to build the Pacific Dunes course because they were the only workforce available in the local area. But, what was an initial disadvantage became an advantage. Many of the crewmembers stayed on, hired as course maintenance workers. They had taken pride in building the course; now, they had pride of ownership. They also knew all the intricacies of the course in terms of what was necessary to keep it in perfect shape for play. Jim viewed it as "the perfect scenario; there's no better way to build a course."

Mike thought of Pacific Dunes as an Irish course. One of the nuanced differences between Scottish and Irish courses is color palette of turf found respectively. For an Irish course, the palette is varied so it's not one color, and variation of vegetation reinforced this attribute.

When I interviewed Tom, I asked him what Pacific Dunes did for his career. Because he'd been around American golf for many years people in the industry knew who he was. He thought a moment and answered: "It turned me from a young guy with potential to a guy who had actually done a great golf course. It was huge; it put me on the map."

THE PUNCHBOWL

St. Andrews has the Himalayas (not the mountains); it's a putting course built as the Ladies' Course in the early 1900s with the strategy: Hit the ball and see how close the ball can get to the flag. Mike believes "it's fun and quirky." After visiting the putting course at Pinehurst, in the spring of 2013, Mike decided to enlarge the existing putting green at the Pacific Dunes Golf Course. Instead of random putting activity, the course super-intendent and staff can lay out a specific routing plan, although the routing is changeable. The putting course at Pinehurst has been very successful; golfers love it.

By expanding the existing putting green at Pacific Dunes, Tom Doak and Jim Urbina created a three-and-a-half-acre course that opened for one month in September 2013, to allow guests to test out the facility. The turf area is huge compared to a practice putting green, which, most of the time, doesn't typically exceed 18,000 square feet.

Players are limited to a putter only. However, the routing layout on this course can be altered from day-to-day, week-to-week or a special routing for a special occasion. The course can also be divided up. You could have two different eighteen-hole layouts and double up the number of golfers playing on the Punchbowl.

Fig. 11: The Punchbowl

The design of the Punchbowl is different from the design of a golf course. Since the routing can change every day, Tom felt, from a designer's point of view: "It's a little scary. It's like we've built a medium for someone else to lay out a golf course. Where do you cut the holes on any given day?" The reality is someone else is going to position the tee arrows, flags and cut in the holes.

So he and Jim gave up control over the routing(s). And they are OK with this; they are resistant to trying to influence what could happen in the future. However, they do have a maintenance concern: depending upon the popularity of the Punchbowl, wear and tear could become an issue. One way to manage this potential problem is by taking one quarter of the course out of the routing plan. This would allow rotation of areas to give other areas a rest from foot traffic.

Players will probably play the course late in the afternoon, after playing one of the full courses earlier in the day. Tee times may be required and, depending upon the number of tee time requests the day before, this may then determine which layout is available. The concept is appealing to senior golfers, who may not want to play thirty-six regular holes in one day. It also is an opportunity to create different golfing experiences, increasing the variety of play options. It was Mike's idea to build, but it's someone else's idea to manage. Ken Nice and his staff will have to work out the routings and scheduling.

After Mike called, both Tom Doak and Jim Urbina flew out to the resort and spent two days designing and building the Punchbowl. Shaping was easy; the entire course was pure sand—no red shot or clay to hinder the process. The design has lots of undulations with more extreme ups and downs than found on other greens at the resort.

Behind these extremities is the idea of providing guests with the ability to learn more about putting and to improve their putting skills. To make a connection with the regular links courses at the resort, undulations offer different options in lining up a putt. This challenges golfers to use their imagination in deciding how to line up a putt. It teaches them that the different shapes on the green offer different ways to approach the hole.

A typical routing on the course offers six easy putts, six difficult putts and a graduation of difficulty among the remaining six holes. As explained to me by Michael Chupka, golf professional and superintendent at Pacific Dunes, "The course is instructional—golfers are forced to confront unusual situations where the correct line is not a straight line from the tee box to the pin." During the month of October 2013, the course was available for preview play. A single golfer could spend as much time as he or she wanted, to practice. Groups of various sizes came, and, often as not, there were yells and groans as sporting wagers were won and lost. It was a great social experience, with up to fifty golfers on the course at any one time. During the preview there were instances of 150 guests using the Punchbowl.

The course was shut down in November with a grand opening scheduled for May 20th, 2014. Over time, management will need to work out issues related to capacity, flow and a possible fee. But, on micro-scale, standing on the course, a conifer tree line and elevated topography at the periphery of the course convey a pleasant, enclosed quality to the Punchbowl. There is a sense of oceanic rolling waves to the ground plane.

Above the course, the patio at the Pacific Dunes clubhouse has been expanded. It has become a popular overlook to watch the action below and later to watch the sunset over the ocean. A few guests always remain to have another libation—an offering to the Golf Gods that watch over these proceedings. Many linger and huddle around the new rectilinear fire pit as twilight turns to darkness and a night chill settles over the patio.

When questioned about the Punchbowl, Tom Doak recalled how he and Jim had actually suggested a much larger putting green when they worked on the Pacific course. He knew the potential was there to do something cool. When the Boora clubhouse design was scrapped, and plans for a different clubhouse got put on hold, Tom thought, "We'd better not do anything in the open sand dunes because they might need to go through there for access to build a clubhouse." And then he forgot about it. The opportunity lay dormant, only to resurface later.

But before the Punchbowl was built, four other courses were playable at the resort. The third course built at the resort was Bandon Trails, and it tested the integrity of the resort master plan.

BANDON TRAILS

S and Hills captured Mike's imagination. There he had admired the golf course design by the firm of Coore and Crenshaw. For the third course he hired Bill Coore and Ben Crenshaw. The Trails course was supposed to be a woodlands course—a course out of the wind. Not all golfers enjoy playing in the wind; it beats you up.

Mike invited Bill to come and visit the resort and look at the proposed site for an interior course. When Howard picked Bill up at the North Bend Airport, Bill immediately felt comfortable with him. Once at the resort, Bill met Troy Russell, the golf superintendent. Troy approached Bill, welcomed him and mentioned he was looking forward to working with him. Bill was surprised, because he was only at the resort to look things over; he'd not yet been offered a job. Troy shook his head, smiled and responded, "Yes, indeed. I'll be working with you. It's obvious. Of all the people who have looked at the site, you're the only one Howard has picked up at the airport."

As they struggled with the initial routing plan, Bill remembers telling Mike, "We are working on the wrong property." Bill was referring to the land north of the Pacific Dunes course that later became the Old Macdonald course. Mike's response was, "Anybody could do that course." Mike's direction was: "You can choose any acreage over there [in the woods]."

But that changed. Mike asked Howard, pretty please; can we move a few of the holes to the ocean side of the ridge? Mike remembers Howard's sharp response: "It doesn't fit the master plan." So Mike gave up. He just wanted a course out of the wind.

Mike and Bill were both thinking about a golf course in California called Spyglass Hill. It had holes in both a forest setting and a coastal setting. Mike liked Spyglass, but he didn't want this design to be another Spyglass. Mike didn't want to fight about where holes should be, but Bill Coore did.

Over the next three or four days, Bill and Howard discussed the design parameters for the Bandon Trails course. They reviewed the approved master plan and the illustrative concept plan that depicted the course layout intermingled with private homes and a chain of water features. That plan also envisioned a nine-hole golf course and more residential buildings scattered over the west slopes of the South Ridge. But that plan changed.

Rising early each morning, Bill walked out to the course site to get a feeling for what a golfer would see for an early morning tee time. Each time he walked through the dunes, then across a native grass meadow on the ridge slope facing the ocean, and finally up and over the ridge top and down to the wooded site on the east side. During these walks, a recurring thought entered Bill's mind: "why isn't the golf course in the dunes?" And he would also think: "this is a links style golf resort; why are we only in the woods?" These thoughts prompted Bill to ask Howard if it was possible to build a few holes on the west side of the ridge.

"No," was the immediate answer; "the meadow is sacred." During the master planning effort, we discovered it was a historic landscape, and we wanted to preserve it. The dunes were also off limits because we had zoned it as a conservation area for the protection of a threatened duneland plant species—the silvery phacelia.

Over late night dinners, they continued discussing the matter (Bill thought of these conversations as negotiations). At this point, both Mike and Howard were insisting the course should stay in the woods. Bill was persistent; he argued there was a way to put a few holes in the meadow and in the dunes. He also felt construction costs could be lowered by connecting to existing infrastructure already in place for the Bandon Dunes course. As Bill continued his arguments, Howard's typical answer was, "You can't do it, you can't do it." Little by little, Bill chipped away at Howard's resistance and, little by little, Howard conceded it was a good idea but, at the same time, he was conscious of the fact that the underlying master plan might need serious revisions. He didn't relish the idea of going back to the county for another approval.

In Mike's mind, the Trails course was going to be different. Ben Crenshaw felt he wanted "something different; a course that had appeal to a group of golfers who wanted to explore a different type of territory at the resort."

Mike initially thought that the Trails course could become a "winner" if it was designed in the manner of the West Course at the Royal Melbourne Club in Melbourne, Australia. Mike had played this course and liked the look of the course, since Alister MacKenzie, one of Mike's favorite golf course architects, had designed it.

However, Bill and Ben believed the "raw topography and distinctive character" of the site presented an opportunity to "showcase" a course that complemented the existing courses but reflected the natural attributes found at this wooded site. Both architects, although design minimalists at heart, sought a design solution that would "emerge from the character of the land. They let the ground dictate the concept and approach while lightly putting down golf holes people can enjoy." Ben thought of this commission as a "leap of faith" on Mike's part.

Mike did have a serious design concern: putting some of the holes on the ocean side of the ridge would split up the character of the golf course, as was the case with Spyglass Hill. Spyglass starts in the woods, goes to the dunes, but ends in the woods. Mike thought this was a big letdown. Bill's solution was a simple variation on that theme, and so Bandon Trails starts in the dunes, goes to the meadow, to the woods, back to the meadow, but ends in the dunes. That's a Big Difference.

As the routing plan coalesced, Bill wanted to put more holes farther north of the meadow. He and Howard met in the field with a topography map. As the discussion heated up, Howard emphasized his position by saying, "No, No, No!" He pointed at the map and said, "Can't you read?" Bill looked at the map but couldn't see anything in particular, given

Howard's state of excitement. Howard then put his finger on the map. At the end of his finger was a note printed on the map. It indicated "Dense Trees." The trees remain today.

Mike got comfortable with Bill's approach, and today Bill feels blessed that he had a client who took the time to listen to his ideas. Mike won't always take a consultant's recommendation, but he will listen to the argument.

As Bill refined his design, another problem came up. A critical piece of the course layout ended up on top of a major scenic drive. Bill asked Howard, "Can we move it?" Maybe. Howard then asked me for my opinion, and I said, "Sure, but relocating the roadway will put it on top of a wetland." We decided to move the roadway and had to hire a local wetland consultant, who prepared a mitigation plan. It was submitted to the state authorities and approved. Bill Coore and Ben Crenshaw were able to design and build the layout they wanted, and now all the courses at Bandon Dunes are linksland courses with oceanside holes.

To achieve this end, Bill and Ben had to overcome several design challenges. By far, their greatest challenge was in creating a course that was worthy of being at Bandon Dunes. David had created a superb Scottish links course, and Tom's design had measured up, and some say surpassed it. The last thing Bill and Ben wanted was to create "an inferior course people didn't want to play because it didn't measure up to the first two courses." Bandon Trails had to complement and enhance what was already there. In doing so, it had to embrace " a spirit of togetherness," according to Ben.

As Bill worked out a final routing plan on the ground with Mike, the specter of Spyglass hung over them. Every time they walked the layout and left the second green, Mike voiced his concern: 'what will you do to make a golfer want to continue into the forest, when most of them will want to turn around and go back to the ocean?' Instinctively, Bill knew the design had to give the golfer some reassurance that "you knew you were coming back to the dunes, you just had to know it" in order for the golfer to continue his or her round into the woods.

There were other challenges as the design progressed. Since the layout traversed different environments, the design needed to "blend them together in a seamless fashion so you didn't feel like you were playing three different courses." Golf balls needed to run on turf in a similar fashion throughout the entire course, and a golfer also needed to have golf shot opportunities that were consistent throughout all eighteen holes, irrespective of whether or not they were playing in the dunes or in the woodland setting. To achieve this required solving a technical issue.

Everyone thought the entire property was underlain with sand. Not true. The soil east of the South Ridge was clay. David Kidd had already faced and solved a similar problem on the terraces adjacent to the bluffs. Fortunately for Coore and Crenshaw, only the golf holes located east of the South Ridge needed to be sand capped with sand excavated from elsewhere on the resort property.

There was one more critical challenge: they had to figure out how to get golfers over the ridge to the woods and back to the dunes. A tunnel had even been discussed, but it was rejected. Returning to the dunes after playing the 13th hole in the woods was the more difficult problem to solve. The basic problem was the vertical change in grade at the toe of the ridge on the east side. From the 13th tee boxes, the top of the ridge towered over the natural grade at the green. To diminish this impression, the architects decided to raise the green thirty feet higher than the existing grade. This made the "walk off" from the green to the top of the ridge acceptable. The ridge trail passes by an understory including native Rhododendrons. During seasonal bloom, it is a "magical, enjoyable nature hike."

Bandon Trails is a nuanced course. Bill's view is that "it's a course you have to play a number of times to appreciate the experience." And it contains what golf writers feel is a very controversial hole. The 14th hole, a short par 4, has been written about and compared to the 18th hole at Cypress Point and others as one of the worst holes in golf. But, it has also been said to be "the worst hole on the best course." Mike doesn't mind a bit of controversy, but, over the years, the architects have made the green two yards wider and have cleared out some of the hillside trees on the left side of the green, easing past difficulties with approach shots. It's still a demanding hole, testing a golfer's skill on short play.

The biggest changes have been on the 18th hole. In summer, the north wind was always a major factor in the approach to the original green. Typically, balls ran out thirty yards if you missed the green. Mike requested a change, and the architects lowered the green by three feet. The cut sand was pushed out to soften the natural fairway contours, forming an approach to hold balls that didn't reach the green.

Golf courses are natural, dynamic creations that are subject to natural forces that can introduce change. Man can also intervene. Bill and Ben's design philosophy included the notions of "observing, learning and adapting" their designs over time. The Bandon Trails course is the better for it.

OLD MACDONALD

A coastal gorse fire burned down most of Bandon in 1936. We always mentioned that fact during the public hearing process. Then we followed up by emphasizing that the removal of gorse to build golf courses resulted in excellent firebreaks. In December 2007, the north end of the resort property was ablaze. An uncontrolled beach fire had started at a public beach access area at the end of Whiskey Run Road; it had gotten out of hand, and had spread onto the resort.

Fig. 12: Gorse Fire on Old Macdonald Site

I was on-site that day when a resort employee drove by and yelled, "There's a gorse fire up by Whiskey Run." I got in my vehicle and drove up the maintenance road to the top of the ridge. Looking through the windshield, I saw a wall of flame and smoke across the north end of the resort property. It was a gorse fire. Gorse is extremely flammable due to its high oil content.

I knew that if the fire reached the conifer forest along the east edge of the property, it would soon spread to the adjacent rural subdivision. So I headed back down the road and drove over to Brown Road, a local road that led to the subdivision. During the next twenty minutes, I drove around and warned local residents that there was a fire on the resort, and that they needed to be prepared to evacuate their homes if the fire expanded into the tree line bordering their homes.

Firefighters from Bandon and the Coos Forest Protection Association arrived within minutes after the alarm was raised. Three engines, two bulldozers, three helicopters and one reconnaissance aircraft were mobilized. A firebreak was quickly established, and the fire contained. About 110 acres of gorse burned. The vegetation blazed, smoldered for a while and, eventually, several hot spots were completely extinguished the next day. Only charred plant material remained, scattered over the burned ground. It's not the recommended way to remove gorse, but it is very effective.

Mike invited Tom Doak and Jim Urbina back to design the fourth course—Old Macdonald. Walking the site, they encountered acres of partially charred ground. Nature had already started to produce new ground cover, and the gorse was attempting a comeback.

Gorse plants produce a prodigious seed bank. Typically, there are millions of seeds per acre, and they are viable for two decades or longer. The coastal fire destroyed about seventy acres of gorse, while at the same time activating the underground seed bank. Fire cracks the seed casing while also removing any surface organic material. Thereafter, the gorse quickly recovers. One way to prevent re-growth is to establish a grass cover crop, or, in the case of the resort, build golf courses.

The architects had to contend with gorse hedgerows as tall as they, while portions of the site were devoid of gorse. On one field trip, Jim, eyeing a particular opportunity, remarked, "Look at that green. When we came out here after the gorse fire, it was just sitting there waiting for us, a sweet little private bowl, with these hills surrounding it— how could we not use that!"

The design approach used for the Old Macdonald course was different than what had been used for the previous courses. One of the first ideas was to replicate the Lido Golf Course, which C.B. Macdonald had built on Long Island.

George Bahto is the person who came to Mike with the idea of reproducing the Lido Course. The course was completed in 1915, then it disappeared off the map during the Depression. The Lido has mythical status as a lost treasure—a course that was the equal of Macdonald's National Golf Links course. At the time, Mike was intrigued with the idea because he loved Macdonald courses.

Mike called Tom Doak and asked him to look at George's preliminary routing plans. Tom was skeptical of the idea, principally because the site at the resort was so totally different from the original Long Island site. The latter was lowland situated by the ocean and an inland coastal waterway, while the site at the resort was an elevated marine terrace 150 feet above the beach. The Lido had been built as a very small, compact course with a much smaller golf playing audience compared to contemporary times. To even consider reproducing it today, it would need to be expanded in areas to accommodate more players. Tom's comment was: "If you are going to reproduce it as close as possible, and you can't really achieve a design close enough to the original; don't try to sell it that way, don't do it."

George's plan was a paste-up. He had cut out all the holes for the Lido and had pasted them up on a site map where he thought they fit, to form a routing plan. Tom told Mike: "that's exactly what Macdonald did." Macdonald had a series of favorite concepts taken from existing golf courses in the British Isles. He simply copied some of his favorites and pasted them up where he thought they fit the ground he was working on at the time. That's why many of his courses seem similar.

At some point, Mike abandoned the idea of replicating the Lido course. Instead, he and his advisors (at one point, Mike had twenty-odd architects offering suggestions) agreed that the design should be a collection of golf holes using Macdonald's design principles. Mike knew Tom had studied Macdonald courses and most of all the classic links courses in Scotland and Ireland as a young man and as a caddie in the British Isles. Tom went from critiquing someone's ideas to being asked if he and Jim could design Old Macdonald. At some point, Mike asked Tom, "Can you do that?" "Ya," was the reply.

In making this decision, Mike had to weigh the conventional wisdom of using a different architect in order to get extra PR for the resort. But in the end, Mike went with Tom Doak and Jim Urbina because he knew their work firsthand.

Jim had been Tom's shaper on the Pacific Dunes course. Now he was a full associate and would receive equal recognition for the design of the Old Macdonald course.

Tom and Jim met Mike's challenge. They successfully created golf features in the spirit of classic holes reminiscent of C.B. Macdonald's past designs. To achieve this, they had to reverse their normal design approach; instead of searching for "natural" golf holes suggested by the existing landforms, Tom realized he was actually trying to find locations that allowed him to insert classic golf holes Macdonald had used in the past.

The Old Mac course at the resort is an homage course to the father of American Golf. C. B. Macdonald founded the Chicago Golf Club in 1892, built a nine-hole course the same year and, the next year, built the first eighteen-hole course in America. For Tom and Jim, the honor of designing three courses at the resort was beyond belief at times. Reflecting on being called back a second time and then, to have a third opportunity build the Punchbowl, Jim Urbina remarked, "This reward has no price-tag."

LIQUID GOLD

Water in the West is like liquid gold. Resorts and golf courses can't be built without access to water. At Bandon Dunes this meant drilling wells. However, links style courses use substantially less water than conventional American golf courses. We were extremely fortunate: we found good producing wells both for irrigation and potable water use.

The resort is rich. It sits atop an ancient valley—the Coquille Formation—formed in the past during the four major glacial stages that occurred in North America. Geologically, that portion of Whiskey Run Terrace located between Whiskey Run Creek and Cut Creek is known as the "Elk River Beds."

Multiple wells were drilled to draw this water up to the surface. One of the first engineering tasks was to design and build reservoirs with a pumping and water distribution system. However, over time, as more golf courses were added at the resort, the system was expanded.

The water destined for irrigation use had to be pumped out at night so enough would be available to water the golf courses in the early morning. This required building multiple reservoirs. Eventually, four reservoirs were built. All this sounds simple and straightforward; it's not. You can drill the well, but you need a permit to use the water. Mike owned the land, but the state owned the water. The state Water Resources Board issues permits for water use; I have a four-inch-thick file containing correspondence from the consultant the resort hired to shepherd the paperwork to and through the board. I don't even want to think about how many or thick their files are for the resort's water rights applications.

Having multiple wells and multiple reservoirs complicated the distribution of irrigation water. Typically, the permit system assigns quantitative flows from each well to each course. In our situation, we ended up with a hybrid system. It's kind of like a circular merry-go-round with water flowing into a system of reservoirs that then pump the water into a distribution system via pipes. Computers then ration and record water usage to particular courses while monitoring the inflow and outflow of water from different sources. In this manner, we comply with regulatory reporting requirements.

This system also allows the managers to constrict and stop irrigation at specific courses seasonally. The one good thing about links golf is that the courses don't have to be obsessively green all the time; brown and muted grass is OK.

Opponents considered golf courses water wasters. We pointed out that irrigation water would be applied at agronomic rates—exactly the amount of water the turf needed, with little waste. Moreover, seasonal rainfall is high in the Pacific Northwest, in contrast to golf courses in the Southwest and California. On the Oregon coast, Nature waters the courses in the late fall, winter and early spring.

A NEW MECCA

Mecca: a place that attracts people of a particular group or with a particular interest. Each of the four eighteen-hole courses possesses individuality. Ben Crenshaw would characterize this as the way the ground moves, its undulations. Among the golf courses at Bandon Dunes there is a common attribute: the ground presented at each course keeps moving; it is never static. This is what makes each of the golfing experience at the resort different, yet inspiring.

Game changer. This term came up several times during my research interviews. I liked what Ben said about how it applied to the resort: "Golfers used to talk about making a pilgrimage to St. Andrews or the British Isles to see where the game originated." Bandon Dunes became a new beacon of light for the golf industry in America.

Chapter Eleven

Building and Landscape Architecture

If you build it and it's good enough, they will come.
—George Peper

DESIGN AND MORE PERMITTING

We had an approved master plan, but Howard and I had been thinking all along about architecture. Now we had to build and construct a destination golf resort. Guests could come, but they needed a place to sleep, a place to eat; a place to buy golf equipment and clothing (many would need rain gear); and, most importantly, a place to have a drink. A round of golf doesn't end on the 18th hole; you have to experience the 19th hole to relive and understand the attraction of the game.

Besides building habitable structures, we also needed to provide a potable water supply system as well as a wastewater treatment plant. We had power, but we would need to upgrade the capacity several thousand-fold. Building serviceable roads, laying miles of underground utility pipes, clearing forested areas for construction sites, constructing irrigation reservoirs and moving lots of cubic yards of sand: all these activities had to be discussed, designed, coordinated and supervised to erect a complex enabling guests to actually stay and play golf. To build these facilities and improvements we needed specific construction permits.

As part of our re-zoning approval for the property, we had proposed—and the county had accepted—the notion of the two-step permitting process. Critics of our initial proposal had suggested we provide detailed building designs as part of the resort master plan. This was unreasonable. We needed flexibility, and the two-step permitting allowed us to discover new planning and design opportunities that were not obvious in earlier years. As we built more golf courses, we needed more lodgings. We became captives of customers' demands. But again, this produced a better design and operational product.

On the other hand, the dual permit requirement meant more paperwork. Each new phase of development required another submittal to the county—a document referred to as a final development plan. In a way, this was like a mini-environmental statement that demonstrated how the proposed phase of work complied with the conditions of the approval permit. By 2014, the resort had submitted eleven final development plans. It would take almost a decade and a half to build out the physical fabric that defines Bandon Dunes as a resort.

Although architects often create and emphasize forms and objects that are renowned for their visual appeal, architecture is actually about creating places based on three fundamental purposes. Vitruvius, in *De architectura*, defined architecture thus: "Well building hath three conditions: firmness, commodity, and delight." In modern English, this translates as "the ideal building has three elements; it is sturdy, useful and beautiful."

Although delight and beauty are weighty considerations, the heart of the matter is the place. Architecture is not simply about making beautiful objects; it's more about making places for people to enjoy and marvel at how different a place can be. What is essential is what people experience and take away from the place.

The translation of the design program and the master plan into real buildings, roads and the other utility improvements became a team challenge. We were no longer dealing with abstract ideas and soulful thoughts. Now came the test: can these concepts and plans be transferred from paper to events on the ground?

Everything we did in the early years was a direct response to a perceived need. The overlay was placemaking: we wanted to create the atmosphere of a village and an ambiance that was memorable. On top of this, we had to fast-track our work schedule. We tried to stay one step ahead of Mike and his new ideas, although sometimes it felt like we were two steps behind.

The preliminary design program used during the master plan phase included estimated square footage requirements for buildings. In many cases, these were minimal and did not allow for expansion. As a result, we undersized facilities, like the kitchen and retail shop at the main lodge. No one realized, least of all Mike and Howard, how fast the resort would grow. It was hard to program space needs when we didn't know what the actual demand would be.

THE BUILDING ARCHITECTS

The resort resembles a small village. It's self-contained. It's also a place where architecture and landscape design are interwoven. We took pains to ensure the buildings fit into the landscape, preserving the pre-existing landscape character. Ultimately, four different architects were responsible for the building designs at the resort. However, it took one architect to take what others had done and create a definitive architectural style and motif for the resort. Several years had to pass before we achieved that outcome.

First we had to design and build a main lodge. Howard and Mike had talked at length about this building. Mike liked Stanford White's beautiful clubhouse for the Shinnecock Hills Golf Course in Southampton, Long Island, New York. The building, a classic shingle style structure, was built in 1893 and is acknowledged as the first golf clubhouse built in America.

So, early on, Howard worked up some preliminary ideas with Mike's model in mind. Howard could have been the architect-of-record for the building, but that wasn't his primary role or responsibility. Instead, he hired Bill Church, a Portland architect, to design the lodge. Howard knew Bill understood the collaborative design approach. Howard was not going to be a passive observer.

Bill had designed several special recreational homes at Cascade Head, a popular scenic area on Oregon's North Coast. He had built a series of simple multi-story cabins there in the 1970s. Every time Howard had driven into Cascade Head, he had seen Bill's slender, tall structures nestled amongst a mature Douglas fir tree line at the edge of a meadow. At night, the windowed façades of these buildings glowed like lanterns in the woods. He was impressed. This remembrance convinced Howard that Bill was the perfect choice to design the lodge.

Bill had over forty years of experience. A native Oregonian, he knew the coastal environment intimately. He was also well-versed in green architecture and had co-authored a handbook for Multnomah County on energy conservation and had led several solar workshops for architects. Howard knew energy conservation and sustainability were important design issues, and Bill's expertise in these specialty areas would be useful. Mike, however, was puzzled by Howard's choice; Bill didn't play golf, and he had never designed a clubhouse. But Mike went along with Howard's choice.

The chosen location for the lodge and clubhouse was perfect for the building Mike had in mind. The site was flat and at the same grade level as the first fairway and putting green that were under construction.

Bill's design for the lodge was similar to White's building. Both are horizontal-appearing structures, although the Shinnecock clubhouse is a one-story building, while the Bandon Dunes structure is a two-story building. The form and silhouette of both buildings are accentuated by their relationship to the ground plane. Bill sheathed the building in wood shingles, like White did, but he left off the white paint used at Shinnecock to highlight the window frames and other architectural details. The resort lodge is all weathered cedar.

The selection of building materials was important to Howard. As the design for the lodge progressed, he found a source for Port Orford cedar, a locally available wood that was used to detail the interior of the structure. In making this choice, he advanced the idea of "sustainability" into the design and construction of resort buildings. Furthermore, he added a fourth axiom to the previous three: Do not compromise on building materials and design quality.

Once the building shell was enclosed, I began to think about some form of paving around the building. We knew there'd be a lot of foot traffic with golfers, caddies and other visitors walking about. We considered designs more elaborate than what is there now. In the end, we simply installed large, square concrete slabs separated by grass strips as a transition between the building and the golf environment. It was a perfect, low-key solution; it didn't detract from the landscape beauty as the eye followed a rolling carpet of golf turf to the ocean view. As the guest population grew, we just laid down a few more squares to make an outdoor patio. When the sun shines, you will find a few souls sitting on the patio, watching the passing parade of golfers or watching the sunset dipping into the horizon.

RESORT VILLAGE CENTER

The resort master plan has a heart—the Resort Village Center. But as the various lodging complexes—Lily Pond, Chrome Lake and The Grove—were built, it became obvious these were all spatially detached from the resort core. The core consists of the main lodge and clubhouse and other key amenity service buildings. As the "village" grew, it didn't quite feel like a village. The facilities were scattered; there wasn't much connectivity in the early years.

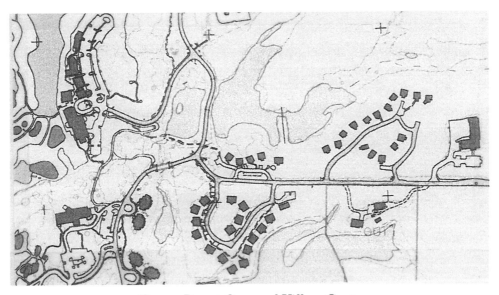

Fig. 13: Resort Core and Village Center

As Bill Church refined the design and construction documents for the main lodge, a program question arose: How many rooms should be in the building? This provoked another question: How many floors should the building have? Howard and Bill thought two additional floors of lodgings were needed in order to have enough guest rooms. This meant building a three-story structure. Howard liked this design for its unit cost efficiency.

When David Kidd heard about this idea, he was flabbergasted. He believed a building that tall would tower over the golf course and be too visually dominant in relationship to the golf course. Upset, he had construction workers erect vertical poles (they used two-by-fours nailed together) to demonstrate the eventual height of the roof peak on a three-story structure. This allowed Mike, Howard and others to walk out on the golf course at various locations and judge the visual impact. The lodge is a two-story building.

Fig. 14: Main Lodge

As the design work began, Howard was also thinking about construction. He wanted to bring a general contractor on board right away. He wanted advice on construction practices in a marine environment and budget cost estimates sooner rather than later in the design process.

He selected Walsh Construction, Inc., a Portland-based company, to be the prime contractor. Having cost estimates early allowed preliminary concepts to be vetted. This provided Howard with real budget numbers he could discuss with Mike so there wouldn't be any uncomfortable surprises later.

The initial project budget was "tight" because Mike was funding the project out of pocket. Even though the budget had quadrupled due to additions Howard had made to the original design program, Howard had to cope with budget limitations when it came to designing and building the first structures. These limitations would have an unforeseen effect in future years.

Howard and his team were now under a time crunch. Mike wanted to open the resort as soon as the first course was ready for play. At this point, the success of the resort was still in question; there were no thoughts about future expansion. If we built it and opened, would golfers come? They did, in increasing numbers.

In 1999, the resort management estimated the resort might do 10,000 rounds on the first golf course. By 2004, the resort recorded slightly more than 80,000 rounds on multiple courses. In 2008, while the national economy was still in the doldrums, more than 100,000 rounds were played on a total of three courses. By the fall of 2011, about 130,000 rounds had been played on all five courses, and it looked like there would be more rounds played in 2012.

Sitting at a window table in the Gallery Restaurant at the main lodge, one can look down the 18th fairway and see the ocean. The view can be grand just before sundown on a sunny day. Fog associated with marine air movement often will move out over the ocean and form a low bank. As the sun begins to dip into the ocean, the light will create a glow on the underside of the fog. It's spectacular. Or a guest can eat breakfast and, as the fog lifts, the large putting green next to the main lodge glistens with dew. It's a fresh, untouched scene until a guest approaches the green with his or her putter. That's just a reminder to guests to quickly finish breakfast so they can practice a few putts before their tee time.

Besides providing guests with their basic needs—a place to sleep, to eat and to drink—there's also a sauna, Jacuzzi hot tub, fitness workout room, as well as the Bunker Bar, at the lodge; those four amenities are located in the basement.

Fig. 15: Sunset from the Garden Room

But Bill Church added something special. Passing through the entry doors, many a guest is intrigued by the presence of four stone columns in the reception foyer. There, centered in the two-story space, are four basalt columns at varying heights reaching for the sky. As a young man, Bill had traveled to the British Isles to visit Avebury and Stonehenge. In his words, "I was obsessed with stones."

The columns are basalt stones quarried and transported to the resort from Eastern Washington. He and Howard traveled to the quarry, inspected and selected the stones. The day the stones were installed found Howard, Bill and me huddled together as a crane lowered each stone into the foyer. The subfloor had been beefed up with concrete and special brackets would be used to securely attach the stones to the floor slab. We actually spent a couple of hours shifting the stones around to get the right composition. Howard and Bill had agreed on a plan orientation that reflected the four quadrants of the compass with a slight offset. The big question was concern about which stones went where as each was of a different height.

Originally, when the building was completed, the stones rested on a custom-made carpet. The carpet had an undulating wave-like pattern that suggested water or sand exposed at low tide. The installation of these stone columns had been a bit tricky, but the carpet installation was an amazing sight to behold.

And what a task it was: the carpet was installed over the stones. On that day, at least thirty people gathered at the stones. Having raised the carpet, they then, standing on stepladders, ever so slowly—a few inches at a time, in order to prevent a tear—lowered the carpet until it nestled flat on the floor. Today the carpet is gone, worn out by the myriad footfalls that left their imprint on the wavy pattern that had been woven in. A more serviceable floor treatment, combining stone paving and new carpeting in a quadrant style pattern, now covers the foyer floor.

The stone columns dominate the foyer space; you can't avoid seeing them when you enter or leave the reception area seeming to possess a magnetic attraction. Many people approach the stones, stop for a moment and touch the column faces. Some people actually put a hand on the columns and appear to push. Or maybe they just want to get a tactile feel of the surface.

OPENING DAY AT THE RESORT, JUNE 1999

On the Grand Opening for the resort, the main lodge was still in construction. This didn't diminish the enthusiasm brought to the festivities by the locals who showed up. Many had thought about this moment for five years. They had sat in Old Town, drinking coffee or a beer, talking with their golf buddies about how great this moment would be. They had believed in Keiser's folly from the beginning; it was no longer a folly. They were eager to play golf.

In advance, Mike Keiser had chartered a jet to ferry a bunch of Chicago golfers to the resort for a pre-opening event. They were here to support and celebrate with Mike; many had been to the resort in earlier years to test-drive the courses during construction. They all stayed in Bandon at the Harbor View Motel, as there were no lodgings at the resort. But that was OK. They were among the chosen.

Many local golfers came. They had been bystanders over the years. Many had sat through the public meetings during the permitting proceedings. All had anticipated this day, and now it was here. They loved the game. After today, they would have a tale to tell to their grandkids. Playing golf on an opening day is a one-time experience. That's serious bragging rights.

It rained opening day, and Mike stood out in the rain and shook the hand of everyone who stepped up to tee off. Each foursome had their picture taken with Mike. This became an opening day ritual for every course that opened at Bandon Dunes.

The lodge finally opened a month later. There was still a lot of staff to hire and other buildings to build. Howard and his team would have another decade ahead of them to build out a resort with enough facilities to support another three eighteen-hole courses and eventually a fifth course. But at this moment, Howard had fulfilled his original mission— he'd turned a dream and a vision into reality.

Open for business, and what a business year it would be. No one really knew how many rounds would be played that first year in 1999. The low estimate was around 10,000 rounds. Josh Lesnik, the resort general manager, had worked out a breakeven point at about 12,000–13,000 rounds. Someone else predicted 18,000 rounds. In the first year, about 24,000 rounds were played. Ah, the sweet smell of success.

The year before the resort opened, design and construction of additional guest rooms were underway at what became known as the Lily Pond Cottages. We also built the first structure to house maintenance equipment and accessory uses. Later this building and several others formed what is known as the Agronomy Center. Over the next fifteen years between twenty and thirty more buildings found a place at the resort. Expansion was driven by the resort's success. As more people became aware of Bandon Dunes, the reservations poured in and more rooms were needed. More guests overwhelmed available tee times that signaled to Mike that more golf courses needed to be built to satisfy demand.

THE LILY POND COTTAGES

A s site planning progressed it became obvious that more guest rooms would be required than we could provide at the main lodge. More rooms meant more cars, and there was no more room for parking at the main lodge. Therefore, a site away from the resort core was needed.

Nearby, the topography sloped down to a lovely lily pond. Nestled against the backdrop of a stand of tall Douglas fir trees, this was an enchanting setting. But there was a problem: the resort master plan didn't indicate any direct vehicular access to this promising site.

A proposed major interior road linked the resort core with the south entrance to the resort. This road was routed along the west side of Round Lake. We needed direct access to these future guest accommodations, so we shifted this major road alignment westward so it passed by what became the Lily Pond complex.

Fig. 16: Lily Pond Cottage

The existing ground slope gave us the opportunity to build two-story structures (like a daylight basement) partially into the earth. From the roadway, the buildings appeared to be only one-story in height. On the backside of the building, elevated balconies would give guests an enjoyable view of the pond and the native waterfowl that frequently glided across the water surface. Initially, six buildings were considered; four were built. At the time, we didn't realize how spatially detached the buildings were from the resort core.

As we built more and more lodging facilities, we continued this pattern of lodging facilities that appeared to be detached from the resort core. A guest could walk to and from the main lodge to their lodgings, but a sense of physical separation from the resort core remained for several years.

In 2006, Howard McKee made a decision that changed this perception; it would take us several years to realize a true sense of the village center concept.

THE PRO SHOP

Fig. 17: Pro Shop Entry

The building appears to be sunk into the ground because of the earth berms that slope up against the exterior walls. A one-story building with exposed concrete walls, it is a departure from the shingle style architecture of its neighbor next door. It also has a pyramidal-shaped roof with a cupola. For many years, it was the only building that used concrete as a material for an exterior wall, and it was the odd duck out. Occasionally, guests would remark that the building appeared unfinished. And Mike was less than fond of it. But a lot of merchandise was and is sold there.

This perception changed when Don Stastny began designing buildings at the resort. Don embraced concrete as a building material. Further building additions and renovations at the resort core and at other locations now exhibit concrete wall treatments. The Pro Shop now appears to fit in at the resort core.

MCKEE'S PUB

No golf course is complete without a 19th hole. From day one, there were two bars in the lodge. However, Howard thought we needed an authentic pub in the style and spirit of an English or Irish pub. And it's named for him—McKee's.

To achieve this, he needed a pub designer. He found that talent in Ken Hattan, a Portland architect. Ken had designed hotels and pubs for the McMenamin Brothers, Portland-based developers.

In 2001, Ken was at work designing the McMenamin's Rock Creek Tavern when Howard called. Howard got right to the point: "Would you be available to design a pub for Bandon Dunes?" He would and he did.

Howard originally thought of the pub as a one-story building containing a bar, a few tables, a small kitchen for burgers and hot dogs, and restrooms. Well, the restrooms are there, but the design requirements changed: the structure is two stories. The ground level is a pub, and it has a big kitchen, lots of seating, a great fireplace, a long bar and lots of single malt Scotch to choose from. Scotch eggs are on the menu. If you don't know what they are, try them with the sweet potato fries.

Mackenzie Hall, an upstairs dining room, is an events room used for special occasions. Windows line the sidewalls. It's one of the few places on the resort where you can get a good view of the ocean while dining. While designing the building, Ken also converted a portion of the adjacent building into the St. Andrews Center, a venue for mini-conferences and events requiring a big screen.

Architectural design always requires drawings, and Ken remembers having to draw the building elevations about twenty-five times before Howard said, "I like this one." While working out the building details with Ken, Howard expressed the desire to create an outdoor courtyard for use by pub patrons. I was asked to join the conversation.

Fig. 18: Courtyard at McKee's

The pub is adjacent to the first fairway on the Bandon Dunes course. Topographically, the level of the pub is about ten feet below the grade of the fairway, which required construction of concrete retaining walls. Soon the three of us were batting ideas around, trying to define the space. We focused on how to build some retaining walls that would play off the adjacent flat façade of the pub. How about adding a fireplace? OK. Maybe we need some trelliswork to support vines to soften the concrete walls? At one point, Howard and I were arguing over how to stagger the walls to create more interest in relationship to the flat plane. Ken suddenly interrupted us; he quickly sketched out a plan on tracing paper and said: "Here's what you guys are bickering about." That's collaboration.

Almost every day, a roaring fire is built in the courtyard fireplace. In the evening you will find a bunch of golfers sitting or standing around the outdoor fireplace, drinking and sometimes smoking a cigar well into the night. Inside the pub over the fireplace mantle is a picture of Howard. He still watches over the festivities.

THE CHROME LAKE COTTAGES

The shoreline along the south side of Chrome Lake and the upper reaches of Cut Creek, the stream that fed the lake, was an appealing site for lodgings. However, our field reconnaissance indicated there were severe building limitations. There was little flat ground to build on. The site was very narrow in width and long in length, paralleling Randolph Road. But this meant there was good, direct access for vehicles.

Another positive aspect was the fact that this linearly-shaped site was elevated above the lake and watercourse. A dense stand of mixed conifer trees grew out of the steep slope between these water features and potential building sites.

I don't remember who came up with the idea, but as Howard, Bill Church and I stumbled and pushed our way through the forested understory, out popped the words—"Tree Houses." Given the limited space between the edge of the treed slope and Randolph Road, we also decided to build several small cottage-like buildings instead of structures housing several guest rooms.

We couldn't really build houses in the trees. Instead, we elevated the buildings. By raising the first floor three feet off the ground, the design accomplished two things. 1) The exterior building walls were cantilevered three feet away from the foundation and footing walls. This allowed us to save many fir trees that grew next to the new buildings because we didn't have to disturb critical tree root zones. 2) Since we ended up building two-story buildings, the views of tree foliage and views through the foliage to the lake and stream were great.

Fig. 19: One of the Cottages Overlooking Chrome Lake

A total of twenty-one buildings were built, each building having three units. Two side-by-side units were on the lower floor level. The end walls were designed with large floor-to-ceiling windows and wide sliding doors on the sidewalls.

The upper unit was special. Two separate bedrooms flanked a central common living space. These units became very popular since they allowed two guests or two couples to enjoy separate bedrooms and bathrooms. Opening a glass slider, leaning and stretching a hand out, you could almost touch a tree trunk or fir bough (there was a handrail across the opening). There was the sense of being in a tree house.

After the cottages were finished, guests who drove by or walked by the buildings kept inquiring: they wanted to know when we were going to finish siding the buildings. The buildings have a black finish, and guests thought this was tarpaper. Bill had decided to sheath the structures using an architectural metal siding. The material was manufactured on site (the resort bought a machine to custom make the material), and it was black in color. All the trim is Port Orford cedar. The cottages blend wonderfully into the forest setting.

THE GROVE

It's not the Bohemian Grove with encampments, which began as a private men's art club. But, at its heart, the resort is sort of a club—a golf club. And I don't consider it a campground. Instead, guests camp out in luxurious accommodations, some of which are in The Grove at the resort.

As time went on, we still needed additional lodgings. After building two previous complexes for guests, besides the rooms at the main lodge, we built more lodgings on a wooded site directly across from the Chrome Lake cottages. This site also fronted onto Randolph Road. In this instance, we had to build a loop road in order to provide access to the sixteen cottages that made up the Grove complex.

It was an odd piece of ground. Spindly tall trees, mostly fir, grew out of a ground plane almost devoid of understory vegetation. The ground, generally flat, was carpeted with deadfall, decaying organic material, moss, lichens, and a few ferns. No tree exceeded fourteen inches in diameter. Worst of all, the trunks were lacking branches and needle foliage for the first thirty to forty feet above the ground. Unless one looked up, walking through this stand of trees was like walking in a forest of telephone poles. I thought of it as a dead zone.

Fig. 20: A Cottage in the Grove

Howard and I looked at each other and smiled. There wasn't a lot to damage or get upset over, even if we had to clear the site. And we didn't. But there was going to be a cost penalty associated with creating a land-scape setting that complemented the future lodge buildings. It was perfect for a group of cottages that would turn out to be a variation of the upstairs unit plan in the Chrome Lake complex.

Somewhere and sometime during his Russian travels overseas, Howard made a sketch of a slightly squarish-shaped building. Echoing the upper floor units at Chrome Lake, he started with a social living area as the central element. Thinking about a golf foursome, he added four bedrooms, one at each corner of the plan. Each bedroom had a private bathroom sharing a common wall. For good measure, he threw in a foyer and an entry niche. It was a simple building, but an elegant solution that became The Grove complex.

It was the ultimate accommodation for four golf buddies—a detached cottage for their private use. Corporations loved these accommodations. They sent groups to the resort, treating their employees and preferred clients to a special golfing experience.

On a trip to Portland, Howard gave the sketch to Ken Hattan, the architect who had designed McKee's Pub. Ken then refined the concept and started working on a set of construction documents. I was engaged in figuring out how to provide an access road and see how many of the cottages I could fit on the site. The solution for vehicular access became readily apparent; it could be accomplished by building a loop road in from and out to Randolph Road.

I quickly drew up a preliminary sketch plan that distributed sixteen cot-tages along the loop road. As the site plan evolved, I was able to locate several of the cottages so they had peek-a-boo views of Round Lake.

A centerline for the road was quickly staked in the field, trees were felled, construction equipment brought to the site, and, in short order, a road corridor was cleared and base rock installed. Later the roadway would be paved. As a bonus, the clearing opened up the tree canopy. Previously the overhead canopy had severely reduced the amount of sunshine that reached the forest floor. Sunlight could now reach the ground, so new landscaping along the roadway could survive. Per a set of construction drawings, Walsh Construction cleared and leveled building sites and began forming and installing concrete slabs for building foundations.

However, one of the crew's first tasks was to remove all the organic material on the ground. In places, it varied from a foot to nearly two feet in depth. As one walked around, one sank into the ground. In the winter months, a footprint slowly filled with ground water due to a high water table.

Construction continued—the buildings were framed, roofed and sided—and within a few weeks the building envelopes were completed and weatherized. The area began to take on the appearance of a small subdivision that had been parachuted into a forest setting.

Soon there were seventeen buildings splayed out along the roadway. We had added a two-story structure to serve as a reception facility. During the design of the Grove complex Howard had decided our old Design center on Round Lake had seen better days. The second floor of the reception building became a new design center for the consultant team.

Next I turned my attention to devising a landscape plan to restore the natural forest setting using native plants. I had worked out a preliminary planting plan, but it would be expensive to install. Howard convened a meeting with Eric Stevens—the Walsh Construction project manager, Doug Spiro—our landscape contractor, and me. Originally about $100,000 had been budgeted for landscaping. After much discussion about what could or could not be accomplished for that figure, I flatly stated that this figure was insufficient. If Howard and the design team wanted to recreate a natural woodland appearance, the figure would have to be doubled, and it was.

The backbone of the landscape design concept involved planting native trees along the loop road to re-establish a tree canopy along and over the roadway. I also wanted to have some native cedar trees, but Doug convinced me to plant Hogan cedar trees, as they aren't susceptible to the local root rot disease. To establish the understory, I used native shrubs—Pacific Myrtle, Salal, Huckleberry, Flowering Currant, Douglas Spiraea, Western Sword Ferns—and a sprinkling of ornamental ground cover plants. The latter were installed near the entrances of each cottage for accent and seasonal color. I interspersed a few Vine Maple trees along the loop road for their red color. They brighten up the landscape in the fall. Guests now comment on how natural the area appears to the eye.

The Grove buildings were simple in form and somewhat nondescript; they blended into the woodland well—very subtle architecture. Ken appreciated Bill's use of metal siding, so he used the same custom architectural pattern but changed the color from black to dark green. He also articulated the building entries in a special way: the building form is big; the entry nook small. Scaling the entry to human proportions, the architect also gave the entry a mini-cathedral look. Lined with wood, the entry cavity is very inviting.

All previous lodge buildings had a defined and articulated entry that took the focus away from the larger building form. At the Lily Pond, there was a boxy, foyer space surrounded by glass walls. Inside, a two-story interior courtyard with bamboo plants provided a gracious entry experience. It was a way to eliminate long hallways to the individual rooms. Lit up at night, the entries became "light boxes," beacons guiding guests to their sleeping quarters. The Chrome Lake cottages also had an attached entry enclosure that contained a stairwell to the upper floor. Providing a transitional space to enter a building is important in architecture; it elevates the human experience.

THE INN

It was 2006, and Howard had an idea for a guest lodge that would be an annex to the main lodge. In the 1980s he had met Lucien Lagrange, another architect with whom he had worked in the SOM Chicago office. Both had left SOM in the early 1990s to establish their own practices. Lucien had a large architectural office in downtown Chicago. When Howard returned to Chicago, he saw Lucien from time to time. So, he engaged Lucien's firm to come up with a design concept for the annex.

There was a ready-made site for the annex lodge across Cut Creek from the main lodge. We thought of it as an "infill" project. Howard proceeded to get Mike's approval, and the project moved ahead. In addition to guest rooms and a commons room with bar service, Howard programmed in a new fitness center with a spa in the basement level.

Howard flew back and forth between Chicago and the resort as Lucien's office produced a building design that had an unusual V-shaped footprint—

like a chevron. After several months, Howard brought drawings for a four-story building design back to the resort for review. Four stories: this raised a red flag immediately with Mike. How visible would it be from the main lodge, especially the garden dining room, which looked directly at the proposed site?

Mike thought four stories might be too high. The main lodge had previously been reduced from three to two stories; Howard was now advocating a building twice as high. Ken Hattan suggested we prepare a drawing to illustrate the visual impact of the proposed building. He drew up an elevation of the proposed building, scanned the drawing and digitally inserted it into a photograph that had been taken from the main lodge.

The composite drawing pictured a four-story building towering over the tree line along the creek. The design was put on hold while Mike and Howard carefully reviewed the building floor plans. They decided a chevron-shaped footprint was an unacceptable design, and the project was shelved for the moment. A couple of years would pass, and Howard would come up with another design idea as demand increased for more guest accommodations.

Mike now acknowledged that the undeveloped land by Cut Creek was a prime site for another building that became known as The Inn. Howard the initiated a design; but, as his role at the resort waned, another architect—Don Stastny—took over Howard's role on this project. Ken, working under Don, designed a conventional box-like structure that used rectilinear geometry, in lieu of the chevron-shaped building plan. It was a big, two-story building, comparable in length to the main lodge. It was really part of the resort core, given its proximity to the main lodge.

As with all the lodging facilities, the building conformed to a progression of spaces at its entrance. Guests would arrive under a covered roof, and then enter a boxy reception and sitting space with a high ceiling. After check-in at the reception desk, the progression continued into a spacious public space that contained several pieces of artwork. Off a central hallway, the commons or lounge room offered guests an informal place to meet and talk. At the end of the room was a fireplace flanked with windows. Outside, guests on a paved patio could see the main lodge, the 18th fairway and green, and the putting green of the Bandon Dunes course. On warm days in the late spring through the fall seasons, guests sitting on the patio could read, chat or just enjoy the sunshine and peaceful setting along Cut Creek.

The overall building design mirrored the design features at the main lodge. Ken used wooden trusses and a high ceiling, similar to the lodge reception area. Using exposed wood for the ceiling made the interior space very inviting. Some architects forget that the ceiling is a "landscape" that can be manipulated to achieve special qualities and experiences. Ken knew that.

The Inn was carefully positioned to preserve a group of Madrone trees and Manzanita shrubs nearby; these two plants were found only occasionally on the property, so I wanted to save them as a landscape feature. It's difficult, if not impossible, to transplant either one of these plants. Moreover, they are extremely slow growers.

After parking their cars near The Inn, guests would have to walk through this garden to reach the building entrance. Besides the native trees and shrubs we saved, the walkway was lined with deciduous Azaleas that were added to introduce seasonal bloom and a bit of color. Accent up-lighting under a few of the plants added a dramatic visual effect to the arrival experience at night.

Fig. 21: The Arrival Entry at The Inn

The Inn changed the perception that there were different groups of buildings scattered all over the resort. The resort village center became a more defined "place" architecturally after The Inn was built.

There were other beneficial consequences. The design and workmanship at The Inn raised the standard for public spaces and raised the bar for the standard of design quality. This fulfilled the fourth axiom to successful project development: Don't compromise on building materials and design quality. People comment on The Inn's functional and attractive qualities.

Renovations and refurbishing of older buildings now became the target of Don's work. Over time, renovations at the main lodge resulted in both the main lodge and The Inn sharing more of the same aesthetics. At the lodge, Don added wood ceilings, better lighting and more durable floor materials and coverings in the reception area.

THE PRACTICE CENTER BUILDING

After Schuman logged a forested portion of his property, he didn't clean it up. Going into bankruptcy, he probably needed all the cash he had! What remained was a wasteland of tree stump and slash. As Howard and I walked about, it felt like we were on a trampoline; there was a springy matt of debris everywhere.

We cleaned the area up, since Mike had decided this was the right place for a driving range and other practice facilities. Mike brought David Kidd back to look over the site, and he and David worked out a design that consumed forty acres. There were multiple driving ranges with greens and flags at a variety of distances, an over-sized putting green (it was huge), and separate chipping and sand trap practice areas. Guests and the caddies could spend hours there, honing their game. The center also had a nine-hole practice course laid out by David Kidd. Known as Shorty's Course, no reservations would be needed to play the first short course at the resort. The local high school golf team also used this course for practice.

When Mike acquired the Fahy property, he and the resort inherited Shorty Dow, the property manager. Shorty quickly became a valuable asset, given his intimate knowledge of the property. The consultants and Howard gained a better understanding of the lay of the land, its pluses and minuses, by simply walking around the property with Shorty. This nine-hole course was a tribute to Shorty's contribution.

We needed an operations service building at this practice area, so we installed a small temporary building. It was basic: a changing room with lavatory and toilet facilities, ball dispenser and vending machines.

As with most of the temporary structures at the resort, it took a few years to replace it. Worn out, Don Stastny designed a replacement building. A simple, compact, mixed-use structure, it was made up of two separate building elements separated by an open-air passageway. A continuous roof connected and unified the structure into a single architectural statement. A cupola sat atop the roof, a recall to a similar feature on the Pro Shop.

The south half of the building was a windowed snack bar, providing patrons extensive views of the practice facilities. It would also prove a great place to drink coffee, have a libation and watch practice balls and time fly by.

Fig. 22: Replacement Practice Center Building

The other half of the buildings had public restrooms and two offices. One of the offices now belongs to Grant Rogers. Grant was working at the Salishan Resort before the resort opened. He'd always liked links golf. He'd made many trips to the British Isles to play there. When the resort opened, he started driving down to play the first courses. He liked what he saw, returned again and again, and, in due time, was hired and became the Director of Instruction. If you look for Grant in his office, chances are you won't find him. Most of the time, he is elsewhere, moving about the resort, doing what he does best: helping guests improve their game.

Grant is a PGA Master Professional, and he's been called a Zen guru. Having taken classes from him, I can attest to the fact that his teaching methods are unconventional. He has many good points as a teacher, but what I liked most was that he only gives you what you need at the moment. He uses a building block system very similar to martial arts instruction. He was a student of Karate.

I remember having a class with him. I was moving one of my feet when I shouldn't have. Grant interrupted my practice swings and told me a story about Bob Johnson, a mutual friend of ours.

Bob, who had been taking a personal class from Grant, had been making the same mistake as I. Grant had pointed out the mistake. Then he had to mention it again. Softly, but firmly, Grant told Bob (Grant was holding a three iron at the time), if you move your foot again, I'm going to swing this three iron and plant it on top of your foot. Bob's foot never moved again. I didn't move mine either.

Grant is responsible for creating strategies to teach guests how to play links courses, how to play particular shots in specific situations (like getting out of a links style bunker or approach shots for big greens) and creating program events for special guest groups. He thinks his approach to teaching is "kind of like being a guide to better golfing."

He also organizes corporate "social" events, like night golfing with illu-minated balls. If you ask him what he likes about his job, his response will include the word "interactive." He likes to work with people, whether in a threesome group or one-on-one, and likes to interject humor into his lessons and the game. He discourages players from worrying about their score; he thinks keeping score should take second place behind having fun.

When playing a lesson round, sometimes a player will mutter a comment about their bad shot, and Grant will respond by saying, "There are no bad golf shots; there're only golf shots." When a player gets disgusted because the ball goes astray, Grant will say, "It's there because you hit it there." The message he is conveying is "don't make it something that it isn't."

What Grant appreciates about the resort is the variety and contrast among the five courses he has to use as teaching venues. Combined with the X-factor, the wind, he can accelerate a student's learning process by using the differences among the course layouts, hazards and variations in environmental conditions to teach specific golf skills addressing what a player needs to deal with each problem situation. There are eighty-one holes available at Bandon Dunes (excluding Shorty's course and the Punchbowl). Each hole is extremely interesting to play. Each is a teaching venue.

Take putting, for example. Grant encourages golfers to use their putter when they get within fifty yards of the flag. It's a simple club choice. More importantly, it's a fun shot; it's easy to do. At the Old Macdonald course, a player needs a good putting game. Getting on the greens is usually not a problem for experienced golfers because several of the holes have greens that are oversized. But it can be a problem when the wind or rain showers engulf the course. However, to have a chance to putt out in one or two strokes, a golfer first needs to hit the ball into the right area of the green in order to have that chance. And, once on the green, the golfer needs to use his or her imagination. The golfers who find their way to the Punchbowl, the three-and-a-half-acre expanded putting green built in 2013, will learn what imagination has to do with putting, especially at Bandon Dunes.

Since the resort's brand is an expression of the guest's experience, the form of instruction available at Bandon Dunes is all about elevating that experience by showing guests how to play links golf. And, just maybe, they'll walk off the 18th green with a good scorecard, assuming they even kept one.

To be a good instructor, one has to be a keen observer of human behavior. An instructor can't suggest a change in technique or golf strategy until he knows the golfer is making the same mistake over and over. Then the instructor can step in and say 'this is what needs to change. Here is how you correct the mistake.' Grant also believes part of his job is to instill in the golfer the view that he or she should always strive to improve.

As an instructor, Grant is fortunate in that the resort courses are playable year-around. Even though it rains a lot along the Oregon coast, the courses are very playable because the sandy soil and the underlying drainage system allow easy percolation and disposal of rainfall. When I interviewed Grant, I ended by asking him what golfers need to do to learn to play links style golf. His view is: "Everyone should first come and play here; stay as long as possible and return as often as possible."

Obviously, this is commercially rewarding to the resort. But there's another point of view to consider. Remember, Grant was—and still has the spirit of—a martial artist; there are only two secrets to success in the martial arts: finding the best instructor and practice. Bandon Dunes has an excellent instruction program and it's a great place to practice.

PACIFIC DUNES CLUBHOUSE

Each course has its own clubhouse. Each has its own character, and all have halfway houses. The Preserve Course and the Punchbowl share existing clubhouse facilities. At Pacific, there have been two designs; only one was built. And, in between the two designs, a temporary clubhouse—a doublewide mobile home—was used quite successfully.

The first design was appealing and promising. A Portland-based architectural firm, Boora Architects, came up with an interesting concept: a building that grew out of the sand dunes. Mike and Howard approved the design concept, design plans and construction documents were prepared, a big hole was dug into the sand dunes to accommodate a two-story structure, and then the design turned to ashes.

Several features of the building were problematic. The west side of the building had a vertical glass wall that tilted out from the roofline; it had associated technical issues. There was a sod roof with no perceived utility or visual benefit that also portended waterproofing and maintenance issues. There was also a massive concrete retaining wall associated with the building entry. But the real problem was cost. Howard made several suggestions to the architects encouraging them to reduce the construction costs to meet the budget constraints. The architects resisted these suggestions. Their contract was canceled.

We were in a pickle. There was not enough time left to design and construct a replacement building before the Pacific Dunes course was scheduled to open. That opened the door to discuss using a mobile home for a clubhouse.

Luck intervened. Word reached Howard that the temporary clubhouse at Salmon Run—a new golf course just outside Brookings, Oregon—was available. Salmon Run had just opened a new clubhouse. So Bandon Dunes got a used temporary building for a nominal cost. Several days later, a doublewide mobile home arrived at the resort. Unfortunately, this structure was clearly an ugly duck!

It is said that necessity is the mother of invention, or creativity as well. We needed something to take the curse off this building. Unfortunately, once positioned at the Pacific course, the end of the box faced directly at the drop-off area. Somehow we had to disguise the end elevation. Our brainstorming led to a perfect solution: we'd build a tower. A vertical element would draw the eye upwards, thereby taking the observer's eye off the end of the building and the boxy shape. And it worked. We even found a way to build a greeter station and small storage area into the base of the tower.

More good luck was on its way. One day a golfer playing the Pacific Dunes course stopped by and inquired if the resort could use a clock for the tower. He happened to be a sales representative for the Bulova Watch Company. Yes, we could use a clock. A few weeks later, a big, gold-plated clock was delivered to the resort, and it was promptly attached to the top of the tower. That gold clock added a touch of elegance to the tower. Today, that clock is prominently displayed on the replacement Pacific Dunes clubhouse.

Mike loved the temporary clubhouse. He had wanted to use a mobile trailer for a clubhouse when discussing his ideas for the first golf course. Of course, Howard talked him out of it. Having the old clubhouse from Salmon Run validated Mike's initial thought.

Eventually, the temporary clubhouse succumbed to wear and tear. This pleased Howard, and he immediately began thinking about a replacement building. Instead of a building buried in the sand, he thought the building could be a two-story structure that sat on high ground to capture views, with an entry on a lower level.

With these thoughts in mind, Don Stastny came up with a building concept that featured a central light and stairwell in the center of an octagonal floor plan. Dining on the upper floor level provides guests with several view corridors to both the Pacific and Bandon Dunes courses and the ocean.

Being a landscape architect, the building architecture is normally outside of my providence. However, I did make a contribution to the upper floor layout. Don was scheduled to present a preliminary building design to Mike Keiser and KemperSports personnel at the resort. However, he was unable to make the trip due to a scheduling conflict. As I was going down to the resort, Don asked me to fill in for him.

Fig. 23: Pacific Dunes Clubhouse
Photo courtesy of Wood Sabold

Standing before the assembled group, I began to highlight aspects of the building design. As I explained the rationale for the two-story building, Mike interrupted me and questioned the appropriateness of a two-story structure. He thought a one-story building was more appropriate since he believed golfers preferred not to walk up stairs. But I persuaded him that having the restaurant level on the top floor afforded great views in three of the cardinal quadrants; he and the others agreed.

However, an examination of the architect's floor plans (with which I was not that familiar) revealed that the kitchen was located where it obstructed one of the scenic view corridors. So I simply suggested we could rotate the plan to solve the conflict. Problem solved. Returning to Portland, I briefed Don about the meeting. He replied, "Why are you screwing with my plan?" He revised and refined his plan, the building was built, and the views are great. Ever since, he continues a threat to refer any "kitchen design" questions to me.

I often think of this episode as a good example of what we termed the "last man standing rule." We would gather at the resort to meet, discuss, resolve design questions and supervise construction activities. Often there were varying opinions about what was the right solution. Everyone got their say, but if you left to return home before others did, or if you found yourself the only person on site when a decision had to be made, the last man made the final decision.

The later addition of several wall art pieces and some custom-made hanging light fixtures in the central light and stairwell turned the building into a jewel.

BANDON TRAILS CLUBHOUSE

The clubhouse at Bandon Trails is distinctly different from the others. The structure would feel comfortable in a Japanese Garden. Before succumbing to the weather, the newly installed copper tile roof glowed in the late afternoon sun. The metal roof, darkened with a patina of age, provides a nice contrast and adds to the simple elegance of the building.

Fig. 24: Trails Clubhouse

Guests either walk up a sloped, paved walkway or are dropped off by a shuttle bus at the entrance portal and storage area for golf clubs. You only get a glimpse of the building at the drop-off area; you have to pass through an arched gateway and walk by an entry garden that features native pine trees to reach the clubhouse. And there's no obvious entry door in sight.

Bill Church, the architect, wanted a surprise arrival experience, not unlike the arrival to a Japanese teahouse. The building—a long, skinny building—is perched on a narrow strip of high ground. The entry is along the side of the building. The location of the entry divides the building into two halves—a dining area and a pro shop. An outdoor terrace allows golfers to look out over the 18th green and enjoy the dune-land scenery.

Here Bill also added a special feature. A detached, roofed gazebo, enclosed on three sides with glass walls, sits on a wooden deck next to the clubhouse. The glass provides needed protection from the wind and rain. A fire pit sits in the middle of the gazebo. Ringed with short basalt columns, remnants from the stones used in the main lodge, naked gas flames provide warmth and a fireside setting for diners day and night.

Fig. 25: Gazebo Fire Pit

In 2004, Mike, Howard, Bill Church, Ken Nice and others had stood on this narrow ridge overlooking the preliminary construction work for the Bandon Trails course. We were assembled to evaluate whether or not this was the best site for the Trails clubhouse. Ken had joined the group because he supervised all the golf course superintendents and had overall responsibility for turf conditions at the resort. Looking due west, the view from this ridge was commanding. You could see where flags had been stuck in the ground for proposed 1st greens and tee boxes. The view from the ridge took in rolling sand dunes, the ocean and a horizon that stretched for several miles up and down the coastline.

It was a natural location for the clubhouse, but there were access limitations. Construction would be difficult, but, in the end, a construction road was built and eventually converted to a vehicular drive and drop-off for guests. There was no room for parking by the clubhouse. Golfers would either walk up the hill from the parking lot at The Inn or ride the resort shuttle bus.

OLD MACDONALD CLUBHOUSE

Fig. 26: Old Mac Clubhouse

The simple, compact clubhouse for the Old Macdonald course was not the only design considered for the structure: an earlier attempt by Larry Booth, a Chicago architect, was the first design. Larry had designed the clubhouse for Mike's first golf course in Michigan, the Dunes Club. The design for Old Mac was promising: a one-story structure perched on high ground would have overlooked the first tee boxes and the 18th green similar to the clubhouse at the Trails course. But it was not to be; timing and cost intruded. Mike settled for a smaller, less expensive building.

Don Stastny had done several architectural building studies for the Old Mac clubhouse, but Mike, being cost-conscious, had doubts about these initial schemes. However, there was an old, dilapidated open-air horse barn near the golf course site. Its condition suggested it was a candidate for a tear-down.

Looking beyond the run-down building's condition, and with some imagination thrown in, Don preserved the basic pole structure of the horse barn and turned it into a charming contemporary cottage-like structure.

It required removing almost everything but the wood posts, pouring a concrete floor, framing and sheathing walls and capping it with a simple roof. Don then called it good. Concrete pavers were laid to form an outdoor dining patio. The finished building serves as a check-in facility for golfers. Although there was limited space, Don found room for a very small retail shop and a grill that supplies hamburgers and hot dogs for hungry patrons.

What's interesting about this clubhouse is its relationship to the golf course. At all the other clubhouses, the course is visible. Here, the course is out of sight beyond a rise. Walking to and over the rise, a surprise awaits. A wide, wide undulating carpet of turf, flanked on both sides by tree lines, fills the viewer's picture frame. The first fairway elongates, stretching out forever; the 18th fairway contracts bringing the eye back to the 18th green. These fairways are twice as wide, or wider, than any of the other fairways at the resort; this is great for hackers, but a loss for the pro shop in terms of ball sales. Other surprises await the golfer. When they get to the 8th hole, a Biarritz hole, the putting green is huge, almost 100 yards of running surface.

LANDSCAPE DESIGN

During forty years of practicing landscape architecture, I knew that building architecture usually got first preference. However, from the onset, we had decided that the architecture would be subordinated to the landscape setting. I was also acutely aware of coastal environmental conditions on the South Coast. Primarily because of the salt air and wind conditions, native plants—almost exclusively—formed the landscape palette I used in restoring disturbed ground.

Although the soil profile throughout the property had a top or mid-layer of sand, there were instances where other materials, including clay, were present. In upland forested areas, nature had formed a thin layer of organic material over the ground plane. The dunes were pure sand with a sparse mat of native plants scattered about. If we disturbed this soil, we had to plant something or nature would assume the role and responsibility to re-establish vegetative cover.

Dealing with wind was the landscape challenge. The winter storm winds off the ocean are harsh, and, as a result, the exposed Shore Pines have sculptured forms depending upon their degree of exposure. The warmer summer winds can also be a problem. Both can and will desiccate the foliage of new plantings if water is lacking. Providing irrigation, at least to establish new plantings, was mandatory.

Once the shell of the main lodge was enclosed, and weather-tight, and the parking areas were completed, I drew up several landscape plans to discuss with Howard and Mike. One proposal featured paved terraces facing the golf course in conjunction with landscape planters extending outward from the lodge. I also suggested installing lots of Shore Pines around the parking areas to visually screen the vehicles. Mike thought this approach fussy. It was also costly.

Taking a cue from the nearby golf environment, I then suggested a different approach: let's plant more grass—ornamental grasses. The idea was to surround the building with a "grass garden" setting. Three varieties of ornamental grasses were planted on the entry side of the lodge. These grasses added a change of texture and color, seasonally. They also tend to brown out in the fall and blend in with the grasses on the courses. The grass garden provided a unifying theme, and it was a very cost effective solution. I'm not sure what Mike thought about it in the beginning; he may have been a bit uneasy about the solution. But the plantings are still in place today.

Springtime brings fresh, bright green stalks of *Pennisetum orientale*— Oriental Fountain Grass—emerging from the earth. The grasses mature through the summer and, in the fall, turn a deep tan with a yellowish hue. The reddish tint on the tips of *Panicum virgatum 'Haense Herms'*— Red Switch Grass—provides a touch of color in the fall. In the late fall or early winter, the grass is cut down nearly to the ground; what you see for several months are round brown dots, floating in a dark field of mulch. What's best about the design is seeing the tall grass in the summer gently shimmering in the ocean breeze.

This dead winter landscape renews itself in the spring. It's a sustainable landscape that requires a one-time pruning effort and, sometimes, replacement of a dead plant or two. It provides a nice visual transition from the natural woodland that guests pass through as they enter the resort property on their arrival.

Having established a landscaping approach for the resort that featured restoration of the native plant community as the standard, occasionally I added heather to the palette. I used this plant around the main lodge and the 18th green of the Bandon Dunes course. Heather added variety, texture and seasonal color. People liked the look (it's Scottish), and it stands up to the wind and salt air and does a good job as a ground cover. At The Inn, heather found a place flanking the building entry as well as the entry drive intersection with the South Scenic Drive.

I knew from our initial site survey that the natural landscape was very fragile. Disturbance and the removal of existing vegetation gave weeds and exotic plants a chance to establish themselves. Once the ground was disturbed, it was sometimes difficult to get plants established, and the wind and salt spray in the air took a toll on new plantings.

New plantings needed water to root and acclimate in order to survive the first year. Both drip and pop-up spray systems were used. After the landscape had grown in, these systems could be shut off year-around. However, they are maintained in case of a summer drought.

I also realized it was imperative to limit the extent of site clearance in advance of new construction. If we didn't disturb a forested area, we didn't have to re-landscape the area.

Chapter Twelve

A Change of the Guard

Get the house in order.
—Howard L. McKee, Portland, Oregon

THE UNDERSTUDY

Around 1997, Howard had been diagnosed with colon cancer. Chemo treatments had checked the disease, and he had been in remission for half a dozen years. Now it was back, and Howard was running out of energy and time. He and I discussed the situation, and I suggested he find a replacement.

So, around 2003, Howard decided to search for an understudy. He needed someone with a specific set of skills and talents to carry forth his and Mike's vision. Such an individual, an old friend and colleague, unaware of this fact, was waiting in the wings.

When Howard lived in Portland during the early 1970s, Don Stastny had met Kennon, Howard's wife. She had served on an advisory committee for the design of Portland's Pioneer Courthouse Square. Don had been in charge of planning, programming and organizing the design competition for the square. In the local architectural milieu, he knew Howard by reputation and, in time, became an acquaintance, then a close friend.

Donald (Don) Stastny was trained as an architect and urban designer. Like Howard, he also grew up in a small town, population 596. Born and raised on a ranch, Don grew up in Malin, Oregon, graduating from high school in a senior class comprised of thirteen students. He went on to study architecture at Oregon State University and the University of Washington, with graduate studies in Architecture and City Planning at the University of Pennsylvania. By 1976, he was a practicing architect in Portland, Oregon.

In 2003, Don found himself in Chicago, organizing a design competition. The project, sponsored by the Salvation Army, was being funded by a Chicago foundation. Don was told the foundation's founder wanted him to meet with an architect friend of his. Apparently, the founder wanted to make sure things were to his liking. To Don's surprise, Howard McKee was the architect.

They met: first chatting about the Salvation Army project for a few minutes, and then they launched into hours of conversation about professional interests and the parallels between both their careers. Then the conversation turned to Bandon Dunes. Howard informed Don that his cancer was back, and he was looking for a replacement. Did Don have any ideas about someone who might be a good candidate? Within the blink of an eye, Don said, "How about me?" The ensuing conversation moved from Portland to an on-site visit with Howard and Mike. Howard now had an understudy.

Asked why he thought the project was of interest, Don's answer was: "Howard kept mentioning the word 'vision.'" The 1970s saw a movement in the fields of city planning and urban design, both at the city and regional levels, that sought to refocus long-range planning around the concept of "visioning." This basically entailed thinking about things comprehensively and conceptualizing scenarios that provided alternative plans and policies for long-range planning. Critical to the process was community participation that usually took the form of community workshops and meetings with a variety of interest groups: residents, business owners, environmental activists, representatives of regulatory agencies and officials. Being active in the urban design and community planning fields, Don was a true believer and an advocate for projects anchored in a vision.

As an understudy, Don's initial job was to observe. He had no specific responsibilities. Howard had him attend all the design and construction meetings. But, as Howard remarked to me several times, "What can I give him to work on?" For a year or so, Don accompanied Howard and me on trips to the resort. In this manner, Howard eased him into the dynamics and flow of the design and construction work at Bandon Dunes. But, the answer to Howard's question soon became obvious; his health declined, and he didn't have the energy to handle all his responsibilities.

When Don replaced Howard, he faced three main challenges. The first had to do with design. Everything that had been accomplished up to that point had been done very quickly. What was built met the initial design program and specified square footage requirements. It was good design, but it didn't address future needs or expansion issues. There hadn't been enough time to think out and project future space needs or shifting market demand. As Don recalls, "Up until that point, there had been a great deal of value engineering and trying to develop the best product for the cheapest price." And that drove a lot of the design decisions. The general contractor was focused more on delivery than on craft design execution. In the beginning years, we always felt we were behind schedule, and we were just trying to keep up.

The Inn project changed our perspective. The level of design was elevated, but we were still tied to the idea of programming space use to its perceived use in the immediate future. Future building design would incorporate more flexibility into the process.

The second challenge was that we were in a recession. All of a sudden, demand went away, funding for new facilities became sparse, budgets became drivers of decisions, so there was a reflective period about sustaining the operations of the resort until the economy recovered.

Don would also replace a number of temporary buildings because of their short life cycles. The resort now has several new halfway houses on the golf course. Don also took on a project that Howard had started but never completed.

In past years, Howard had advocated for a separate facility to house a fitness center. Various ideas had been put forward. In one instance, he tried to incorporate an expanded fitness center into a proposed lodging facility. Another time he had preliminary plans drawn up for a fitness center that took the form of a series of interconnected pavilions on the shores of Round Lake. When Mike Keiser reviewed the final drawings, he asked Howard what the cost was. "About 2.5 million." Mike replied, "Well, we won't do that." Cost was not the only reason the scheme was rejected by Mike. The design had incorporated a spa, and Mike felt a spa was not really compatible with the resort image.

The demise of the pavilion scheme was a loss to Howard. What to do now? A few weeks later, this issue was discussed in a design team meeting in Portland. There was a heated debate about the fitness center and other resort projects that were in design or in construction, but there was a sense that things were not totally under control. Howard—who always projected a sense of stability and calm, even when things were frayed—was at a loss as to what to do next. At this point, his illness had diminished his ability to manage the project as effectively as he had in the past.

The meeting adjourned with few resolutions, and Howard appeared tired. We had met at my office, which is on the third floor of the building. As Howard left and started down an exterior stairs, it was evident he needed help. With Don's assistance, Howard made it down the steps. At the bottom, Howard turned to Don and said: "Get the house in order." Don was now officially in charge.

MEMORIAL SERVICES

Howard died in December 2007. Two memorial services were held—one in Chicago and later one at the resort. I flew to Chicago and, in St. James Cathedral, we remembered the path we had walked with Howard—"our companion, brother and friend." Howard, true to his nature, had designed the service.

Looking over the service program, I saw a quotation attributed to Janet Rogers, a good friend of his: "And so I am thinking of us like wild geese, with the whole flock that loves you moving across the sky, calling and calling, hearts to hearts, back and forth, to stay in touch even as wings are spreading and lifting into a new lightness for a new morning." Janet had penned these words "for Howard, who hears wild geese call and already has wings."

These words touched my heart. I had known this man for over forty years. I thought, as old men—hell, we were only in our mid- to late sixties—at some point in the future, we would stand in the dunes and survey what we had accomplished. This was not to be.

Back in Oregon, I found myself driving to the resort for another memorial service. It was held in the Mackenzie Hall, the upstairs dining room at the pub Howard had convinced Mike to build. On a bright sunny day, the assembled throng climbed the stairs to the second floor. The tabletops were gone, replaced by rows of folding chairs. Light flooded through side windows lining the length of the room, and music filled the room.

An empty podium stood silently at the front of the room. I hadn't expected to be here. After Chicago I felt drained emotionally. I didn't think I could attend another service. But Hank Hickox, the resort general manager had called. When I told Hank I was not coming, he was aghast. 'Not coming? You have to come. You need to speak.' So I went.

As I made my way up the aisle to a place in the front row, I glanced about and saw many familiar faces. There were exchanged smiles and nods, but the room felt compressed with emotion. Thankfully, live string music from two violins and a guitar drifted over the room, softening reality.

Then Hank was at the podium. He spoke about Howard and his contributions and went on to say, "He is still here, in the building and on the grounds." Then Hank introduced several speakers. Warren Felton spoke first, and he reminded us that Howard spoke very much to the point. Howard didn't waste words.

As I sat listening to speakers reminisce about Howard at one point during the service, someone said, "Howard knew everything." This was not quite accurate. He was knowledgeable, but he didn't know everything. However, he was always enlarging his base of knowledge, and he always took time to personally connect with others. Those who spoke, spoke for themselves and others when they said, "he changed my life."

Don Ivy had worked with Howard to resolve Coos-Coquille Tribal concerns. He pointedly spoke about several personality traits that captured Howard's essence: "He was engaged and thoughtful all the time. He was careful in how he dealt with people and what he said. He was trustful, honorable and respectful of the things that were important to the Native People. He was alert and aware of what was going on, and he was sensitive to others. He was unassuming and principled."

Don also said that Howard took up space. People sometimes say that about someone who is physically large or heavy. But that's not what Don meant. Don was thinking about how Howard reached out to people and engaged them in conversation. He related to their world and brought them into his world. It was a Big World. His knowledge was expansive and his personal experiences were down to earth. He was comfortable with different kinds of people. This talent was immensely helpful in engaging and communicating with the people he contacted when explaining the proposed resort and in asking for outside opinions and suggestions as the project developed. For Howard, what he did at Bandon Dunes was heartfelt and a soulful journey.

The more I thought about this attribute—taking up space—I realized there was more to it. We all take up space, but how many of us really contribute to the conversation? Making a meaningful contribution means you have to care about what you say and do. So caring is really about personal risk; you have to put your beliefs on public display. To contribute makes one vulnerable to criticism and rejection. That's what Don sensed about Howard, and that's why Howard took up space in a meaningful way.

Bob Johnson, long-time friend of Howard, spoke next. He fondly recalled the "family of friends" Howard had created at the resort, his "incredible commitment to environmentalism," and the wide and "wonderful web of relationships" that had grown up around him, and that Howard "always brought out the best in everyone."

Al Johnson followed and ended his tribute by saying, in the words of another: Howard was the kind of person "to do things that outlast us."

Don Ivy's interpretation of Al's tribute to Howard is worth remembering: "It's what we leave to the future for others." And he went on, "It's really an opportunity for others" to build on and carry forth. Janet Rogers built on this theme by noting that "we [at the resort] are carrying on a legacy that began thousands of years ago with the Native People." She continued in her belief that Howard's work at the resort was "his intent to be of the place and in the spirit of the place."

Amid the solemn atmosphere, levity leapt in. Howard had had difficulty coming to grips with management's request to add TV sets in the pub. Howard didn't want the pub to resemble a sports bar. One of the other speakers said, "I can see you (Howard) redesigning heaven; but, God would have asked him to leave the TVs till the Super Bowl was over." Peals of laughter were heard, but none compared to the throaty, hardy laugh we used to hear from Howard.

Now it was my turn to speak. I had strong feelings about the loss of a good friend I'd known for four decades. Looking at the assembled group and remembering how he lit up a room with his personality and charm, I said, "He looked forward to the personal interactions he had with people; he sought out people, asked about their lives, their families, how they were." At the resort, "there was never enough time in the day [for talking with staff and friends]; his dance card was always filled."

As the project architect, he was always on center stage, in the spotlight. But he "had a unique capacity to put the spotlight on others. He could move it around and let each person [on the consultant team] play his or her role on stage."

In speaking about our personal and collective loss, I went on to say: "In the end, each of us has our personal experiences with Howard. We should hold these close to our hearts. They are precious memories. We should (and can) take comfort in the fact our life paths crossed Howard's."

Don Stastny had the last word. He spoke about their relationship and their common professional value system. He mentioned his previous work for Native People, and the fact the Elders had shared some of their wisdom with him. They, he and Howard also "listened to the land."

Everyone has a personal view about the legacies associated with the resort. Don believes Howard's legacy is simply that "he touched so many lives." Don went on to read *A Time of Longer Shadows*, a poem he had written:

This is your time
A time of longer shadows
Cast by the afternoon sun

Shadows that others feel
Shadows that outline who we are
Shadows that guide others

Youth is a morning shadow
Moving quickly, free
Shadows without impact

Work hard, evolve, and grow
Noon shadows, parents
Patterned and dark, denser

Older, wiser, accomplished
Others watching your shadows
A person affecting his time

This is your time of longer shadows
You gave what you could
We live as you taught

And soon things will change
The shadows fading
Your spirit remains, reminding

Of your shadow in our lives

Don ended by saying, "We're not stopping; we're carrying on," and we did.

L ooking back, as Howard's physical capacities diminished, there was a paradigm shift when Don Stastny took over the leadership of the team. Howard had begun work with a blank slate; with Howard gone, Don had to finish what was left undone. To do this, he needed to channel and interpret Howard's planning and design intentions. This was Don's big challenge.

The assortment of architectural buildings also became a challenge. Don was the architect who pulled together the coherent collection of buildings that comprised the built-out environment. To achieve this goal, the architectural style of the resort evolved based on three fundamental design principles he espoused:

- Structures would be located and built so they were of the land or built into the land so they became part of the landscape setting.

- Structures would reflect agrarian style buildings. They would be simple in shape and form.
- The material palette would essentially come from mother earth—wood (siding), metal (roofs and siding), concrete (walls) and glass.

Besides completing the work Howard had begun, a lot of Don's new work focused on the renovation and repurposing of existing buildings.

NATIVE AMERICAN ART

Howard and I both loved art, and Don made it a threesome. When the resort opened, the walls in the Lily Pond Cottages were bare; the décor of the guest rooms lacked visual interest on wall surfaces. We needed some wall art.

Howard had an artist friend, Frank Boyden, who lived at Cascade Head. After a visit to the resort, Frank and a small group of artists produced a series of black and white prints that were installed throughout the Lily Pond complex. Over time, other works of art—including paintings, bronze reliefs and sculptures—were hung or placed in public spaces at the main lodge.

When Don took over, he took the idea much further. He had worked with many Native American artists during his work on museums. This gave him access and the ability to buy artwork directly from the artists.

Building on what Howard had done earlier, Don began formulating an art program that would expose and educate guests to artwork by Native American artists. The Inn offered him the opportunity to present Mike with a proposal: 'Let's put together an art collection for the resort.' Mike agreed.

The Inn is home to most of this collection. Most of the art is in public spaces, like the hall corridors, the stairwell to the second floor, and a commons room that faces onto an outdoor patio space. Guests can also find other artworks by Native American artists at the Pacific Dunes Clubhouse.

One of the dominant pieces in the commons room is a ceramic face with carved animals and feathers by Phillip John Charette that is mounted on a wall. A carefully positioned spotlight creates an enhanced depth and interest to the sculptural piece titled *They are Gathered Together*.

Fig. 27: They Are Gathered Together

Another interesting work, by Alano Edzerza—titled *Sea Monster Box*—awaits the curious guest who ventures or passes by the second floor hallway by the stairwell. Traditionally, these boxes were made out of wood; this one is cast glass. It is opaque with traditional designs etched into the exterior surfaces. The box has a wooden top with seashells that are embedded into its surfaces. The resort is proud to display this collection of native works of art that "honor those who walked this land before."

As his design work on the building progressed, Don was mentally placing pieces of art in his design drawings. Once construction was completed, he went back and placed the art in virtually the same locations he had imagined. The public spaces in The Inn have become an art gallery. Don had the collection photographed, and it has been published in book form.

PRIVATE HOMES

There are no condominiums, time-shares or fractural home owner-ships of any kind at Bandon Dunes. Mike believes the resort is not a second home resort; it is not a traditional golf resort community and seasonal, part-time or full-time residents are deemed unnecessary at this time. The resort was designed and is solely managed as a golf experience. This keeps the Brand pure. Providing private housing might jeopardize the resort image, identity and, therefore, the Brand.

A consideration to use any of the available residential permits raises several questions: Should private residences ever be built at the resort? Why build any? If built: where and how many are appropriate? And, more importantly, how would it affect the guest experience at the resort?

Looking at the financial picture and profitability is intriguing. Bandon Dunes has the right, in perpetuity, to build up to 600 private residences. What does that mean in financial terms? Let's do a calculation. Assuming the lots are worth at least $100,000 each in 2013 (that's probably a low-ball number), that works out to about sixty million dollars. Assuming an average residence could be sold for $750,000, and ascribing twenty-five percent of that value to each lot, that's another $112.5 million. The potential gross revenue associated with 600 private homes is $172.5 million. There's a lot of potential profit in that number.

Currently, the local demand for second recreation homes or for private residential development on the Oregon coast is still suppressed. There's also no economic incentive to build any private homes at the resort.

However, at some point there will be a recovery in the housing market. Alternatively, the resort owner may decide to build a few private homes for a special reason and market. Then there will be other questions. But the key question is: What would happen to the resort's brand image if you built any private homes or even established a limited residential commu-nity consisting of less than the maximum units allowed?

Under Mike's watch, it is unlikely that private homes will ever be built. Although he will admit, if pressed, that if he wanted to build a few private homes, there are potential home sites on the east side of the Bandon Trails course that might be acceptable.

The 2003 revised master plan identified three mixed-use centers in addition to the main resort village center. The Madrone Center was envisioned as a complex focusing on the Madrone reservoir. This concept was abandoned when the Old Macdonald course and clubhouse were designed and built. However, there is a possibility that a few detached residential buildings might be built on an open meadow located between the existing putting green and the east toe of the North Ridge. The site is visually hidden from the golf course activity.

The revised graphic master plan also illustrated another mixed-use complex—Randolph Center—on the high knolls at the north end of the property. Multiple-story structures were originally proposed, to take advantage of the only site at the resort where ocean views for residential uses were possible. If the first principle of not seeing any non-golf-related structures from any of the golf courses is respected, the Randolph Center will not be built either.

There is an isolated portion of the resort property located along the south shore and southern tail of Fahys Lake. Completely invisible to any golfing activity, this location is suitable for lakefront residences, as the structures can be accessed off of Fahy Road without causing any traffic congestion internal to the resort core.

However, after a decade of resort operation, the assumptions regarding private housing have morphed, primarily in response to how management advertises the resort. Don Stastny believes, "any private housing now would be more about golf. It would have to work operationally with the Bandon Dunes golf brand." Instead of conventional condominium ownership, the residential use might take a time-share form. This is changing the operational form and not the physical form. At this point, construction of private homes is a consideration for the distant future. But Mike could change his mind at any time.

Chapter Thirteen

Beyond the Village and Fairways

The resort has evolved into a multiple layered
set of experiences—recreational, social and spiritual.
—Don Stastny, Portland, Oregon

SCENIC DRIVES AND TRAILS

A close examination of existing trails on the property, especially old logging trails, became a template for the provision of a simple circulation system for the resort. The addition of base rock, asphalt, concrete, pavers, and wood timbers embedded in the ground, and bark chips at selected locations with a bit of on-the-ground engineering to adjust alignments resulted in a simple, direct circulation system. As the master plan was built out, the system of roads, walkways and hiking trails expanded to allow guests and visitors to explore and enjoy a variety of experiences. While substantial portions of the property were converted to golf course use, the overall feeling is of openness. At and within the resort village center and the scattered guest accommodation areas, views are contained and localized. Away from these areas, large portions of the property remain in the natural condition we first encountered, with broad vistas and panoramic views from elevated heights.

The resort's open space system consists of forestlands, wetlands, dune-lands and a few open grasslands, as well as the golf courses. A minor fraction of the property was used for building sites that needed to be connected by roadways. But, in our situation, we wanted scenic drives instead of urban or suburban type streets. The road network we devised allowed for a circulation pattern that left the bulk of the natural environment intact as a visual amenity.

Since we didn't want a lot of guest vehicles driving around the resort once they got here, we designed and built a system of walkways and nature trails to encourage pedestrian foot use instead of vehicular use. As a further incentive, we provided a shuttle bus system to ferry golfers and other guests to outlying facilities and places of interest.

I n the fall of 1996, after Coos County approved the development permit for the destination resort the consultant team began the detailed design for the resort's roadway system. Locating the interior roads was actually pretty easy; connecting them to an entrance off Highway 101 was a challenge. This highway is a heavily traveled scenic coast route, and the Oregon Department of Transportation (ODOT) limits access in order to control congestion. We needed their permission to get access to the highway. First we had to commission a traffic study to determine projected traffic loads. Our consultant's findings recommended dividing arriving and departing resort traffic loads among three access points. Now we had to negotiate with ODOT for a permit.

Tor Flatebo, the team's in-house engineering consultant, coordinated this effort. The department wanted improvements to an intersection at Seven Devils Road and Highway 101. The department believed some of the resort traffic would use this local road, and ODOT wanted the existing intersection, that was acutely skewed, redesigned. They had us over a barrel, so we complied. How could you build a resort if no one could get to it? But, at the same time, we had to decide which of the three roads to designate as the major entrance to the resort.

An existing gravel road, Randolph, was rejected as the main entry road because of its rifle barrel alignment. The other disadvantage was that two-thirds of roadway on both sides was owned by others. Among the three choices, the southern route, which was the longest, had an existing logging trail that traversed exceptionally scenic woodland.

I had discovered this old logging road, the alignment of which was reasonably in intact, during my field investigations. The road passed through stretches of Shore Pine forest filled with interspersed stands of Madrone and Manzanita, seasonal wetlands and there were glimpses of sand dunes along the route.

Howard and I proceeded to drive the logging road. It was a scenic route, and we liked it. With some grading, easing of tight turns and bumps, this could become a spectacular entry drive. Our excitement diminished a bit when I did a code check on the county's road standards. The code mandated extensive rights-of-way. Compliance would open up huge cleared corridors in the scenic woodlands. I needed to find out if standards could be relaxed.

Under the Coos County code classification for road standards, the entry road was considered to be an arterial road. The standard required a sixty-foot right-of-way and a twenty-four-foot-wide paved road with drainage ditches on both sides of the road. Clear-cutting a road corridor that wide would have been a travesty. What we wanted was a scenic drive, not a narrow highway.

After discussing the situation with Howard, I decided to get in touch with the county road master. She went by the name of Boots. I called her up later that fall and invited her to come out to the resort and look at a proposed roadway alignment. A couple of days passed and, on a bright sunshiny morning just before noon, Boots and her assistant arrived to meet with us. Instead of sitting down in the design center conference room, I suggested we take a drive in my beat-up 1987 Toyota Land Cruiser.

As we drove along the logging road, between bumps, I explained how we felt that twenty-four feet of asphalt paving was a bit oversized for this situation; perhaps twenty feet of paving was more appropriate. I emphasized the fact that we wanted to build a winding road and keep traffic speeds much lower than what an arterial road standard accommodates. And, if the road width could be reduced, why not reduce the right-of-way width as well.

When we got to the end of the logging road, Howard chimed in: "Boots, what do you think of our idea?" She smiled and agreed with our suggestions. She didn't say it, but I think we all felt: why would anyone want to spoil this lovely scenery?

The right-of-way requirement was reduced to fifty feet. More importantly, we only had to clear thirty-six feet of vegetation in the right-of-way corridor, and we built a twenty-foot-wide asphalt roadway. Eight feet on either side of the roadway proved to be sufficient for a drainage ditch, gravel shoulders and the necessary grading to allow for cuts and fills on embankment slopes. Sometimes it pays off to object to a regulatory "code standard" that may not fit a particular situation.

For several of the early resort years, the South Scenic Drive was our main entrance road. Guests liked the slow, curving road alignment that wandered through the Shore Pine dominant forest in the sunken interdune valley. Because of the wet soil conditions and exposure to strong coastal winds that shear the treetops, the pines have a stunted habit and form. The presence of Madrone trees and Manzanita shrubs intermingled among the pines create an attractive contrast between the conifer and broadleaf evergreen tree species. Many guests thought of this resort entry drive as a "decompression" experience after either a long drive or an airplane ride to get here.

Today, the South Scenic Drive has occasional use. Drivers returning from the City of Bandon will pass the south entry and take the Randolph Road entry of Highway 101. For those who decide to use the south entry, it may be a little more time. However, the landscape has more visual appeal than the rifle barrel alignment of Randolph Road. If you happen to drive the South Scenic Drive just after it rains, the beauty of the setting is heightened. The exfoliating bark of both the Madrone and Manzanita vegetation exposes a red coloration. When wet, the tree and shrubs trunks and limbs glisten and shine in contrast to the green needle foliage of the pines and dark, evergreen shrub leaves in the understory. Guests or day visitors who decide to take the South Scenic Drive, especially after a rain shower, can take another experience home with them. Whenever I have an extra half hour on my way back to the resort from Bandon, I still prefer this route. Driving slower allows one to take in the scenic qualities associated with the setting. The drive is a big reward in exchange for a slightly longer trip.

This South Scenic Drive intersects Randolph Road at a turn-off to the main lodge, but it also continues beyond the Resort Village Center as the North Scenic Drive and continues north, terminating at the Old

Macdonald clubhouse. Adjoining roads provide access to the Caddy Complex, the Agronomy Center (the main maintenance shop facilities and offices), and the Pacific Dunes clubhouse. Eventually, the road may continue farther north and connect to Whiskey Run Road; this would give the resort a third way to access Highway 101.

🌑

Aguest or day visitor can explore the resort property without playing golf. A system of trails provides access to nature in abundance. Five trail loops invite discovery. Paved walkways and soft paths loop around the Resort Village Center, connecting all the lodging facilities with the resort core. A Beach Trail about three miles in length allows people to hike out to the ocean. The Ridge Loop Trails begin at the main lodge and goes north to Madrone Lake, while the Dune Trail follows the ridgeline south, turns west—crossing the south entry drive—and then traverses a precipitation ridge until it reaches the sand dunes. Wooden poles mark the trail in the dunes so hikers can maintain their orientation as the trail meanders about.

Fueled with an early breakfast and with a break for lunch at either the Pacific Dunes or Trails clubhouse, an entire day can be spent hiking around the resort. Numerous birdhouses have been set out, so birders can see an assortment of birdlife, including wood ducks that tend to settle on many of the coastal lakes and irrigation reservoirs that dot the property.

Birders should also be aware that Bandon Dunes is located on the Oregon Coast Birding Trail. The diverse habitats at the resort are home to about two dozen bird species; among them are various species of warblers, sparrows, hawks, and thrushes; Pileated Woodpeckers, Hummingbirds, Grebes, Ospreys, Kingfishers and Flycatchers.

Within close driving distance, birders can also find more bird species at the Bandon Marsh National Wildlife Refuge and an addition to the marsh known as the Ni-les'tun Unit. The former is located off Riverside Drive south of Bullards Bridge (over the Coquille River), and the latter is located just east of the north end of the bridge. Together with the resort, these two locations offer tremendous birding and hiking opportunities.

SUSTAINABILITY

When the resort master plan was prepared, natural resource conservation was the watchword. Sustainability, including green building practices, became the architect's watchword when applied to the design and construction of the resort's infrastructure and buildings. Over time, resort managers established many policies and practices in the daily operation of the resort to support this worthy goal.

Sometimes it's difficult to know exactly what sustainability is about. It is one of the new marketing terms, like "green building, green construction, sustainable building." For everyone who worked on the consultant team—designers and otherwise—and the resort staff who manage and operate the resort, this meant taking responsibility for the planning, design, construction and management of the Bandon Dunes Golf Resort from the beginning forward. These policies and practices were applied on both a macro and a micro scale.

Besides constructing buildings that fit and complemented the landscape setting with a minimum of disruption to the natural setting, this approach also required being resource-efficient in the selection and procurement of building materials. At the micro scale, it means informing guests that they can use their bathroom towels a second or third time; they didn't have to have fresh towels and washcloths every day.

All the architects, starting with Howard, embraced a "green" approach to their architectural work. Local wood products were sourced and used in many of the buildings. As construction started on the main lodge, one of the resort staff told Howard about a lumber supplier in Myrtle Point that milled Port Orford cedar.

This cedar is indigenous to the Oregon coast and is excellent for construction in a coastal environment. They were able to mill and supply clear finished grade material. Myrtle Point is a stone's throw from Bandon, so the shipping cost was nominal. The price was a bargain. Port Orford Cedar became the standard trim material both for interior and exterior applications. Sometimes the local building material quotes were unreasonably high, so materials were procured from Portland.

Howard also instructed Walsh Construction to use as many local construction workers and subcontractors as possible. The ironwork handrails in the lodge were fabricated by a local craftsperson. Later, Howard engaged a local company as the prime contractor to build a housing complex for caddies.

Attention was specifically paid to energy use. Both Howard's and Don Stastny's architectural designs for the resort emphasized energy conservation. They also insisted on strict evaluations for window selections to ensure they met or exceeded insulation standards. The choice of windows at the resort was critical; they needed to stand up to driven rain conditions.

In 2011, Don investigated the feasibility of using solar panels on an old barn that was being converted into an equipment storage building for the Old Macdonald course. The cost of the solar panels was about $200,000. However, almost half of this cost was returned to the resort as a tax credit. A local engineer was retained to design the panels and to determine the estimated energy output.

The results were outstanding from a sustainable perspective. The panels were fabricated locally and installed using local labor. There was even a surplus of energy that was sold to the regional energy grid.

Time and use have been hard on some of the buildings, as many were temporary with short lifecycles, due to wear and tear. Some simply didn't meet a current need or the resort outgrew their usefulness.

Don designed a replacement building for the Practice Center and a new halfway house for the Pacific Dunes course. Based on his experience incorporating solar panels into the renovation of the Old Mac Maintenance Building, he had solar panels installed on the roofs of these two new buildings. Incorporating solar collectors meets one of the resort's sustainability goals. Over time, it pays for the installation and will generate revenue.

The resort generates a lot of wastewater. The closest available public wastewater treatment facilities were in Bandon. Before committing to on-site treatment, Howard conducted a feasibility study to determine what it would take to connect to services in Bandon. The study concluded that a very long, large-diameter pipe would be needed to connect to city services. But there was a major problem at the Coquille River: the pipe would have to be tunneled under the river. The cost was prohibitive.

Howard then engaged a special consultant to look at on-site treatment options. One of the seemingly feasible green options was to use a man-made lagoon-style wetland and native plant material to treat the effluent waste materials. Investigations were made, and the idea seemed to make good sense. A local contractor came out and dug a big, rectilinear hole in the ground and plants were installed. This occurred in the fall. Unfortunately, this solution proved unsuitable during the winter season, due to nitrogen take-up problems. The wetland treatment idea was abandoned, although it's still there and can serve as a backup system in an emergency. The resort replaced this "experiment" with a new wastewater treatment technology from Japan—the Kubota membrane system.

This system is a very efficient treatment system. All the wastewater from resort buildings is piped to the treatment plant. After processing, the water is recycled and reused to irrigate the golf courses. In this way, potable water from on-site wells is returned into the ground water system. This wastewater treatment approach is a key component in Bandon Dunes' water conservation program. The Kubota system was also chosen because it is a modular system. It allows additional capacity to be added as needed as the resort grows in the future.

Howard and I both felt we had another overriding responsibility as we went about our mission and work. We embraced the idea of stewardship from the very beginning and did our best to prevent environmental degradation. Before existing forest areas or other natural landscape settings were disturbed, care was taken in the site planning work to ensure sensitive natural resource areas were avoided. Where it was necessary to remove existing vegetation, we preserved important stands of trees and restored environments to maintain the character of the landscape setting.

The golf architects were also sensitive to the landscape. In fact, they sought out and designed golf courses that, in most cases, fit into natural landforms. That's not to say they didn't push some sand around. But the feel of the landscape has been preserved. The Pacific Dunes course follows the windblown troughs of sand to such an extent that very little grading was necessary to realize this nationally ranked course.

Opponents attack golf course development for many reasons. Among them is the reliance on and heavy use of fertilizer and pesticides. A common objection is over use of wasteful irrigation practices. In addressing these concerns, the industry has changed many of its practices and has embraced several different kinds of 'stewardship' programs. Kemper-Sports recognized this issue years ago and became sensitive to sustainable practices they could implement in their management practices. By 2009, they had formalized their approach in the form of the Green To The Tee Program. This is a set of environmentally friendly practices that were implemented at all the facilities that the company manages throughout the United States.

The program is an on-the-ground awareness approach that provides managers and staff how-to guidelines on golf course maintenance, water conservation, energy use, recycling, habitat restoration and other "green" practices. The program is implemented through staff education and training. Ken Nice, the Director of Agronomy, and all the golf course superintendents employ these practices on a daily basis. The program uses four levels of awareness and commitment to determine how successful the program is at any point in time. The levels range from Level 1, which reflects a state of mind regarding awareness of the problem or issue, to Level 4, which requires some form of certification.

In addressing Level 4, the resort has sought certification in the Audubon Cooperative Sanctuary Program. This program, administrated by the United States Golf Association and Audubon International, has issued two certifications for the resort. One covers the Bandon Dunes and Pacific Dunes golf courses and the resort's common grounds (certification for the Old Macdonald course is in progress). A second certification that will cover the Bandon Trails course and the Preserve Course will be added later.

The concepts of conservation and sustainability were built into the project from day one. Howard and I took these two concepts to heart: they became fixed points of reference in our everyday dealings with everyone we spoke to about the proposed resort. Embodied in the master plan documents and set forth in all written documents submitted to the county and verbally underscored at all the public hearings, Bandon Dunes was already committed to implementing these concepts as on-the-ground practices once the development permit applications were approved by Coos County. However, applying them on a day-to-day basis is always the measure of Bandon Dunes' sustainability.

Another sustainability-oriented program is the LEED program for buildings. Although none of the buildings at the resort were built under the LEED program, many of the guidelines and requirements were used in the design and construction process. Economic sustainability was a major concern in 2003; the economic success of the resort was not assured at that point. Mike had purchased additional land for expansion. Howard and Al knew they had to seek a revision of the original destination resort development permit from Coos County. We had to state a purpose and rationale for the revision.

The resort had received some national attention and international acclaim. But would this success be short-lived? To assess the situation, Mike had an economic assessment made by the firm, Economic Research Associates. Their report "identified and confirmed the need to broaden the range of recreational pursuits available to future resort guests." The resort expanded, adding more golf holes and overnight lodging facilities, resulted in the number of guests who came to the resort. It also created more jobs for local residents, more tax revenue for the county, and it created entre-preneurial opportunities in Bandon. If sustainability can be defined as a composite of resort development, operations and maintenance practices that meet their needs and are ultimately profitable without compromis-ing the ability of local residents and future generations to meet their own needs, then the resort has been on the right track.

Sustainability can mean lots of things. One can consider expand-ing after-hours opportunities at the resort a form of social sustainability. Guests who still have energy left over from playing golf can relax in the main lodge bar, the Bunker Bar, or the McKee's Pub. The Bunker Bar is always a good choice. There, one can play pool or play poker with golf buddies. There's always the chance to win back any money you might have lost playing golf, or you can lose some more money.

However, an opportunity exists to expand this network of after-hour pleasures to include the halfway houses on the golf courses. The halfway houses could invite and offer informal gatherings. They could be venues for barbeques to see sunsets when the weather and sun cooperate. The attraction of a special cuisine or entertainment could attract some guests to venture out for a different experience. It might also be music or story-telling by local individuals, including Native People with knowledge about natural or cultural history. Only management programming and their imagination limit the opportunity.

THE LABYRINTH

There is mystery in the game of golf, as there is mystery in life. The Labyrinth at Bandon Dunes, dedicated to the memory of Howard McKee, reminds the golfer of that mystery. It resides, hidden off a path, in a dense forest setting. It is an artifact denoting spiritual power, healing and well-being. Beyond its physical presence, the labyrinth augments the *genius loci* at the resort. In a wonderful way, what Howard and I first recognized when we walked the land, the intangible quality and spirit of the resort is now manifested in the build environment.

Fig. 28: McKee Memorial Labyrinth

As the planning and design for the resort progressed, Howard began talking about having a labyrinth at the resort. Because he thought of his work as soulful, he was also thinking about a labyrinth as a symbol—an active symbol to represent all the work and energy he and others were putting into the project. Evidence of this attitude is the personal attention accorded the installation of the labyrinth under the conscientious supervision of Tom Jefferson and Calvin Gederos.

Resting in a shallow depression in the earth, a replica of the Chartres Cathedral labyrinth in France (a design from the 14th century) awaits the seeker. The design pattern was formed using laser cut Turkish limestone pavers in contrast to a path made of black basalt chips. The contrast between the dark and light materials seems to elevate the surface of the labyrinth so that sometimes it appears to float.

A stand of conifer trees forms a vertical cylinder of empty space above the labyrinth. When the sun shines, sunlight filters through the trees, highlighting the surrounding trunks, laying an alternating pattern of light and shadow over the surface of the labyrinth. A night visit, when the sky is clear under a full moon, is magical. Flooded by soft moonlight, the space and labyrinth take on an ethereal glow. A visit in the morning, when the site is shrouded in fog, is a different experience, especially if one waits until the fog lifts, revealing the pattern as if for the first time.

The labyrinth is a spiritual container; it holds energy. I dowsed the site in order to determine the orientation of the entry to the labyrinth. This alignment connects the entry to the circular and spiraling pattern of the earth's energy. As more people come, walk and experience the meditative spirit there, the labyrinth will give rise to more spiritual power.

I have walked the labyrinth many times. Walking a labyrinth is an intentional act. One needs to bring a personal intention—a question—to the experience. I once walked the resort's labyrinth with a friend, who had told me he had been experiencing a lot of impatience recently. Approaching the labyrinth, I entered first. Along the way, I encountered a slug crossing my path. I stopped. My friend asked, "Why have you stopped?" I said, "I stopped to let a slug pass the path; we're not in a hurry here." During our journey into the center of the labyrinth and back, I stopped twice more to let slugs pass our path. Each time my friend was frustrated with the holdup. After completing our walk, we chatted by the labyrinth. At one point, my friend remarked, "Maybe I've been too impatient lately; perhaps I need to become more patient."

Although Howard is gone, his spirit resides at the resort. A guest may not be aware of Howard, but the quality of their stay and experience reflects Howard's attention to detail and how they experience their stay.

If guests choose to visit the labyrinth, they will share in an experience Howard felt manifests itself in how to approach life. In 2007, as he lay in hospice, when asked what he thought about the labyrinth, he replied: "Let it be a happening in the landscape, anonymously created, that impacts people as it might, much as the standing stones do in the lobby." It's not all that anonymous. But you have to make the effort.

H. L. MCKEE PRESERVE

Significant portions of the lower half of the resort property are sensitive habitats. Howard and I were always thinking about how to protect these natural resource assets in the long-term. Before he died, he asked me to look at the possibility of creating a preserve for sensitive habitats we had discovered during the early inventory work. After his passing, about 200 acres of open space were formally designated as the H. L. McKee Preserve. Paired with a labyrinth, both memorialize Howard's contributions.

The preserve is made up of land predominately in the southern half of the resort. Sand dunes, a major interdunal wetland, a Port Orford cedar stand, the south ridge top, coastal lakes and creeks make up the principal features in the preserve. The restoration of Fahy Creek for Coho Salmon was one of the first active conservation improvements associated with the McKee Preserve concept.

Another important endeavor was the resort's participation in a comprehensive inventory of the silvery phacelia population on the West Coast by the United States Fish and Wildlife Service (USFWS). In 2008, the resort conducted a detailed survey of the silvery phacelia plants in the dunelands south of Cut Creek. Together with ongoing restoration and abatement measures, one of the long-term goals is to expand suitable habitat for the threatened phacelia plants at Bandon Dunes.

The McKee Preserve also includes an extraction site—a sand pit. This site has been mined over the years to facilitate golf course construction. Now the sand pit is near the end of its useful life and is scheduled for closure in 2015. Reclamation will follow.

Reclamation is an opportunity to expand the habitat for long-term survival of the phacelia species. The reclamation plan could also include a new trailhead. Establishing a trailhead along the South Scenic Drive would allow guests to access the sand dune landscape and interconnect with Dunes Trail and the Beach Trail. Of course, the resort's trail system permits foot access to almost all resort lands.

As I thought about the resort trails and natural areas we preserved at the resort, I was reminded of what one of our critics once had to say about the property. He suggested the owner donate the land for use as a public park. I'm not sure what he had in mind. Neither the state nor the local community had the resources to manage or maintain this acreage. However, on principle, he believed golf was absolutely the wrong use for the land. Besides objecting to a resort as an irreversible land use, I think he envisioned a use where the land would have been accessible to a wider range of public users, and that's a good thought.

Although the McKee Preserve occupies a fraction of the resort property, it does preserve, in perpetuity, critical natural resources that previously had no stewardship and little accessibility. The public now has convenient access to a wide variety of landscape and habitat settings. The preserve and other portions of the resort have become the parkland a concerned Bandon resident envisioned when he suggested Mike donate the property as a legacy for use by future generations. Both active and passive recreational users have benefited from what is available at Bandon Dunes.

Chapter Fourteen

KemperSports

Brands are created in the mind.
—Walter Landor

MANAGEMENT AND STAFF

R e-zoning the property, erecting buildings and infrastructure is one thing; running the place is another. Operating the resort requires management. KemperSports (based in Northbrook, Illinois) fills that need. They were brought into the project at the very beginning to provide advice during design program discussions. In doing so, they were an essential part of the consultant team.

Every company has a flagship property—Kemper has Bandon Dunes. The fact that the resort is profitable reflects their commitment to the unique brand of hospitality found there. The company successfully weathered the financial and economic downturns from 2008 forward and came back economically stronger than before. They have, through innovative turf management policies and practices, influenced standards and practices in the national golf industry. Bandon Dunes is recognized as a game changer in the American golf industry; everyone wants to build links courses now.

The resort's success is also due to KemperSports' marketing approach; much of it is based on third party endorsement. Word of mouth is every-thing. Mike likes to refer to this as the use of "Bell Cows." Farmers sometimes put a bell around the neck of a dominant cow in a herd. When it's time to bring the herd back to the barn, the bell cow leads the way.

By interacting with select individuals in the industry and individuals who "influence" others, the resort gets the word out to the golf community. These influencers may be golf writers, ranking panelists, or simply the guy in charge of a local country club. A local club leader or organizer, who may not even be the most skilled player, will be the one most traveled and passionate about the sport. At any moment, they know what's happening in the industry. The bell cows are the guys who introduce other golfers to dream golf and continue to bring them back to Bandon Dunes.

Kemper doesn't spend tons of money on advertising, but they do court and entertain the media. They know once someone experiences Bandon Dunes and becomes infected with the passion of "what golf was meant to be," they become their best salespeople.

As the resort concept and master plan developed, the director in charge of marketing at Kemper was Josh Lesnik. As soon as Coos County approved the development application, Mike knew he needed a general manager right away. Without hesitation he called Josh (Josh had never met Mike). He told Josh he wanted him to come out to Oregon and visit the resort. Next, Josh flew out to Oregon with Mike and drove down to the resort in a rental car. On the way, Mike asked Josh to consider becoming the general manager. As Josh recalls it, Mike then suggested he think about the offer. Hell, Josh hadn't yet seen the property. In reality, Mike was interviewing Josh, and he had planted a seed.

Arriving at the resort, Josh found himself in a construction zone. In short order, he was playing the Bandon Dunes course. Near the tees for the 17th hole, he stood on a bluff overlooking the ocean beachfront. To say he was impressed would be an understatement. That day, Mike offered him the opportunity to manage the resort. One of Josh's first thoughts was, "How am I going to sell this move to my wife?" He did, and Josh became the first general manager at the resort.

Josh's first task at Bandon Dunes was to build a staff to service the resort. He needed good people. Over time, he hired key managers to handle specialty functions, people to run the reception area, clubhouse sales staff, bartenders, a chef, cooks, a wait staff, and many others to operate what, in time, became a small city. Josh also knew he needed a caddy master, as Mike had prescribed that all the golf courses would be walking courses. No carts or cart paths are allowed. Instead there is a caddy corps. Golfers can use a caddy or a pull cart, or even carry their own bag. But, a caddy can provide essential advice the first time a golfer plays golf at the resort.

Matt Allen had heard about the resort, and he contacted Josh to find out about a possible job. Matt grew up in Portland. Golf was not one of his interests until he was a freshman in high school. At the age of thirteen, he took up the game, in part because his father was a golfer. When school ended and summer vacation arrived, Matt found he had been signed up to attend a couple of golf camps. By fall, he was back in school and a member of his high school golf team.

During his high school years, he got a job working in the bag room at one of the local golf course clubhouses. There, he caught the attention of one of the golf pros, who helped him obtain a Chick Evans Caddie Scholarship to attend the University of Oregon.

This scholarship program offers financial aid. It is a one-year scholarship that is renewable for four years and can represent a source of college funding worth up to $50,000. The program is available at designated schools with significant populations in every state in America. The Evans Scholars all live together; this connects young men and women together in a discrete golf industry network useful to a golf-oriented career.

After graduating from college, Matt was offered an internship with the Oregon State Golf Association. Working with the association gave him access to news about what was happening in the golf industry. Becoming aware that a new golf course was under construction in Bandon, Matt called up Josh. After exchanging several telephone conversations, Matt drove down to Bandon to meet Josh. This was only a month after Josh had arrived as the new general manager.

When they first met, Josh immediately thought he had found someone who could fill the role as caddy master, but he didn't offer him the job initially. He and Matt talked about the resort, and then Josh invited Matt to play golf on the Bandon Dunes course that was still in the grow-in stage.

Initially, Matt wasn't eager to work at the resort. But he felt he'd made a connection with Josh and that the chemistry was good between them. Over the next several months, they continued to talk by telephone, and a few months later Matt got a call from Josh offering him the position of caddy master. The offer was a surprise to Matt. He'd gotten his current job with the golf association right after he graduated from college and was in a good position to advance, working with the association. He also had no real experience working at a golf course. At the time, Matt hadn't thought about changing jobs yet; working at Bandon Dunes would be a lateral move, but the offer was intriguing.

Matt considered the caddy master offer but decided not to accept it. Instead, he told Josh, "I can do more." After some negotiation, they worked things out. At the tender age of twenty-four, Matt Allen became the first director of golf at the resort. He started work February 1, 1999. Now Josh had someone to help him build a staff.

Critical to the operation of a golf resort is the tee time reservation system. For the resort to make money, they needed to fill tee times. The system started with a couple of people simply answering the phone when it rang.

Good fortune always seemed to smile on Bandon Dunes. *The Oregonian* newspaper had published an in-depth article on what was happening at the resort. Immediately, the telephones started to ring. Josh and his small, growing cadre of workers were inundated with phone calls. Everyone pitched in to take the calls and make reservations until a dedicated reservation system and staff could be put in place. In time, it would require specially designed software to coordinate reservations by determining availability for both room and tee time requests. Since the system uses live operators, it has evolved and reflects the small-town atmosphere that permeates the resort. Guests now call up and ask for a specific reservation agent with whom they have a relationship.

Matt Allen, recalling the atmosphere his first year on the job, said, "It was wild." For him, it was a rich and rewarding experience to see the resort take shape in the early years before it opened for play. But there were serious tasks: they had to purchase a point of sales system for retail sales in the pro shop. They also had to begin ordering merchandise.

For Matt, it was just the beginning of a career in the golf industry. A decade later, he left Bandon Dunes in order to become the general manager at the new Chambers Bay golf course. For those who show promise, Kemper promotes their employees, and Matt exemplifies how far one can advance within the organization.

Josh still didn't have a caddy master. He found one in Bob Gaspar, aka Shoe. Shoe was a local resident who worked in the cranberry bog industry.

He'd been around Bandon forever and knew everybody. When the local newspaper ran an article about Bandon Dunes, Shoe knew his future was at the resort.

Before Matt joined the staff, Shoe simply showed up one day and asked if he could help out. He was Josh's first hire. Matt had turned down the caddy master position, so Shoe took the job. For a while, he did whatever else was needed. In fact, he took the first reservation call for a tee time that the resort received.

In 2013, he was still at the resort, as he's the official greeter at the main lodge. As a guest pulls up in a personal vehicle, the resort's shuttle bus or a commercial shuttle van from the airport, Shoe is always standing by to answer a guest's question or direct them to wherever they need to go. No one has a more gracious smile or bigger heart than Shoe.

Josh managed the resort for only two years. Hank Hickox took over the managerial reins in September 2000. Previously, he had been the chief operating officer for the Oneida Indian Nation in New York. Early in his career, he had worked with John Gray, a prominent Oregon developer who had started the Salishan Resort in 1984. Hank joined John and became the president and CEO of the company. Hank then went on to conceive the Skamania Resort and Lodge project in Stevenson, Washington.

When the Skamania Resort was sold in 1996, Hank spent the next four years as a consultant with a number of American Indian groups. When Josh returned to Chicago, Hank was recruited to fill the position. This was his opportunity to return to Oregon. Like Josh, it was too enticing an opportunity to pass up.

Several key managers, who couldn't imagine working anyplace else, support Hank. One of them is Kristie Jacobson. She was one of the first administrative people to be hired in 1999, so, by 2012, she was an old-timer. Initially, she worked with Josh and was responsible for finding new hires. Except for a few special hires, most of the employees from the beginning came from the surrounding area.

A small town tends to breed a particular atmosphere among its inhabitants. Since they see each other a lot, they are friendly and good conversationalists. This warm disposition is a genuine quality that is refreshing to guests. This small town spirit is also infectious. Resort guests, encountering this type of friendliness, immediately feel welcomed at the resort.

The Randolph Center, located near the resort's main entry perimeter, is home to administrative staff. Besides housing administrative offices, it also contains warehousing space. As the resort expanded, the presence of delivery trucks, including semi-trucks and trailers, in the resort core became a major congestion problem. After putting up with the congestion and inconvenience for several years, management finally decided the situation was intolerable. What was needed was a warehouse where supplies and goods could be delivered and broken down for distribution. Coincidently, there was a need for more administration space.

The resort architect at the time, Don Stastny, combined these two functions into a single building. The offices are spacious, and all have views of the forest setting. It's a very peaceful place to work, away from the hustle and bustle of the resort core.

The office building has a special feature in the reception area. A huge, wall-sized photographic mural dominates the reception foyer. Twenty feet long, it extends from floor to ceiling. The mural is a landscape image depicting one of the golf course holes on the Old Macdonald golf course.

As construction on the building neared completion, Don remembered that there had been extensive visual documentation of the construction process associated with the Old Macdonald course. Wood Sabold, a local photographer, had taken photographs during the entire construction process. He had also interviewed Mike Keiser and Tom Doak, the principal course architect.

Don approached Wood and asked him to develop a mural display for the entry of the new office building. Drawing upon the material he had previously photographed, Wood came up with the concept of a mural that would cover an entire wall. He then decided to superimpose small photographs that showed men and equipment engaged in the construction of the Old Mac course on the mural.

What Don had in mind was a "surprise." It was specifically intended for Mike and for others who would come to the building in the future. The size and scale of the mural is impressive, but there is also a subconscious message attached to the mural. It's a reminder that the people who work here helped build the resort, manage it, maintain it, and they are exceedingly proud of that fact. It also conveys a subtle message to people who come to apply for a position at the resort. What you see or will see if you work here is more than what you may initially think. There's history here, a legacy, and you will be part of it.

Ken Nice believes he is at the resort for a purpose. He is in charge of all the golf courses—a super superintendent of sorts. His official title is Director of Agronomy, and he is one of Hank's key managers.

Ken ended up in the golf industry because he was fascinated with the history of links style courses before he ever started playing golf. Asked what was the fascination, his response is, "The seascape, brown grass and the firm, fast turf conditions associated with links golf."

Earlier in his life, Ken had a landscaping business in Seattle. At some point he decided to go back to school, and he enrolled at Oregon State. He got a degree in turf grass science and got his first job at the Astoria Golf and Country Club. Troy Russell, a previous superintendent of golf at Bandon Dunes, recruited Ken. He met Howard McKee one day while walking one of the golf courses with a group that included Howard. During the walk, Ken found himself with Howard somewhat detached from the group.

Given the conversationalist Howard was, they talked as they walked. Howard brought up the subject of soul work. This subject resonated with Ken. It spoke to Ken's belief: "If you have true intention in your heart, doors do kind of open up for you." Ken has a true love and authentic passion for the landscape settings home to links golf. For that simple reason, Ken feels "I am here [at the resort] for a reason." He, like others who worked on the project from day one, truly understands the owner's vision, and how Howard, while accommodating golf, also embraced a conservation ethos. Ken understands the resort's mystique. So Ken joined the ranks of people with a dream job. As a bonus, it was in his home state.

Ken deals with problems day in and day out and has faced many challenges and obstacles. He is responsible to ensure all the golf courses are playable all the time. As problems occur, he and his staff inevitably solve them. However, there is one obstacle he will probably never overcome— the invasion of Poa grass on the resort golf courses.

Most turf specialists consider Poa a weed that can't be contained. The first course at the resort used a blended mixture of grass with some fescue. Old Macdonald was all fescue. But, over time, Poa crept into the mix. You can't keep it out, but you can delay its infestation. Links courses are not uniform mono-stands with one color. However, the characteristics of Poa—clumpy, disease susceptible, lots of flowers and of poor color—are not desirable. In its earliest stages of invasion it can be hand pulled. As it multiplies exponentially, it quickly becomes part of the turf mix.

Five golf courses at the resort means there's lots of work for the maintenance staff. Additionally, there are extensive grounds and landscaped areas that also require maintenance. Storm winds blow down trees on walkways and trails. Occasionally, landscape plants die. Lawns need cutting. Shrubbery needs trimming. In extremely hot weather, landscaping needs watering where there is no irrigation.

To deal with these issues, the resort needed a grounds maintenance supervisor. This is Tom Jefferson's role, and his real challenge is just keeping up with the work. There's always more to do than there is time to do it. Up until 2012, he was also responsible for installing landscape plantings as new buildings and improvements were undertaken. Sometimes we used outside landscape contractors. At other times, it was more cost effective to use resort staff.

As the resort prepared to open, new opportunities emerged for the local workforce. Besides being beneficial to the local economy, it would open up opportunities for high school students who didn't have lots of choices for summer jobs.

In 1999, a young, local woman found summer work as the first hostess in the Gallery Restaurant at the main lodge. After graduating from high school, she went on to college. But she would return summers to work at the resort. Later, she opened the new pro shop at the Pacific course.

Continuing her college career, she eventually graduated with three degrees. Moving on, she found a position with one of the big accounting firms based in Portland, Oregon. A few years later, the resort's general manager, remembering her work ethic and previous accomplishments at the resort, recruited her for a key management position. Today, Breanna Qualttrocchi is the resort controller and is in charge of four administrative departments. Sometimes you "can go back home" and find success and happiness.

THE BRAND

You can imagine a golf resort, you can permit it, you can build it, but to succeed you must operate the facility and please your clientele. Today, product branding usually leads to success.

At Bandon Dunes, the customer experience is the Brand. All decisions made by the owner and KemperSports are based on how the decision will affect the Brand. Will it diminish or enhance the Brand? All proposed improvements, buildings or new activities have to pass this litmus test. The concept of branding at the resort permeated the design of the resort, and how the resort is managed by KemperSports.

What is "Branding"? According to Walter Landor, "products are made in the factory, but brands are created in the mind." At Bandon Dunes, branding is the total effort expended in creating an experience the golfer and other guests take away from their stay at the resort. It's not so much about what it is, but rather how you feel about it, and it has to have lasting and memorable value. That's what brings them back.

Before the recession in 2008, the resort had 500 employees. During the downturn, staff levels dropped to 350 employees. Bandon Dunes, like many businesses, had to tighten its belt. Some people were let go, but all key core staff personnel were retained. This required staff to do other tasks beyond their normal responsibilities in order to keep the doors open.

The belt tightening that came with the recession actually benefited the resort. Adjustments to staff assignments and responsibilities led to more efficiency and productivity. But, more importantly, core staff members were retained. However, as demand returned, staff levels grew. By early 2012, KemperSports employed 509 employees. For the resort, business was back and better.

Together, Mike and KemperSports have established a unique Brand. It's one of the most talked about places in the golf world. Unlike most other golf courses—especially those built in the 1970s, 1980s and into the early 1990s—golf at this resort is not a real estate business. In previous decades, golf courses were not built for the love of the game. Instead, they were being built to sell homes. If a developer could find 600 acres or more of undeveloped land near a metropolitan area, he bought the land, built a golf course and then subdivided the remaining land for residential development. Residential development was not part of Mike's golf vision. He loved the game, and he wanted to build a golf resort that offered a different experience to the public. And this meant public golf courses, instead of private golf courses.

As soon as Josh Lesnik got back to Chicago in 2000, he had to decide what his role was going to be. It was easy: he became the brand manager. As he and Mike discussed how to advertise the resort, they realized two simple facts.

They needed publicity to market the public courses, and the more they could get the better. The first course generated lots of buzz in the industry, so they both knew they had a great story going for them. Then Mike realized, "the best way to get publicity is to be willing to talk to writers." Previously a somewhat private person, he needed to change. Out went his private persona; in came a more public-oriented persona. Mike became the face of the resort and started traveling and giving public speeches. This approach was more effective than buying advertising in golf magazines. In fact, once they saw photographs of the first course, the magazines were dying for stories.

Mike was bombarded with: Why are you doing this? What is it going to look like? What are the ingredients of success? Why do people come all the way to play golf here? But in the end, the resort still has to deliver on the promise of the vision and the experiences guests take away when they go home.

As the brand manager, Josh is the "spokesperson" for the resort to the golf industry. His primary responsibility is developing and maintaining relationships with media people. As more courses were built, both Mike and Josh realized the great story had become an ongoing story that needed to be continually updated to the media. Now the Brand had to be protected.

Chapter Fifteen

Taking Care of Business

The caddy program is a significant asset.
The added value the program brings to the resort is
a gigantic reason for the success of the resort.
—Ken Brooke, Bandon Dunes Resort

TRUE SERVICE

Underlying the success and mystique of Bandon Dunes is Kemper's management policy of True Service. The policy did not originate at the resort; KemperSports imported it from the Chicago office. The policy consists of seven teaching modules, and all new employees are required to complete all the modules. The policy acquaints new resort employees with a service mentality that instills in them an attitude, as the human resources director states: they are "here to serve the guests."

This manifests itself in the way staff sometimes goes out of their way to assist guests by doing little things that are beyond the normal expectations of guests. Realizing a staff person has done something special that they didn't have to do, that's memorable. This tends to foster a distinctive remembrance guests take away besides their golfing experiences.

When the resort first opened, employees were told to make direct eye contact with guests. This behavior, coupled with the small town ambiance found at the resort, establishes more personal relationships with guests.

One of the best examples of this true service is a story about what happened when a guest arrived late at the resort. It was during the winter, when services at the resort and in Bandon close by eight o'clock at night. All the resort's restaurants were closed. One of the staff members took the late arrival home and fed him. That's personal service!

One of the best examples, where resort guests experience "True Service," is in the dining facilities at Bandon Dunes. Service begins with the hostess, then the wait staff and the kitchen staff. Another influence was present several years ago. A former food and beverage manager, who had worked in a premium Las Vegas restaurant for seventeen years, instituted an interesting wait staff-training program.

As the manager for the Gallery Restaurant and the resort's wine expert, he oversaw the wine program and among his tasks was the education of the wait staff. As he used to say, "The more you know [about wine], the more you can sell."

When a customer wants a Pinot Noir with a fruity nose or shades of a particular fruit, or from a particular part of the country or winery, the server needs to be knowledgeable. They need to know the terminology and the taste profile of different kinds of wine; how else are they going to know what "earthy" means? They need to have a basic knowledge of wine, and the characteristics of all the wine on the resort's wine list. This will allow them to recommend appropriate choices that will appeal to a particular customer.

What does the resort do to educate its wait staff about wine? It selects staff members on a rotating basis and sends them on a trip to the Napa Valley and Sonoma wine country in California.

They go to these locations because they are set up for educating people in the industry about wine. Over four days, staff will be exposed to about 120 wines. Plus, the people on one of these excursions also get exposed to upscale environments and the ambiance associated with premier resort facilities. The training process also includes meals. The wineries host breakfast, lunch and dinner events where staff members learn about wine and food pairings. Moreover, these experiences also give the Bandon Dunes servers a chance to see how other servers perform their duties. When you have knowledge, you have confidence. This is mentoring at its best.

In a manner, one can think of the dining room servers as being in the "entertainment business." People want to feel good when they're dining, and not just eating. The resort servers are prepared for anything. "'No' is not an acceptable answer to a guest's request or question at Bandon Dunes."

The Bunker Bar has always been the after-hours action spot at the resort. Located in the basement of the main lodge and clubhouse, it is the only place where smoking is allowed indoors. This is where cigar aficionados congregate. For guests who don't want to retire early, want another drink, and want to smoke a cigar with their golf buddies, play poker or shoot pool, this is their hangout. It's a small room, and it's usually smoky. Enter at your own risk.

But you can always smoke outdoors. Walking one of the golf courses, you can always find a cigarette butt here and there. But, it's been reported that one cigar aficionado, when asked where's the best place to smoke a cigar at the resort, replied: "No matter where you light up a cigar on the Bandon Dunes property, it's the greatest place to smoke."

Some people like to take the short pathway up to the overlook on the ridge top just above the parking lot at the main lodge. Just before sunset, when it's not raining, the view is magnificent. The water is lit up with brilliant rays as the sun begins to dip below the horizon. Golden light bounces off the waves as the ambient light dims, and the veil of night settles over the buildings below. Elevated above the crowd below, if you stay till the night sky turns black, the stars in the heavens twinkle and sparkle in the overhead darkness.

THE CADDIES

A caddy at Bandon Dunes probably contributes immeasurably to the guest golfer's experience. Guests spend more time with the caddies than with any other staff person. A caddy spends at least four and a half hours with a guest on a round of golf. If they partner up for the duration of the guest's stay, they can provide the most lasting impression of the guest's experience. At Bandon Dunes, a caddy can be a true professional. By the nature of their work, many caddies are nomads. However, many who came to Bandon Dunes stayed and have now taken up permanent residence.

All the courses at Bandon Dunes are walking courses. A few carts are available, but only for use by handicapped golfers.

Because the caddies are familiar with the courses, having a caddy can make the difference between having an enjoyable round or a frustrating round. Usually a caddy can assess the strengths and weaknesses of the player by the third or fourth hole. Then the caddy can tell a golfer what club to use and how to play the shot based on the golfer's ability. He can also offer advice regarding optional "lines of play" to take to reach the green.

The resort caddy corps resembles a big family. There is a strong sense of camaraderie, and many of the caddies have known each other for years. There is also the recognition that management values the face time caddies have with the guests. Caddying is a customer service job.

Outside of any personal differences in age, gender or profession, the caddy and the golfer have a common objective. The focus is always on how to hit the ball and get it in the round cup with the shortest number of strokes. According to Eric Rackly, "Golf is always the common thread" that connects golfer to caddy for four to five hours. Eric—or Rack, as he is called—was the first caddy at Bandon Dunes.

Rack first came to Bandon in 1997 and worked as a chef in several of Bandon's restaurants. He had visited the resort when it was under construction, just to see what everyone in town was excited about. He'd played golf and had caddied a bit but had never entertained the idea of being a caddy.

Days later, he got a call from a friend's wife who worked for David Kidd. The resort needed a caddy because Steve Lesnik, then the President of KemperSports, was going to play golf with Mike Keiser and others, and he had an injured back. He needed someone to carry his bag. Rack said OK. He continued to cook, but when a golf magazine writer came to visit, Rack addressed the call again. The next thing he knew, he was a part-time caddy.

When the resort opened, Rack became a full-time caddy. In the beginning, there were about thirty to forty caddies, and Rack remembers, "We played a lot of darts." As business picked up, there was a real need for more caddies on a regular basis. Things got real busy, caddies started "double bagging" (carrying the golf bags for two players), and they made serious money, getting cash for their services.

At the resort, the caddies are independent contractors; they are in charge of their own financial affairs. This creates an opportunity for them to present themselves as professionals—someone who could make a living doing their job. In many ways, caddies are like gypsies—they have a nomadic lifestyle, especially if they go on the Pro Tour. It's an ideal job for a single guy or woman. However, at Bandon Dunes, a caddy can give up the nomadic lifestyle and have a stable family lifestyle.

The work is seasonal. A caddy can take off three or four months in the winter and begin work in early spring. Summer is the money season. A hardworking caddy can make $5000 a month from May to October. A serious caddy can make $400 a day double bagging two eighteen-hole rounds a day.

If you asked Rack, 'what's it like to caddy at Bandon Dunes,' he'd say, "We're living the dream." What makes caddying at the resort a "dream"? One of the main reasons is the fact that the resort built a special facility just for the caddies. The caddies have their own building to hang out in while waiting for their assignment. Their "caddy shack" has a waiting area with a big screen TV, and food is delivered daily from the main kitchen.

Another reason is that the caddy program is run professionally, and the program uses an electronic scheduling system. Ken Brooke, the caddy master, and his supportive staff get high praise from the caddies. Each course has its caddy manager. These managers answer questions and provide feedback before and after a round. Each caddy has an e-mail account for digital scheduling on- and off-site. A caddy can schedule his or her available time months ahead.

Some golf resorts and courses require the caddies to assemble early in the morning for assignments by word of mouth. Bandon Dunes' digital system allows the resort to pre-schedule caddies with specific guests and groups. Likewise, the caddies can pre-schedule private reservations ahead of time. Many caddies have a list of clients who return to the resort and only book with them.

The resort has a caddy-training program administrated through a local community college. This class uses films to instruct caddies in basic skills and etiquette. After completing his training, a caddy has to caddy for a senior caddy. This is one-on-one mentoring. Shadowing comes next. A caddy will accompany a senior caddy on a round. The shadow doesn't carry a bag; he's just an observer. This allows him to see a real caddy in action. And the learning process continues informally in the caddy shack.

Sitting around, waiting for work, caddies constantly talk about what it used to be like in comparison to what it is like today. If a golfer asks a caddy about a particular hole when they're on the course, the conversation might begin, "This is the way the hole looks now; it used to look different." Caddies are part-time historians. They have the opportunity to pass on to guests the background and value system that underlies the course design philosophy.

The caddy corps has evolved at Bandon Dunes. In the very beginning, the caddies wore a shirt printed with the slogan, "Show up, shut up, keep up". You don't see that shirt anymore.

What makes a good caddy? Number one is personality. There are different personalities, but they all have to have the technical knowledge about shot-making, and they have to know each course like the back of their hand. Besides that, they wear many hats: tour guide, historian, often times comedian, storyteller and sometimes mommy and daddy. The good caddies, the ones who make the best money, are excellent psychologists: "You have to know your customers." Some golfers want your life history; others want no verbal interaction.

The caddies have access to the practice center at any time. And the caddies can play any course if there's an open time slot. One caddy told me, "It's a one-of-a-kind. Nothing like it in the whole wide world."

Ray Bursey—aka Ray B—is a professional caddy at the resort. He started as a caddy in 1981. He's worked the Pro circuit, but, in 2002, he found his way to Bandon Dunes to check things out. His intention was to stay two weeks; he's still here in 2012. He simply "fell in love with the place." From Ray B's perspective, the resort is "altogether different from any other place [he] caddied at in the past." At Bandon Dunes, you can't memorize things; every read on a green is different. If you move the pin one inch, the whole read will change. The condition of the greens changes; each day is a new challenge to a professional caddy. He also believes, "You're not going to get bored; you will have to work at your job. It keeps you young." Ray B is sixty-seven years young.

Caddying can also be a humbling experience because of the weather. Wind and rain, they are the major forces that shape the golfer's strategy at Bandon Dunes, and a person must have fortitude to play on a given day when the rain comes down horizontally. You can play in the rain in the morning and play again in the afternoon with sunshine, and you will have two different, wildly different, golf experiences.

Ever the philosopher, Ray B wants to continue to caddy as long as he can. He just wants to leave the course with a smile on his face. A tip helps, too. He always carries a rain bag cover with him when he caddies. If it rains, he can protect his client's equipment. But if he goes down and stays down, he's planned ahead: "Put me in the bag, put the bag in a sand trap, and keep on playing."

What advice do the caddies have for golfers at Bandon Dunes? Ray B was caddying for a golfer playing in the mid-amateur tournament. When they got to 14 on Trails, he asked for a club recommendation. Ray suggested a 4 or 5 iron. The golfer declined the suggestion; he wanted to use his driver. "No," Ray B said. "Never use a driver in competition here. It's a potential train wreck out there." The golfer blasted the ball. It went over the green, and they're still looking for that ball. Ray has several other kernels of wisdom.

- On putting: Even the downhill putts need to be hit firm to stay on your line. The greens at Trails and Old Macdonald are fast. The greens at Bandon and Pacific Dunes are slow. Some of the courses are dominated by Poa grass on the greens that slows the ball down.

- On a read: Go with what you see. Go with it. If it is wrong, you will learn from making a mistake. Don't question your first instincts.

- On character: You can tell a man's character by the way they react to a bad shot. You will hit more bad shots in golf than good shots.

Is there a secret to playing golf at Bandon Dunes? Ray B says, "Hit it where the lawn mower goes." Sometimes that entails putting the driver away and taking an iron out of your bag, or maybe a 3-wood. It's not about distance; it's about keeping the ball in the fairway. If you have the ball in the fairway, you will get an additional twenty yards with the roll. You need to play the topography. If it's windy, you don't or shouldn't use a lofting club. Keep the ball low. The faster you get the ball on the ground the better.

What's the last word on the caddies? Ray B has been asked by many of the younger caddies about caddying on the Pro Tour. His reply: "If you caddy here and make it at Bandon Dunes, you can caddy anywhere."

SUCCESS AND LEGACY

I've often been asked the question: Why were we so successful in this endeavor? There are many answers, but two key factors stand out in my mind. Mike Keiser let Howard and his consultants do what they did best with relaxed oversight. Politically, there was a receptive climate and, more importantly, no major forces united to oppose the application.

Not least of all was the fact Mike did not depend upon conventional financing—he used his own pocketbook. He solicited founder subscriptions and, when things got tough during the recession, he invested more of his own money.

We also found a way to successfully work within the land use planning system in Oregon. Many believe the system is broken and needs fixing. Others believe it can't be fixed.

In 2006, an exchange of e-mails on which Howard commented took up this issue. Al began the dialogue with the statement: "This weekend, amazing what an exception [Bandon Dunes] to statewide land use goals can do." It was followed by the comment: "One can only ponder why economic development of this nature in rural Oregon is an 'exception' in the first place." Which then prompted this comment: "Balance suggests carefully considering all the needs of the rural environment and society—for too long, the land use process has been too restrictive to be truly balanced."

The then-executive director of 1000 Friends of Oregon commented: "It would be difficult for Howard McKee to see it this way because he had to fight his way through it; but from one perspective, the Oregon land use process did produce Bandon Dunes. Land that had some potential for forestry use, but was not being put to that potential and was not contributing to the community's economy, was transformed by the imagination and vision and investment of Howard, and Mike Keiser, into something that neither state or local planners and leaders could have contemplated fifteen years earlier when the plans for that land were adopted. Fortunately, the plans—and the state's regulations—provided a mechanism for visionaries to make a case for something better, something smarter, something more valuable than waiting for the timber to grow back (on the property). And that mechanism ensured that other community values would be protected from harm in the process of allowing the good idea to go forward."

Bill Grile, the former planning director for Coos County, disputed these comments. He argued that the previous owners of the property had tried to develop the property but were unable to do anything that would have provided them a reasonable economic return.

Howard had the last word, and it is as good a summary statement today as it was back in 2006: "I have enjoyed the exchange of emails speculating on what might have been, what should be, etc., etc. Bill Grile pretty much sums up my view of the process. Unfortunately, the 1000 Friends of Oregon dealt themselves out of the process early on despite repeated invitations to participate in the creative stages of the project when concepts and principles were the main discussion items, not the myriad regulatory hoops and research efforts required to demonstrate the obvious. Instead, the organization conspired with the DLCD staff to change the rules on destination resorts midstream, fearing the project might win approval and thus set a bad precedent.

"Al Johnson successfully rebuffed this tactic by exposing the scheme at a planning commission hearing when the 'new rules' were introduced into the record by the DLCD without any discussion with him even though we had been in constant communication with the department throughout the pre-hearings process. Once approved by the Coos County Planning Commission and the County Commissioners, 1000 Friends of Oregon chose to appeal the project to LUBA. Subsequently, they withdrew their appeal only after it became apparent they would likely lose. Thus, the state of planning in Oregon!!! At times it is hard to tell the difference between the staffs of DLCD and the 1000 Friends. Bob (Stacy), I know this all happened before your time, but it should be a call for reform."

For Mike and his band of golf course architects, who together created this marvelous series of golf courses, Bandon Dunes was about Dream Golf. For Howard and all the team members who contributed to the planning, design and construction of Bandon Dunes, it was a Dream Project.

Howard never saw the end of what was accomplished by 2012, but the mystique he felt at the resort remains. Hopefully, the golfing experiences will always be there for new players to discover and for returning players to test their skills and reminisce with their golf buddies.

Resort staff and insiders often chat about the resort's legacy. There's talk about Howard's legacy. Howard's legacy is the built environment, the associated ambiance, and, as Don Ivy said, "the opportunities" he left us. Others and I share this legacy.

The resort legacy is hard to articulate. Are legacies "things"; are they handed out and handed down? The resort is simply a vessel holding potential experiences. Among the recipients, these experiences will vary. It's all part of the resort's mystique.

The resort's true legacy may well reside in the guests. They arrive, experience the place, go home, and then they tell their friends about their experience. Then they and others return.

Mike has his own view: "It's evolving. It's also worth noting that golf is one of the few things in the architecture arena that lasts forever. The old course at St. Andrews has been played since the 15th century. There have been changes over time, but the essence of the course is still the same as it was back then. There's every reason to believe these courses [at Bandon Dunes] and other courses I will build at various locations will be played on for several hundred years."

Are we at the end of the story? No. Mike is always full of surprises; he wanted to build another golf course.

PART FOUR

GOLF AND CONSERVATION

The South Coast is between two worlds:
One is dead; the other is yet to be born.
—Harry Hoogesteger, Gold Beach, Oregon

Fig. 29: South Coast Watershed Coordinator Harry Hoogesteger with a
Spawned-out Salmon on Dry Creek, Sixes River, Oregon.
Pacific salmon die after spawning, giving their bodies up to
the stream food web to nourish the next generation.
Photo courtesy: Harry Hoogesteger, 2004

Chapter Sixteen

The Preserve Course

Real golf on a small scale.
—Bill Coore, Bandon, Oregon

ANOTHER GOLF COURSE

At Bandon Dunes in June 2010, there were four courses open for play, the maximum number we were permitted to build. A year later, Mike wanted another course. He'd never forgotten his first impression of the sand dunes he'd seen twenty years ago. He tried to build there before, but it didn't work out. Now he wanted to try again.

The beauty of this scenic landscape had also impressed Howard. He'd been awed by the grandeur of the setting, but he was sensitive to the threatened phacelia population that thrived in the open sand. During the preparation of the master plan, we had included these sand dunes as a set-aside area. Howard might have questioned building a golf course in a designated natural resource conservation sub-zone. Now, he wasn't around to offer an opinion.

However, Mike had made up his mind, even though a serious obstacle stood in his way: the zoning code for the resort—which Al had written, Howard and I had blessed, and the county had adopted—prohibited recreation uses in a natural resource conservation area. No matter. Mike wanted to look at the possibility of building a Par-3 golf course adjacent to Cut Creek.

The proposed site was limited in size—less than thirty acres. And the site was squeezed between Cut Creek and the Bandon Trails course. To find out if a course was even possible, Mike called and asked Bill Coore to evaluate the proposed site. Bill flew out, walked the site and, after a couple days, had a plan in his mind. He returned home and drew up a routing plan with eighteen potential golf holes. Al and I were unaware of this event.

When we saw the preliminary routing plan, we just shook our heads. About the same time, Mike and several of his retail golfing friends flew out to informally size up the routing plan. Days earlier, it had become obvious that portions of the routing plan were hidden by dense stands of vegetation. Ken Nice solved this problem by having sightlines cleared on hidden holes. As the group walked the layout, everyone oohed and ahhed; the duneland was at a much lower elevation than any of the other courses and the ocean views were "different"—seemingly closer. Everyone thought the proposed course "a winner." They couldn't wait to play it.

Absent Howard's strategy and oratorical skills, the responsibility of finding a way to revise the county's zoning code and comprehensive plan fell to Al and me. We had to come up with a legal argument and a final development plan submittal that would be convincing and appeal-proof. Our challenge was to find a rationale to explain and justify why we were going to take a sensitive set-aside area we had previously zoned for long-term resource protection and allow construction of a golf course on it.

We were faced with the fact that the proposed golf course site contained one of the last remaining phacelia populations on the planet. Protecting this population had been a conservation cornerstone of the master plan.

To find out what impact building a course would have on the phacelia population we needed a plant inventory. After a count was made, we learned that about 4,000 plants were in the proposed area for the course. To determine how many plants might be lost due to construction, I compared the proposed routing plan with a map showing the location pattern of the phacelia plants. This exercise revealed a potential loss of approximately 1,000 plants. To make matters worse, Al reminded me that the land use application process required us to determine if there were alternative sites for this course elsewhere on the resort property. The situation looked bleak.

But, in the end, everything worked out. Our analysis found no other viable sites on the resort. The site's proximity to the existing Bandon Trails clubhouse worked in our favor—we could share services and hook up to their irrigation water system. But we still needed a strong development concept and rationale to justify the zone change.

There's an old saying that those who forget history tend to make the same mistakes again. In our case, we remembered our previous argument for the original re-zoning permit application. We had pointed out that the presence of imported European beachgrass was adversely affecting the ecology of the duneland and destroying phacelia habitat. We were faced with a similar situation.

To see what had happened over recent years on this particular piece of duneland, I reviewed aerial photographs from 2005 and 2009. What had been open sand was now filled with stands of pine trees and native shrubs. The beachgrass accompanied by Scotch Broom and gorse plants had taken over more of the open sand habitat. In essence, the duneland plant community was undergoing natural succession induced by man's intervention a hundred years ago. Unless this trend was thwarted, in another fifty years, the open sand and dunes might be lost forever.

This potential outcome suggested a course design that integrated conservation and recreation uses in a holistic manner. We needed to demonstrate we could preserve phacelia plant material while also encouraging the proliferation of more native plant habitat over time.

Mike supported this approach and also suggested the revenue from the course could be used as a source of funding for coastal conservation action, including habitat restoration elsewhere on and outside the resort. This was also an opportunity to promote an environmental education program at the resort.

With a submittal and legal strategy in mind, we now turned our attention to working with the golf architects to fine-tune the routing plan. I had identified other environment concerns and potential conflicts. One of the first problems with the preliminary routing plan was the number of golf holes: there were eighteen. A close examination of the plan revealed that portions of the course were located in the Cut Creek delta. During seasonal high water flows, the area became inundated. We also knew the delta was a jurisdictional wetland. I informed Mike and the golf architects that the delta was off-limits to any development. After a careful analysis and many walking tours on the proposed site, the routing plan was reduced to twelve holes; the design being a Par-3 short course.

Bill and Ben then got down to detailed design. Besides having a very restricted area to work in, they had to respect a riparian setback from Cut Creek. More importantly, the layout had to maintain a balance between new turf and existing vegetation areas. It all came down to "what vegetation to leave and what to remove."

I n order to minimize the impact on phacelia plants, the golf course architects initially suggested minimizing the amount of turf areas. The result was an innovative course design—a design Al termed an archipelago-like layout. This approach concentrated tees, greens and landing areas on small islands of mown fescue turf surrounded by open sand and existing vegetation, rather than continuous maintained turf fairways. This layout departed from conventional fairway design, where a grassed fairway runs continuously from tee boxes to greens.

To get a permit for construction, Al and I had to make another appearance before the Coos County Planning Commission and the Board of Commissioners. The presentation to the Planning Commission occurred on January 7, 2010, followed by a final presentation to the Board on January 26th.

As in previous public hearings, we had prepped and were ready for any and all questions from the audience. We felt confident we would prevail, as the proposed tradeoffs were understandable and reasonable. Our basic argument traded short-term impact for long-term habitat expansion and survival of a threatened plant species. To our utter surprise, no one showed up to oppose the proposed changes. There were only four people in the audience: three were Bandon Dunes staff and the other person was there to present his own proposal.

Again our reputation preceded our appearance. Over the years, we had always done our homework. At both hearings, Al and I kept our presentations short and to the point. We knew our creditability stood us in good favor. Before voting on the application at the first hearing, the Planning

Commissioners all commended us on our presentation. Both the Commission and the Board voted unanimously for approval.

Shortly after New Year's Day in 2011, construction began on the Preserve Course. Unfortunately, the archipelago design proved unworkable. Upon review in the field, everyone realized golfers would simply walk randomly across the open sand habitat, thereby damaging the population of phacelia plants we were trying to preserve. Therefore, the architects decided to connect all the tees and greens with minimum fairways, thereby defining where golfers were supposed to walk.

To ensure this short course measured up to the other four golf courses, Mike gave the architects a special design standard to meet. He wanted each hole designed so that any one of them could be placed within the layout of any of the four existing golf courses and not diminish the quality of that particular golf course and the golfer's play experience. This was an exceedingly high bar to meet.

As construction proceeded, the architects decided to clear the sloped hillside along the west edge of the site. Cleared of mostly gorse, a natural shelf was revealed. Mike happened to be on-site with Bill Coore when this event occurred. Seeing this previously hidden feature, Bill immediately saw a natural fairway for a golf hole that looked and played directly toward the ocean. He suddenly shouted, "Mike, there's another hole here." The new hole became the 131-yard sixth hole. The course now had thirteen holes; every one a winner, in Mike's eyes.

The evolution of the final design for the Preserve Course focused on the first, second and twelfth holes. To achieve what was ultimately built, everyone had to get comfortable with the proximity of these holes to the first and last holes at Bandon Trails: all were clustered together. The solution also required moving the Trails' putting green. But, in the end, it all came together. Although, at times, Bill thought his task was to put a fifty-pound pig in a ten-pound sack.

The final decision to incorporate fairways into the course layout was also based on considerations for efficient maintenance and long-term protection of environmental sensitive areas. The final layout preserved three major phacelia habitat areas that were present in the original twelve-hole design. Phacelia habitat areas are now defined and protected by hazard fencing around all environmental protection areas. Golfers are allowed to enter these areas only to retrieve their errant balls. Course rules prohibit playing a ball from an environmental protection area. The continuous fairway design gives golfers defined walking corridors throughout the Par-3 course while also protecting the silvery phacelia population.

The removal of the invasive gorse and beachgrass has created new areas of open sand on other courses. Golf course superintendents for both the Pacific Dunes and the Bandon Trails courses have observed the emergence of volunteer phacelia plants where open sand remained, post-construction. Disturbed areas appear to function like "seed beds" for habitat restoration. As Mike Keiser says, "It [phacelia] seems to like golf; Pacific Dunes is covered with it."

This approach—creating more open sand—has resulted in more viable habitat for the phacelia. The larger protected environmental areas will also be enhanced with future plantings. As the course grew in and took on a green look, Bill thought the resulting design effect became something like a "walk in the park feeling."

As construction on the Par-3 short course neared completion, we needed a name for the course. It's called the Preserve Course because it is part of a specially designated conservation area at the resort—the H.L. McKee Preserve.

For me, it was time to leave the project. Howard was gone. Together we had accomplished what we set out to do. The Preserve Course was a surprise. A good surprise; I got to stretch my wings before retiring. It felt good to say goodbye to Bandon Dunes on that highpoint.

OPENING DAY FOR THE PRESERVE COURSE, MAY 1, 2012

Christopher Smith teed up his ball, looked down the first fairway of the Preserve Course and hit a short drive. It was 6:45 in the morning, the sky was gray and overcast, there was a bit of breeze off the ocean, and those assembled at the first tee were wearing caps and jackets to protect themselves from a drizzling rain and the bone-chilling weather. Mike

Keiser and Bill Coore had previously shaken Christopher's hand and posed for a photograph. Mike and Bill continued to repeat this ceremony until nearly dusk, except for a few breaks. So why was Christopher Smith the first golfer off the tee on the opening day for the Preserve Course?

Christopher was there because Mike Keiser has a strong interest in Speedgolf, and Christopher just happens to be the Guinness World Record Holder in the sport, having shot an amazing 65 in forty-four minutes, carrying just six clubs at the Chicago Speedgolf Open in 2005. Over the past decade, Mike has supported this alternative style of golf at Bandon Dunes by sponsoring the annual Bandon Dunes Speedgolf Open in the spring of each year, where twenty to thirty players gather to participate.

In May of 2011, at an event for the Rehab Institute of Chicago, Mike and Christopher discussed the future of Speedgolf. Mike let Christopher know that he wanted to take Speedgolf to the next level, and Mike inquired about how best to do so. The conversation led to the inaugural World Speed Golf Championships at the resort.

Christopher is an award-winning PGA Teaching Professional, long-time consultant with Nike and Nike Golf, and a student and player of the game of golf for forty-plus years. About fifteen years ago, he began playing Speedgolf, a sport where one runs in between shots, as opposed to walking, while carrying only a limited number of clubs. He's preached the benefits of playing in a faster, less deliberate and more instinctive fashion ever since, highlighted in his book, *I've Got 99 Swing Thoughts but "Hit the Ball" Ain't One.*

On opening day, Christopher finished the Par-3 course in about twenty-two minutes and fifty-nine seconds. The first ball he hit onto the course dropped into the cup fifty-eight seconds after leaving the tee. And Christopher parred all thirteen holes. Later in the day, most of the 164 golfers who had signed up to play the Preserve Course took almost two hours to finish.

With the special exhibition finished, Mike Keiser stepped up to the first tee and shook hands with the first foursome scheduled to play opening day. He handed each of them a brass coin to commemorate the event. Wood Sabold, the local photographer, was on hand to take photographs of each group prior to them teeing off.

As the day wore on, Wood needed to change positions frequently. The sun came out around noon and, as it rotated throughout the day, Wood was challenged in his attempts to get good photographs with the first fairway in the background.

Compared to the bleak, gray, rainy morning ambiance that greeted everyone, the afternoon was simply beautiful. The sky was blue; the clouds were white and billowy. Later, as the sun dipped in the west, long shadows played across the course and fairways, shadowing and highlighting the landscape features. At the end of the day, the consensus was that the views from this course outshone most of the views from the other resort courses.

There was a reason for the kudos. All of the previous eighteen-hole courses were built on an elevated marine terrace that is 125 feet or higher at the edge of the bluff overlooking the ocean beachfront. Views from the second hole on the Bandon Dunes Golf Course only provide a glimpse of the ocean and horizon. In addition, portions of the Trails Golf Course are in a forested setting behind a major ridge with no views of the ocean.

The topography on which the Preserve Course was built is quite different. The course extends along and parallel to the south side of Cut Creek. It is basically a sloped plane falling towards the Pacific Ocean. The first tee is about elevation 110, and the sixth hole lies on a narrow sand terrace at about elevation forty or lower. There is no bluff line to interrupt the view. The viewer's eye is carried unimpeded over and down the rolling topography until it rests on a dense Shore Pine forest that recedes until the eye takes in the full expanse of the Pacific Ocean and the horizon, where the sky meets the water. It is a panoramic view that gives the viewer a grand, exhilarating feeling. You feel closer to the ocean than at any other location at the resort.

As opening day continued, Mike and Bill both shook the hand of each succeeding golfer who had signed up for this special day. Besides being wished good luck, each received a scorecard signed by Mike and Bill.

Bill Coore, when asked what was the best hole, replied, "There is no best hole on the Preserve Course, no bad holes, only best holes."

The previous evening in the main clubhouse, Mike had sat at a table, signing cards. He had wanted a head start on tomorrow. There was also a memento for the occasion: each golfer received a small green bag containing a brass coin embossed with the signatory symbol of the Preserve Course. Embossed on the coin was an abstracted image of a four-leaved silvery phacelia flower. The coin also had the image of a cup flag inscribed with the number 13, indicating the number of holes on the course. These coins are collectable.

Over the next twelve hours, 164 golfers would play the Preserve Course. At 7:30 AM, Mike and Bill took a half hour breakfast break. It would be a long day, as play would continue all day until almost 7:00 PM. By nine o'clock in the morning, the rain had stopped, the sun began to shine; it would be a better day.

By noon, the weather changed: the sun came out, there were scattered white clouds in a blue sky, the earlier cutting wind off the ocean had diminished to a breeze, people opened their jackets; the day had blossomed into a perfect day to hit a little white ball around a new Par-3 golf course. Late in the day, a guest having played two eighteen-hole rounds of golf proceeded over to the Preserve Course to play another thirteen holes. Future golfers, after playing eighteen holes in the morning or midday, will probably choose to play the Par-3 course instead of tackling another eighteen holes.

By six o'clock in the evening, Mike and Bill were both tired of standing. They had posed for many, many photographs and had shaken many hands, all the time with a smile and a gentle touch. This is their manner; courtesy is at the heart of the resort's True Service program.

Brian Henninger, a former PGA Tour player, had the best score of the day. His score was a 35, which was four-under for the short course. There was a mix of golfers—men, women and children—playing the course. Everyone had a great time, and afterwards both golfers and guests could adjourn to the Trails Clubhouse for a special treat.

As the day continued, guests and players ate grilled and barbequed brisket, bratwurst and salad. At the main lodge complex, several companies had a tasting area for artisan beers. After a late dinner, many who played the Preserve Course that day went to sleep with a full stomach, a smile on their face, and—in their trouser or jacket pocket or on the bed nightstand—a small green pouch that held a token they could bring out in the future, rub between their fingers and recall the magic of this special day. They could play the Preserve Course again—tomorrow or next year—but it would never be like today, as they replayed the events of the day in their mind before nodding off to sleep.

However, after the last group had finished official play on the Preserve Course, another group found themselves on the first tee. A fivesome composed of Josh Lesnik and BR Koehnemann, Jeff Simonds (all three from KemperSports), and two other individuals—John, a friend of Josh's, and Eric Peterson from Golf Now—approached the first tee box. They teed off, and, as they played, the sun slowly dipped into the ocean.

They played a "skins game." The mood was festive, and the sunset was as exceptional as the Par-3 course. BR would later say, "We had a ball." All agreed the course has "the best views on the property."

Later that evening at dinner, Mike Keiser commented on his sore back. But he couldn't complain too much, for the day was another unprecedented success.

Chapter Seventeen

Speedgolf

Play faster, you'll play better.
—Christopher Smith, Portland, Oregon

FASTER PLAY MIGHT BE BETTER

The established and ancient courses found throughout the UK are different in many respects from their counterparts in the U.S. In the UK, greens and tees are normally very close together, a design element that helps expedite play. Typically, players take about three-and-a-half hours to play eighteen holes, whereas, in the U.S. today, it typically takes four to five-and-a-half hours to play eighteen holes of golf. Playing quickly is not the norm on this side of the pond, nor is it promoted to a large extent, despite ongoing challenges with pace of play. In the UK, you may be asked or escorted off the course, should you exceed the 'expected' time to play. Playing in more than three-and-a-half hours is considered to be "bad form."

So why do American golfers take so long to play a round of golf? First off, it's accepted—the norm; then there's the issue of holing everything out instead of match play that is more commonplace in other parts of the world. Add travel time to and from the facility, warm-up time, the eighteen-hole round itself, social time at the 19th hole, and one is looking at an entire day. Is that what American golfers are really after? Regardless, the five-hour-plus round of golf has become a paradigm in the U.S.

It's interesting to note that the number of golfers in the U.S. has decreased over the last few years. In 2000, there were 28.8 million golfers but, by 2005, the number of golfers had increased to 30 million. The recession of 2007–2008 saw a slight decrease but, by 2009, the number of golfers had bounced back to 28.6 million. Unfortunately, from 2009 to 2010, about 4.6 million golfers left the game, reducing the number of golfers to 26.1 million. Bandon Dunes, like most other resorts, had reduced play during the recessionary period but, by 2012, guests were back and play exceeded that in the mid-2000s period. The industry recognizes today that the game takes too long to play and too long to learn how to play. Both are significant factors in the drop in play. As the popularity of Speedgolf grows, and golfers realize that you don't have to play slowly to play well, the hope is that people will think differently about the pace of play.

Popularizing Speedgolf might just affect and reverse the slow play trend. Asked about how the popularity and potential growth for this accelerated form of golf might be, Christopher Smith's reply was: "It's certainly a challenge, as there is very limited access since the golf course has to be clear of players in front. But the messages associated with Speedgolf—less over-thinking, few, if any, practice swings, heightened imagination and creativity through the use of fewer clubs, no need for exact yardages—can all be integrated into 'slow' or traditional golf." More and more courses are making courses available to speedgolfers, with tee times first thing in the morning or later in the day, when the course is less crowded.

By allowing speedgolfers access to the golf courses at Bandon Dunes, Mike Keiser continues to be a visionary and proponent of influencing the pace of play. The now annual Speedgolf World Championships, held at the resort, showcase the sport's top contenders and help to promote faster play.

Mike has demonstrated his ability and business acumen in getting ahead of the pack, time and time again. His re-introduction of links style golf to the U.S. has changed the complexion of the golf landscape in this country, and beyond. At the resort, a forty-acre practice facility with multiple ranges and target areas, an expansive putting green and separate facilities for chipping and pitching practice is a part of the offerings for all guests.

Christopher Smith believes "the goal of practice must be to learn something, and learning is not about getting the answer right—but rather about figuring out *how to* solve the problem." Of course, it's also important to know exactly what problem you're trying to solve…

You could take the physical fitness component (running) out of Speedgolf and keep the concept of fast play. When golfers practice the golf swing with consequence, hitting shots with different clubs at different distances and using their eyes to judge distance and terrain, they are in the process of building relevant motor memory. To motor learning researchers and neuroscientists, they are creating a new neural pattern that will become an automatic/unconscious response with sufficient focused repetition.

Speedgolf requires less decision-making, due to the fact that fewer clubs are being carried and used. This forces speedgolfers to use their ever-important *imagination* during a round, key to good golf played at any pace. In running between shots, the speedgolfer doesn't have time to over-think set-up, swing or what just happened on the last shot; they are constantly "in the present moment." On to the next shot—and, at the end of the day, one really can't think and act at the same time…

There are no practice swings in Speedgolf, no time to waste precious seconds. By not thinking and/or 'getting in their own way,' the speedgolfer can simply see and react to the immediate situation—the lie, the wind, and the approximate distance—then allow the learnt motor program to fire and do its thing. More often than not, thinking creates indecision and doubt—true killers to the golf swing.

The best example of this is when elite athletes choke. After decades of repetition, practice and play, they have developed what can be termed "unconscious competency," and established neural patterns that allow them to replicate controlled shots again and again. If, for whatever reason(s), they become dissatisfied with their level of play or result, they may revert back to the "how to" stage of learning, consciously thinking about the mechanics or technique of a stroke or shot. This conscious thinking inevitably disrupts the internal neural wiring.

A careful examination of the benefits associated with Speedgolf can show that, from a performance standpoint, playing golf *faster* helps one to play *better*—and everyone wants to play better. The acceptance and promotion of Speedgolf and short course play at Bandon Dunes has been and can continue to be a positive influence in demonstrating new training and learning methods to the retail golf community.

CHAMPIONSHIP TOURNAMENTS

The inaugural Speedgolf World Championships were held October 21–22, 2012, at the resort. Most of the competitors arrived the preceding Thursday for a practice round or two.

Saturday morning at 7:45 AM on the Old Macdonald course, the sun was shining and casting long shadows on a bright green carpet of red fescue grass. A thin, horizontal band of fog hovered just above the ground along the conifer forest that edged the course on the east side. The grass was dew covered, and there was a light chill in the air. The fifteen elite speedgolfers who would play that day were dressed in light clothing, designed for function and speed. When they finished, the steam would rise in bursts from their bodies.

Most of the golfers finished in under an hour. The first golfer to tee off completed the eighteen holes in forty-eight minutes, thirty-seven seconds. The field of fifteen was comprised of fourteen "professionals" and one amateur, a young woman who surprised everyone by finishing in the money.

By 11:30, the day's play was completed; the competitors spent the rest of the day relaxing and recouping their energy for the next day's competition. The sun continued to shine; the day had the feeling of an Indian summer fall day. The contrast of the sun-drenched, golden grass against the backdrop of the dark green conifer forest nearby made for a picture perfect day.

Sunday morning was a different story. It had rained most of Saturday night, coming in waves of drizzle and pelting showers. Luckily, the rain stopped by the time everyone assembled at the Bandon Dunes course to tee off. The elites played first, followed by forty-five amateur golfers. The Bandon Dunes course is an easier layout, to a large extent, compared to Old Mac. Faster times were anticipated, and this proved to be true for most of the players. However, scoring varied: some got better, some got worse.

Chris Walker, a young mini-tour player, won the event, taking home

$18,000 in prize money (his biggest payday ever!) of the $50,000 tournament purse. Eight players finished in the money, with amateur Gretchen Johnson finishing in eighth place. She turned down the $1,000 in prize money in order to retain her amateur status. Many of the amateur competitors had never played Speedgolf before and more than a few people gingerly limped around on sore legs. Looking at the players' scores, an observer quickly realized that Speedgolf has a few lessons to pass on to the golf community: faster play can indeed produce lower scores.

CBS had sent a TV crew to film the tournament, airing the event the following April in a thirty-minute special during their coverage of the Masters Tournament at Augusta National. On primetime television, a national golf audience got an opportunity to see Speedgolf in action—a great bit of exposure for the sport. Speedgolfers featured in the special got some great publicity, while the sport and Bandon Dunes got the kind of exposure that is invaluable in marketing dollars.

T he second Speedgolf World Championships returned to the resort October 26–27, 2013. An elite field comprised of fifty-five golfers from six different countries assembled to compete in the two-day professional event and the one-day amateur competition. In the field were two Olympians: the 2008 silver medalist in the 1,500 meters, Nick Willis, from New Zealand; and the legendary and ageless American, Bernard Lagat, a twelve-time medalist in the Olympics and World Championships, including five gold medals. The previous year's champion, Chris Walker, was back to defend his title. Rob Hogan, from Ireland, led the competition after the first day's play at Old Mac and withstood all challengers on day two to take home the trophy and prize money.

M ike's support of Speedgolf goes beyond the fact that he plays golf at a fast pace, himself. It's a gesture that is reflective of the nature of the man, a pure way to play golf. Or, as the resort's mantra states: "Golf As It Was Meant To Be."

So what's the future for Speedgolf? It's ideal for athletes who are fit and love physical challenges, but the main challenge is in finding a golf course where one can practice (obviously, there cannot be any players in front). If they can get access to an eighteen-hole course, the best time to play is in the early morning, late in the day, or after a shotgun tournament. Ideally, the sport needs a special type of course: a veritable layout designed in a way that is both spectator- and television-friendly.

The future for this alternative form of golf looks promising. The 2013 event at the resort was organized by Speedgolf International and telecast live on Oomba TV. Several other private parties have committed funds to sponsor upcoming Speedgolf tournaments both domestically and abroad. If Speedgolf can secure a big-time sponsor and add an international marketing presence, the sport will literally be off to the races.

Chapter Eighteen

Conservation

Salmon tell you so much about the watershed.
They are the downstream indicator species of
the health of the watershed ecological system.
—Mary Wahl, Portland, Oregon

AN INITIATIVE FIRST, THEN AN ALLIANCE

You can tally a score for a round of golf in minutes, but it takes decades or a generation to see significant environmental changes. Besides being a game changer in the U.S. golf industry, Bandon Dunes has also influenced and changed the way coastal conservation efforts are preceding along the South Coast of Oregon. The opening of the Preserve Course was a pivotal event because it created a new revenue source for conservation efforts. The idea behind donating golf money for conservation had its roots in an experience Mike had many years ago.

After family, children and golf, Mike's passion is philanthropy. Twenty years ago, he met a guy who tried to sell him insurance. Behind the sales pitch was a concept Mike thought was " breathtaking." The salesman said: "I don't make as much money as you, but I make quite a bit, and I am a devout Christian. My family and I, for every dollar we spend on our family, we give away four dollars. And we give time. Right now we are going to Mexico to build houses for poor Mexicans." The insurance product he was selling enabled someone to accomplish this personal goal. Mike never bought the insurance product, but he took away the idea of giving away a multiple of what you spend on yourself. Mike also set up education and scholarship program funds for his employees at the resort and others. It's simply the concept of giving back if you are successful. This is the basis of his and Lindy's community service to the City of Bandon. It also was the idea behind the Wild Rivers Coast Initiative.

The initiative was the coalescence of environmental conservation ideas that had been floating around in Mike Keiser's head since 2008. Mike had always thought of himself as being some kind of conservationist. His father had leanings in that direction because he thought one should always make improvements to a place, and Mike was familiar with that idea. Later, when he owned Cascade Ranch, his view of conservation was aesthetic in nature. Looking back, now Mike would say he "was a passive conservationist."

When Howard proposed constructing a large lake at the ranch, Mike liked the thought of how beautiful and scenic it would appear in the landscape; he didn't think in terms of what kind of habitat it created, or if constructing it would adversely impact any existing habitat. It could have affected fish habitat in a stream over which the location of the lake was proposed, and, in the end, the lake was not built. At the time, Mike simply liked the idea of how the lake would look in the dry, wide-open grassland landscape.

A few years later, Mike became acquainted with Terry Wahl, a sheep rancher who owned property near Cape Blanco, Oregon. A friendship developed over time but, more importantly, Terry, an adamant conservationist himself, began to educate Mike about how the coastal rivers and watersheds along the South Coast play an important role in conservation planning. Terry spent ten years talking Mike's ear off and, in the process, turned Mike into an "active" conservationist.

By 2010, Mike Keiser had decided to seriously embark on a program oriented to land conservation and enhancement along a stretch of coastline known as South Coast. He had decided that about a hundred miles of the Oregon coast from the Coquille River to the California border constituted a priceless coastline that should be preserved for future generations. Much of this coastal landscape was covered with dense forest intermixed with open ranch land, and included several state parks strung out like beads on a string along the coastal highway.

So Mike thought, "let's help preserve more of the coastland and, if it has been abused, restore it." Mike's worldview had changed; it had become much larger in scope. It was more macro than micro in scale. It went far beyond the initial ideas Howard and I had originally suggested when we prepared the original resort master plan. We had had thoughts about a sub-regional approach to conservation centered on the Coquille Estuary and river. The idea was to aggregate designated resort conservation areas together with parts of Bullards Beach State Park and the nearby Bandon Marsh National Wildlife Refuge into a "conservation district" and other properties that could be procured in the future. Mike, on the other hand, envisioned a watershed restoration program targeting 1,000 square miles of coastline. He was thinking way beyond our early thoughts.

During the economic recession, Mike Keiser continued buying coastal land on the South Coast. He was learning more about coastal ecology and becoming more comfortable with the idea of supporting local conservation programs. At the same time, he was thinking about how to set up a private foundation to achieve his goals. He wanted to establish a non-profit organization, but he needed professional guidance to do this.

Arabella Advisors offered the services he sought. Arabella is a Chicago-based company—with offices in New York; Washington, D.C.; and San Francisco—that assists philanthropists who want to make meaningful contributions to society. Mike approached this company in order to develop a strategic plan and to initiate discussions with state agencies, private organizations—like trusts—and local conservation groups and individuals located on Oregon's South Coast.

Bruce Boyd had been a senior advisor for The Nature Conservancy (TNC) prior to joining Arabella Advisors. He is a principal and managing director and manages the Chicago office. With two decades of experience in private, non-profit venture building and his experience at TNC, Bruce took on the task of creating an organizational structure and plan to develop an "initiative" approach for Mike.

In May 2010, Arabella presented an analytical report—*The Wild Rivers Initiative: Conservation, Community and Economy*—to Mike. This report laid out their strategy for how Mike could best use his resources for environmental conservation efforts in Oregon. The report identified the key stakeholders that would need to be involved in this kind of regional planning, the context for action, and a definite set of steps necessary to organize and implement the plan.

With Mike's approval, Arabella established a "formation committee" consisting of selected individuals, many of whom had been interviewed as part of the initial due diligence process. Besides trying to come to grips with the diverse range of ideas on what was of primary importance to future conservation on South Coast, the group also spent two years in a search for an executive director to head the non-profit.

When Mike and the committee were vetting candidates for the directorship of his non-profit, he realized the strategy for the Wild Rivers project had to become an "alliance" in order to succeed. The new name for the organization, Wild Rivers Coast Alliance, reflected both the targeted geography and the need for active participation and commitment by others with interests in long-term conservation along Oregon's South Coast.

Over ninety candidates were identified, and this group was winnowed down to seven or eight individuals. Among the candidates was an ex-employee of KemperSports, Jim Seeley. Mike and Jim had previously discussed the possibility of Jim taking an active role regarding the initiative. Jim had planned on retiring around 2008, but, when the economy tanked, he postponed his retirement. On first glance, Jim's background in the business of golf seemed outside the conservation field. However, he had been involved in operations at KemperSports and had lots of experience dealing with how the company managed environmental issues.

In January 2012, Jim was appointed the Executive Director of the Wild Rivers Coast Alliance (WRCA). This was an opportunity for him to reinvent himself. He immersed himself in the topic of conservation, talked to local people and became knowledgeable about what had been done and what the outstanding regional issues were in Southern Oregon.

One of the primary objectives of the WRCA is to attract other philanthropists and donations to this venture. In some ways, this non-profit is a fundraising organization. In other ways, it can function as a "point" entity, organizing and stimulating the array of diverse local conservation interests that are already at work on the South Coast. It's an alliance because it embodies a wide range of interested participants—environmentalists, ranchers, commercial and sports fishermen, NGOs and landowners. At the heart of this venture is Mike's desire to fund economic development, specific projects, and equity for ownership in what has been a distressed part of Oregon for a couple of decades.

There are three distinctive areas of involvement: ecology, economy and equity. Wherever and for whatever the monetary resources are channelized, the result cannot be just environmental and sustainable in nature; it also has to be economically sustainable. The outcome should demonstrate a real bang for the buck.

Outcomes are important. Lots of public dollars have been spent to protect natural resources from environmental damage without finding an economic description of its value. There needs to be an economic benefit to justify the investment. That's looking at things from a "business" perspective. That could be a good approach in the future. More public and private dollars will be available in the future if tangible results can be demonstrated.

The WRCA is focusing its efforts on an area roughly defined by the watersheds stretching south from the Coquille River to the Winchuck River near the Oregon-California border. One of the first project goals is to take a watershed and improve it environmentally from summit to sea stacks. This would include the littoral zone and marine reserves along the coast. A candidate might be The Elk River Watershed.

To accomplish this goal and others, the Alliance has formed an executive committee. The committee's primary role is to advise and steer the direction(s) that the WRCA pursues over time. They can also be extremely helpful in introducing interested people and organizations to the Alliance. In this way, they can steer worthy projects to the Alliance and also find other funding sources and conservation-minded partners.

The WRCA wants to attract partners like OWEB and others that can bring matching funds to the table. As Jim Seeley likes to say, "The Alliance is not in the business of doing work; we're in the business of finding work worth doing." This perspective "focuses the thinking," allowing the WRCA to stimulate project development rather than implement projects.

The quote at the beginning of this chapter underscores the fact that the Wild Rivers Coast Alliance's mission is just beginning. Lots of conservation work has already been accomplished, but more is needed to preserve habitat for the Coho Salmon. The West Coast Salmon Summit held on May 16th & 17th in 2013, at the Mill Casino and Hotel at Coos

Bay, Oregon was another "call to action" by the sponsors, including the Coquille Indian Tribe; BioEngineering Associates, Inc.; National Oceanic and Atmospheric Administration; the Nature Conservancy; and Englund Marine & Industrial Supply. But, it's important to remember that although conferences and educational efforts are important, what people take away from these events needs to be transformed into on-the-ground projects that are funded and implemented.

LOCAL ACTION

Much has been done; more is needed. Concerned Oregon residents, environmentalists and agency officials agree on the primary long-term goal of restoration of salmon habitat. This work can be accomplished on different scales. On the micro scale, the resort has already restored a local watercourse for salmon habitat. Working jointly with the Oregon Department of Fish and Wildlife (ODFW), Fahy Creek has been improved to encourage a Coho salmon run between the ocean and Fahys Lake. Mike Keiser's notion of a 1,000-square-mile target area is at the other end of the spectrum.

I could write a book about what needs to be done, but three examples illustrate what is possible: Fahy Creek Restoration, Cape Blanco Challenge and the South Coast Watershed Council.

A biologist by training, Janet Rogers had worked for the National Audubon Society and National Park Service. When she and Howard first met (before he became involved with the resort), they both had strong ties near Cascade Head on the mid-coast, where she led workshops for Sitka Center for Art and Ecology, helped establish the Cape Kiwanda Marine Garden and taught at Neskowin Valley School. She moved to Bandon when her husband, Grant Rogers, became the director of instruction at the resort. On arrival, she volunteered with the United States Fish and Wildlife Service (USFWS) on the Bandon Marsh National Wildlife Refuge during the largest estuary restoration project for the state, designed to increase both salmon and waterfowl habitat in the Coquille River Watershed.

At the resort, Janet joined the design team as a naturalist helping design the Bandon Dunes Trail System. This led to involvement in the formation of the H. L. McKee Preserve, where she had two primary focuses. The first was assisting in a USFWS range-wide inventory of the rare and endangered dune plant, silvery phacelia. It became apparent, from the USFWS review, that Bandon Dunes Golf Resort had, as noted previously, the largest existing phacelia population with the northern extent of the plant's habitat range on the West Coast. Key to its survival was restoration and maintenance of early successional dune habitat.

A second focus for the McKee Preserve was the restoration of Coho salmon into Fahy Creek. The resort partnered with USFWS, who coordinated the efforts for habitat restoration from the Coquille River up into Fahy Creek, assisted by ODFW fisheries biologists. A culvert under Highway 101 was replaced, invasive plants were removed, the channel reworked to remove blockages and shores secured against erosion.

The Cape Blanco Challenge began as an informal group of local residents, mostly ranchers and other long-time residents who had grown up on the South Coast in families that made their living off the land from resource-based industries—ranching, timber and fishing. Their values came from living and working on the land. Things tend to happen along the South Coast because of "conversations" that arise amongst locals. Local residents understand the history of the land and know when a problem becomes serious and requires action.

When it is serious, they get together and talk about it, get in discussions with local agency people, perhaps Land Trust people, and then they figure out some way to correct the problem. This kind of grassroots effort began in 2005 and led, eventually, to the formation of an action plan for the Cape Blanco area.

The Cape Blanco Site Conservation Action Plan 2008 is an approach embraced by a consortium of interest groups. An overview of the plan states:

> The Cape Blanco Site Conservation Action Planning process brought together representatives from several conservation groups and agencies to develop a shared vision for conservation and protection of the Elk, Sixes, and New River/Floras Creek watersheds and adjacent near shore environments, and

strategies needed to accomplish that vision. At meetings that were held over the information and data to profile the current condition of the area, defined the desired conditions that team members envision for the planning area, and identified concrete steps that citizens, conservation organizations and conservation partners can take to realize that vision. [sic] Additional refinement and documentation of this work continued through May 2007.

This report outlines the work of the planning team, describing the planning approach the team employed, key concepts and ideas generated by the team, as well as important goals the team set for the planning area. The report details conservation actions and activities that the team determined to be significant for the planning area, thereby providing direction and a common vision for conservation partners in the area.

The planning exercise described in this document is meant to be the starting point for developing a long-term vision for conservation of the Cape Blanco planning area. As our knowledge and experience with the conservation targets grows, the plan will be revised and redirected to accommodate this new information. In this manner it is designed to be a working conservation plan, continually informing and informed by our work on the ground. One overarching conservation strategy for the Cape Blanco site guides our proposed work: Support conservation and restoration-based 'working landscapes and seascapes'.

This overarching strategy acknowledges the contribution that the local community expects to make in the conservation of the existing natural values present at Cape Blanco as well as recognizing the community's dependence on healthy ecosystems for their livelihood and enjoyment.

An excellent example of community involvement was the "wilderness" designation of the upper headwaters of the Elk River. This happened without a lot of controversy. There had been conversations about why it should be done, why it was a good idea; people agreed, and it happened. The result was partly design and partly circumstance, but it clearly demonstrated how knowledgeable, aware and environmentally motivated individuals can successfully influence their environment for their good and the public good.

This local approach to problem solving is a form of "leveraging" people's efforts from a grassroots base instead of complaining about a problem and waiting for the government to deal with it. It's also a good method to ensure the result fits in with local interests and values.

Currently, the approach to conservation by local interests is embodied in what they call the "working landscape." This concept is an integration of land uses (for example, agriculture and conservation) that yield outcomes that are of mutual benefit to both activities. These land uses will be agrarian or natural resource extraction in nature, and typically will be in a rural setting.

Conservation work can be accomplished to produce outcomes, not byproducts. A good example of a working landscape is the Wahl Ranch. They were able to convert 200 acres into conservation use. Previously, 850 acres were used for stocking. Now they have intensive grazing on 650 acres. This approach yielded a 400 percent increase in productivity using intensive grazing versus set stocking. How was this achieved? Intensive grazing required the use of fertilizer and lime on the pastures. Now, this could have been a problem, but they controlled the runoff, and they also had to fence off the production land from the conservation land.

The Wahl Ranch has been in the Wahl family for 130 years. The ranch is one of ten ranches with eight owners located along a sixteen-mile stretch of South Coast from Cape Blanco to Croft Lake. There is an emerging recognition that this place is special because it is undeveloped and still in agricultural production that is economically viable.

There is something else that is special about the South Coast. A short stretch of coastline, about thirty to forty miles long (roughly between Bandon and Port Orford), is dark at night. Pitch black. Sailors traveling the west coast of North America from Canada to Mexico know this place as the Dark Coast. At night, passing ships experience a rare sight, or lack thereof, because there are "no lights."

Why would this be? There are no commercial or residential buildings along this portion of the coastline. Local families have lived in these farmsteads for four generations. Mary Wahl, who grew up on a local ranch, exclaimed, "It's an isolated area with no development. That's the glory of it."

The Wild Rivers Coast Alliance has looked at the Wahl Ranch as a possible case study in how a long-time family owned ranch might be preserved in the long-term for both commercial and conservation uses. Underlying this question is the vulnerability of ranchland when deaths occur and estates need to be settled. The federal tax laws, specifically death taxes, are at the heart of the problem.

One of the available strategies to preserve these local coastal ranch lands is the use of conservation-oriented deed restrictions. This requires pre-planning by property owners and conservation advocates and the use of trusts in some instances. There are related issues: deed restrictions define the value of a property in perpetuity, and there is always the question of how land set aside for conservation purposes will be maintained in the future?

In the past, Metro in Portland, Oregon, had acquired thousands of acres of outlying land for open space and park use. A local bond issue was approved by the citizenry for acquisition of these lands. However, a few years later Metro had to propose another bond proposal to secure additional funds for land improvements and maintenance. At the state level, many Oregonians feel the Oregon Parks and Recreation Department have too much land, a lack of budgeted operational funds, and that they should relinquish some of this land back to the private sector. Ultimately the decision of how much land needs to be preserved and protected for conservation reasons will reflect both public values and the need to achieve a sense of balance between private and public land ownership while recognizing the notion of conserving natural resources for public use and appreciation, future generations and some would argue—the common good—which is highly debatable.

The Dark Coast—it's unique, rural open space—should and can it be protected for the long-term?

❦

Harry Hoogesteger is a macro scale guy. A biologist by training, he is the South Coast Watershed Council Coordinator. Working out of Gold Beach, Oregon, Harry is at the forefront of restoring freshwater habitat on Oregon's wild rivers. If you ask Harry what the watershed councils do, his answer is: "The councils were created to bring everyone to the table to talk about the problem, find common ground and create solutions."

When we think about environmental issues, sometimes our common interests tend to overshadow our differences. Harry believes: "Most of us like to drink clean water, we all want good food, we want our kids to play in good and safe neighborhoods, most of us think an opportunity for a good education is essential, and we want our children to have a good education so they can get a good job. And most of us want to think we are doing 'noble' work. This is work that means something to us and to society as a whole." That's as good a mantra for conservation work as I've ever heard or read.

In interviewing Harry, I asked him what you actually have to do on the ground to achieve habitat restoration. His answer was straightforward: "It involves planting trees along watercourses to shade habitat; having fences built along watercourses to keep animals from destroying habitat; working with timber companies to upgrade their roads, so the roads don't erode or slide down into habitat; opening up fish passages so the fish can get to spawning grounds; removing noxious weeds, and abating exotic plants from invading habitat."

So how does he accomplish this? It's more work than one man can do. Part of Harry's job is to reach out to local communities and enlist volunteers in these efforts while also helping local citizens form local environmental action groups.

So now let's assume there's a local group all fired up to do habitat restoration. How do you organize people to accomplish these tasks? First, you need to have a strategy. One place to start is to allow the salmon to get to where they want to spawn and rear a new population. You need to let the fish have access to the habitat. So, if you have culverts that are barriers to fish movement, you have to inventory the county and identify all the culverts that present a problem for fish access. Then you need to replace the culverts with something that will allow passage of the fish.

Some people wonder why it takes so long for improvements to occur. Again, the tasks appear to be simple. Take fencing. On a 50' x 100' lot, the problem seems straightforward; the scale is small. Now, if you have 10,000 feet of fencing, the scale becomes more complex. So, scale is crucial.

But wait. Remember, Mike Keiser and others, like the Cape Blanco group, are thinking about 1,000 square miles of wild river territory. There are perhaps ten watersheds along the South Coast from Bandon to Brookings. From their headwaters in the coastal range, each can have a twisting, turning streambed ten to twenty miles in length until the watercourse reaches the ocean. Not level land, in many instances somewhat difficult to traverse.

But first, you need to do some table work. You have to sit down and talk with the landowners. Will they let you on their property to do the work? Will they give up the land you fence off so their animals can't get to the watercourse? You're asking the landowners to take some of their land out of production, and there's a cost to them to do that. And, of course, you're also asking them to give up all the free flowing, clean, pure natural drinking water for the stock. Where do they get the replacement water, and how do you get the water to the stock? They would need to replace the "free" water with an off-stream source and maintain it as long as it is needed. The level of complexity just got terribly difficult; the social environment plays an immensely significant role in watershed planning.

Where's the economic benefit to the landowner? You are also dealing with a mindset that says the land is private and mine; the public should stay off my land. Each landowner has a different attitude, different needs. Plus, they don't know what other uses the land may be needed for in the future.

But let's say the fencing got built. Now we want to plant trees for riparian cover to regulate the water temperature for the fish habitat. Seasonally, streams can flood. Who is going to protect the trees? If noxious weeds invade the stream banks, who deals with the weeding problem? And what happens when a winter storm blows down a tree that takes down a section of fence line? Who fixes that problem? Complexity and more complexity!

For each project type, riparian environments are in the middle of the simple-to-complex issue. But the underlying problem is funding. How do you pay for these activities? Then there's the issue of getting the work done. How do you convince a landowner that the construction crew members are honest so he will let them on the land to do the work? The owner might volunteer to do the work, but it will be on his timetable, and that might take a while; the farm or ranch chores will come first. They will do it when they get to it.

Making these kinds of simple, yet complex improvements many times results in payoffs that are "down stream." It means more fish in future years, and this means more sport fishing, commercial fishing over time, more tourism; all of which means more local jobs.

That's quite a story, and it's how Harry thinks about salmon habitat restoration, the local economy and his community. He came to the South Coast in 1977 and, for the last fifteen years, he has worked on habitat restoration. He's a transplant—he grew up in Illinois—but he's an Oregonian at heart.

Harry believes "the South Coast is between two worlds: One is dead, the other is yet to be born. In fact, it's being born as we speak. The mindset used to be, cut every tree, catch every fish." Those good times are gone. Remember, natural resources were abundant to the Native People, the settlers and probably until the 1970s. Technology and the demand for the product intensified the harvest practices. This was before people began to question the practices. It was also before the concept of sustainability began to creep into the lexicon of forest and fish managers.

Historically, from the 1970s into the mid-1980s, the timber and fishing resources were depleted due to overcutting and overfishing. The consequences were realized in a period of suffering, relocation, high unemployment, alcoholism, and economic stagnation. Now we are entering into a period of rebirth. It will take some time, and one of the main goals of the WRCA is to be a key stimulus and to add fuel to this rebirth.

Those industries can come back but not at the same levels. They will come back with established limits in incremental growth. The South Coast wants to grow big trees and big fish. The trees create the watershed; the watershed creates the fish. The quality and quantity of coastal salmon runs is a direct indicator of the health of the upland watershed. The natural landscape is self-perpetuating if we just get out of the way and allow the natural systems to recover. Can we be and act smart?

The good thing about the South Coast is that we still have a chance. The remaining populations of salmon are native stocks. There are no dam barriers for native salmon and steelhead as there are in eastern Oregon, Idaho and on the Columbia. These fish are extremely adaptable to changing environmental conditions. They survived periods of glaciations when they were landlocked. These are smart fish.

Realistically, the restoration approach will be by one neighbor, one landowner at a time, one or more concerned individuals taking "time-out" from their daily lives and work commitments to help the process along. The essence of coastal conservation planning on the South Coast is to get people to work shoulder-to-shoulder to achieve an outcome on the ground. The WRCA can assist by bringing more experienced business-minded individuals into the mix and discussions. In addition, the revenue resources the WRCA can bring to the table are substantial.

On January 25, 2013, Mike Keiser and Hank Hickox presented a check for $510,000 to Harry Hoogesteger, Executive Committee Chairman, and Jim Seeley, Executive Director of the Wild Rivers Coast Alliance. These funds represented the net revenues from green fees collected on the Preserve Course in 2012. Mike had made good on his commitment. By 2013, the Alliance had already invested over $750,000 to South Coast organizations for conservation grants. This commitment will continue far into the future. In fact, the WRCA received another check from Mike in April 2014 for $600,000. The million dollars-plus has been put to good use. You have to pay people to get work done, although a lot of the work by local individuals and organizations is done on a volunteer basis. However, the real success story of the WRCA, over time, will be the relationships and partnerships that will be formed.

By contrast, most of the past funds for coastal conservation improvements were public monies. Some passed through the Oregon Watershed Enhancement Board (OWEB). Formed in 1987, the Board initially had a biennium allocation of about half a million for use in demonstration, education and outreach programs. By 2012, OWEB had an operating budget of fifty million dollars that came from a 7.5 percent allocation of state lottery funds. Additional federal dollars were also available in Oregon, but these funds were dedicated to specific projects, like fish habitat restoration.

If there's a watchword to apply to conservation on the South Coast, it is Think Big. President Teddy Roosevelt thought big, and because of that macro view we have a system of National Parks in the West. Andrew Carnegie thought big, and we have a national public library system. President Eisenhower thought big, and we have the interstate freeway system.

Mike is also looking at the big picture and is thinking about 1,000 square miles of coastland. Can we work, play, recreate and still be stewards of the land and restore the damaged natural resource systems in a way to support that lifestyle? Is the Dark Coast worth preserving for future generations? We need to commit to a long-term watershed restoration program. What does Harry think?: "I'm not sure it will ever be done." But it's time to make the effort.

When I finally got the storyline right for the book, I flew to Chicago to interview Mike again to fill in some blank spots. After his greeting card company, RPG, was sold, he moved his office to the John Hancock Center in North Chicago. The view of Lake Michigan from the thirty-ninth floor is eye-catching. Looking out across the lake, the sky and water meet at the horizon. Mike's eye is on the horizon. He's been heard to say: "I'll keep building golf courses until I run out of money."

APPENDIX

ORIGINAL DESIGN PROGRAM
for
BANDON DUNES GOLF RESORT

(Extracted from the book, *Dream Golf*)

Mike Keiser gave Howard McKee a couple of handwritten pages with the following program requirements:

- Min. 1000 acres
    Best min 5,000–10,000 acres. Land budget $10 MM
- Location: initially, California, Oregon, preferably on coast or with some coastal access
    Would not exclude Monterey south in 1st pass
- Sandy soil/sand dunes on at least part
- Stand-alone water: rivers, streams, lakes, waterfall
    i.e. unusual features a prerequisite
- If parcel is large enough could include a small town
    Regardless, proximity (20 miles) to town or larger "with potential"
- Parcel cannot be flat; further, it must be breathtaking
- Year-round or near year-round outdoor climate
- Sympathetic ecosystems
- Diversity of environment

GO or NO GO within 6 mos
Staged development thereafter, at a planned expenditure rate of max $3 MM/year for 10 years

MIN. Amenities

- 18-hole championship g.c. with extraordinary unique features (sand dunes, waterfall, etc.)
- Room for 2 more golf courses
- Tennis
- Clubhouse
- Guest cabins/lodges
- Natural, easy access to National Forest
- Natural, easy access to canoeing, white water canoeing, mountain and rock climbing, wind surfing, fishing (fly), deep sea fishing, bicycling, jogging, hiking, etc.

BIBLIOGRAPHY

Aikens, Melvin C., Thomas J. Connolly, and Dennis L. Jenkins. *Oregon Archaeology*. Corvallis: Oregon State University Press, 2011.

Alt, David, and Donald W. Hyndman. *Northwest Exposures, A Geologic Story of the Northwest*. Missoula: Montana Press Publishing Company, 1995.

"Appeal filed on Bandon Dunes resort decision," *Western World* (Bandon, Oregon), October 16, 1996: 1.

Bacon, Larry. "Project to go before board." *The Register-Guard* (Eugene, Oregon), June 5, 1996: 1C, 3C.

Bacon, Larry. "Developer calls golf course 'labor of love.'" *The Register-Guard* (Eugene, Oregon), June 5, 1996: 3C.

Bacon, Larry. "Sparks fly at meeting on proposed golf resort." *The Register-Guard* (Eugene, Oregon), July 12, 1996: 1B, 10B.

Baldwin, Ewart M. *Geology of Oregon*. Dubuque: Kendall/Hunt Publishing Company, 1976.

Baldwin, Ewart M. *Geology of Oregon*. Revised Edition. Dubuque: Kendall/Hunt Publishing Company, 1976.

Batey, Tammy. "Commissioners drive divots at hearing." *The World* (Coos Bay, Oregon), July 12, 1996: 1.

Becker, T.J. "Paradise Now." *Chicago Tribune*, January 18, 1998: 1C, 3B

Bibliography

Beckham, Stephen Dow. *Requiem for a People*. Corvallis: Oregon State University Press, 1971.

Beckham, Stephen Dow. *Coos Bay—The Pioneer Period, 1851 to 1890*. Arago Books, 1973.

Berg, Laura. *The First Oregonians*. Portland: Oregon Council for the Humanities, 2007.

Conrad, John. "Making waves." *The Register-Guard* (Eugene, Oregon), April 25, 1999: 1F, 10F.

Conrad, John. "Bandon Trails." *The World* (Coos Bay, Oregon), May 19, 2005: A1, A10.

Cornish, Geoffrey S., and Ronald E. Whitton. *The Golf Course*. New York: The Rutledge Press, 1987.

Douthit, Nathan. *Uncertain Encounters*. Corvallis: Oregon State University Press, 2002.

Gunther, John. "Resort drives for success." *The World Weekend* (Coos Bay, Oregon), December 2, 2002: A1, A5.

Gunther, John. "Bandon Preserve has grand opening." *The World* (Coos Bay, Oregon), May 2, 2012: B1, B2.

Jones, Stephen R. *The Last Prairie: A Sandhills Journal*. Ragged Mountain Press/McGraw-Hill (USA), 2000.

Kocher, Charles. "Developers outline resort plan." *The World* (Coos Bay, Oregon), March 8, 1995: 1, 8.

Kunstler, James Howard. *The Geography of Nowhere*. New York: Simon & Schuster, A Touchstone Book, 1994.

Lichatowich, Jim. *Salmon Without Rivers*. Washington, Covelo: Island Press, 1999.

Mann, Charles C. *1491*. New York: First Vintage Books, Random House, 2006.

Moss Strong, Amy. "Tempers flare in Bandon Duneland hearing in county." *Western World* (Bandon, Oregon), "date unknown": 1.

Moss Strong, Amy. "Bandon Dunes expansions excite golfers and residents." *The World Weekend* (Coos Bay, Oregon), December 21, 2002: A1, A10.

Omstead, Larry. "While Economy Slumps, High-End Golf Resorts Flourish." *Investor's Business Daily*, February 14, 2002: A9.

Peterson, Laura. "Traditional Visitor Centers May Fade as National Park Services Embraces Digital Age." *The New York Times*, June 2, 2011.

Recht, Fran. "The coast isn't safe." *The Sunday Oregonian*, July 6, 1997.

Rybczynski, Witold. *The Look of Architecture*. New York: Oxford University Press, 2001.

Schamehorn, Mary. "Destination resort plans unveiled." *Western World* (Bandon, Oregon), November 15, 1996: 1.

Schamehorn, Mary. "Bandon Dunes project clears one more hurdle." *Western World* (Bandon, Oregon), August 7, 1996: 1.

Tveskov, Mark Axel. *The Coos and Coquille: A Northwest Coast Historical Anthropology*. A Dissertation Presented to the Department of Anthropology and the Graduate School of the University of Oregon in partial fulfillment of the requirements for the Degree of Doctor of Philosophy, 2000.

14579915R00150

Made in the USA
San Bernardino, CA
29 August 2014